War of Shadows

War of Shadows

THE STRUGGLE FOR UTOPIA IN THE PERUVIAN AMAZON

MICHAEL F. BROWN
AND EDUARDO FERNÁNDEZ

UNIVERSITY OF CALIFORNIA PRESS
BERKELEY   LOS ANGELES   LONDON

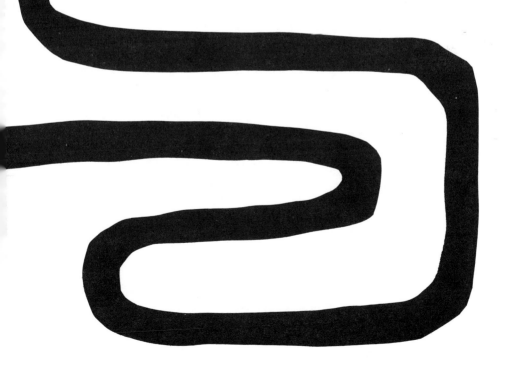

University of California Press
Berkeley and Los Angeles, California

University of California Press
London, England

First Paperback Printing 1993

Library of Congress Cataloging-in-Publication Data

Brown, Michael Fobes, 1950–
    War of shadows : the struggle for utopia in the Peruvian
Amazon / Michael F. Brown and Eduardo Fernández.
        p.   cm.
    Includes bibliographical references and index.
    ISBN 0-520-07448-3
    1. Campa Indians—Wars.   2. Campa Indians—Government
relations.   3. Campa Indians—Social conditions.   4. Nativistic
movements—Peur—Satipo.   5. Indians, Treatment of—Peru—
Satipo.   6. Satipo (Peru)—Social conditions.   7. Movimiento
de Izquierda Revolucionaria (Peru)   I. Fernández, Eduardo.
II. Title.
F3430.1.C3B76   1991
985'.24—dc20   90-26976
                                                                          CIP

Printed in the United States of America
1   2   3   4   5   6   7   8   9

When I wish to evoke the image of the Antis Indians, they very often appear to me in this way: as the Spirits of the Jungle, crepuscular beings, vague forms, Chinese shadows dancing in the moonlight.

Olivier Ordinaire, *Du Pacifique à l'Atlantique par les Andes péruviennes et l'Amazone*, 1892

Contents

Illustrations

Mestizo women on a festive excursion hold Asháninka artifacts. Photograph, entitled "Picnic on the Paucartambo," taken by Fernando Garreaud, ca. 1905. (Courtesy Gastón Garreaud)

Portrait of Asháninkas published in F. A. Stahl's *In the Amazon Jungles*, 1932. Stahl's original caption identifies subjects as "a band of murderers . . . organized for the purpose of stealing children, after killing the parents." Río Perené, ca. 1928. (Courtesy Orlando and Grace Robins)

F. A. Stahl baptizes Asháninka convert near Río Perené, ca. 1928. (Courtesy Orlando and Grace Robins)

Guillermo Lobatón in Europe, ca. 1959. (Courtesy *Caretas*)

Guillermo Lobatón (center) with other members of Túpac Amaru guerrilla column, 1965. To Lobatón's left is Máximo Velando; to his right is Máximo Félix Lazo Orrego. (From Peruvian Ministry of War, *Las guerrillas en el Perú y su represión*, 1966)

Civil guards board transport plane in Satipo during counterinsurgency campaign against Túpac Amaru column of MIR, 1965. (Courtesy *Caretas*)

Luis de la Puente, commander-in-chief of the MIR, at the headquarters of his guerrilla column at Mesa Pelada, Department of Cuzco, 1965. (Courtesy *Caretas*)

Press photograph of bridge partially destroyed by MIR's Túpac Amaru column, June 1965. (Courtesy *Caretas*)

Asháninkas watch parachute training at base camp of the Special Police Emergency Unit, a detachment of the Peruvian Civil Guard trained in antiguerrilla tactics by the U.S. Agency for International Development. Mazamari, Satipo Province, Peru, late 1965–early 1966. (Courtesy U.S. Department of State)

U.S. military advisor with members of Civil Guard counterinsurgency unit during parachute training. Mazamari, Satipo Province, Peru, late 1965–early 1966. (Courtesy U.S. Department of State)

Portrait of David Pent in the Peruvian jungle, ca. 1960, exact location unknown. (Courtesy Joseph B. Pent)

David Pent (in khakis, far left) with unidentified colonists and Asháninkas, ca. 1960, location unknown. (Courtesy Joseph B. Pent)

MAPS

Principal towns and Franciscan missions of central Peru, seventeenth and eighteenth centuries.

Approximate location of the major tribal groups of the central Peruvian Amazon, late nineteenth–early twentieth centuries.

Movements of Túpac Amaru column of the MIR, 1965–1966. Stars mark sites of MIR raids or combat with counterinsurgency forces.

 **Preface to the
Paperback Edition**

If the history we present in this book induced an apocalyptic frame of mind when the first edition appeared late in 1991, the mood can only have been intensified by the Asháninka people's subsequent ordeal. Conflict between Peruvian government forces and two radical guerrilla groups, the Tupac Amaru Revolutionary Movement and the Communist Party of Peru–Shining Path, has transformed the valleys of the Ene and Tambo rivers into a landscape of fear. Reciprocal violence has divided families and cost the Asháninka many of their wisest leaders. The disturbing stories that find their way out of the region are difficult to decode at a distance. What we know for certain is that the unrest has turned thousands of Indians into refugees. Those who stay behind are under fierce pressure to ally themselves with either the insurgents or the army. Other tales are harder to verify: claims that the Shining Path has established indoctrination camps in which Indian children live under inhuman conditions; rumors that despairing Asháninka parents are now killing their newborn babies rather than see them live in a world of such torment.

Sometimes the suffering of a people can be made more immediate by accounts of individual lives pointlessly diminished or lost. One such story: in 1992, the elderly shaman we call Pichari, whose prophetic words close this book, was forced to take refuge in the forest when guerrillas of the

Shining Path invaded his community and marked him for death. During his solitary exile, Pichari—whose real name was Ompíquiri—fell from a palm tree while trying to harvest fruit. Immobilized with a broken hip, he died alone, far from the kinsmen who might have eased his passage into the world of the mountain-dwelling *manínkari* spirits.

The political vision of today's Marxist guerrilla fighters is only the latest in a series of Western programs that would remake native society in an alien image. The Asháninka and other Amazonian Indians struggle to understand and to re-shape these programs to serve their own dreams. We hope this book contributes to a wider appreciation of the creativity of indigenous peoples in the face of these assaults.

M. F. B. and E. F.

May 1993

Preface

The five-year collaboration that led to this book began in the Haití, a café in the Lima suburb of Miraflores. Everyone in Miraflores knows the Haití. Its shabby civility exerts a gravitational pull that seems to hold together a city that would otherwise spin apart from the pressure of its accumulating contradictions.

We met at the behest of friends who felt we should get to know each other because of our common interest in Peru's jungle Indians. After talking business for awhile, we moved on to more informal tale-telling. Against the street noise of Avenida Larco, and fueled by the Haití's luxuriant coffee, Eduardo enfolded us in a remarkable story. During more than a decade of research among the Asháninka Indians of Satipo Province, he learned that in 1965 some Asháninkas had met a black revolutionary whom they regarded as a messiah, as the Son of the Sun. The messiah, Guillermo Lobatón, was an urban intellectual who had studied at the Sorbonne. Lobatón was also a leading member of the *Movimiento de Izquierda Revolucionaria* (Movement of the Revolutionary Left, or MIR), a group of Marxist revolutionaries inspired by the teachings of Fidel Castro and Che Guevara.

Scores of Asháninkas, as well as some closely related Indians who call themselves Nomatsiguengas, took up arms with the MIR when the group commenced guerrilla warfare in the latter half of 1965. Many Indians died as the Peruvian armed forces pursued a counterinsurgency strategy guided by the principle that no guerrilla should be taken alive. Fighter-bombers strafed and napalmed the Indians' villages. Lobatón and the rest of his guerrilla column perished, some hurled to their deaths from army helicopters. Mysterious Americans figured in the story in various guises—as military advisors, missionaries, and even as alleged revolutionaries—though their role had never been clarified in formal histories of the period.

Long before the guerrilla war of 1965, Asháninkas were feared for their stubborn resistance to outsiders. In the 1740s they rallied around a messianic figure named Juan Santos Atahualpa, who called for the expulsion of the Spanish and the creation of a pan-Indian empire reminiscent of Inca civilization. The events of 1965 bore a striking resemblance to their eighteenth-century counterpart, though the duration and scope of the recent uprising were more limited, in part because of the destructive power of modern weaponry. Was it possible that despite the forces bearing down on them from Peruvian national society, the Asháninka people had maintained a tradition of militant messianism for more than 250 years? If so, why had their role in the 1965 insurgency disappeared from conventional histories?

We decided to join forces to explore this mystery. Our principal source of information was to be the participants themselves—when they could be found and persuaded to talk—as well as the popular press, official documents, and scholarly works. As we probed Asháninka oral histories, it became obvious that the Indians' actions in the twentieth century could not be understood without reassessing their long tradition of resistance to Western intrusion. To fathom Asháninka obstinacy, we had to examine in turn the lives of the European, Asian, and North American settlers who helped to mold the Amazon's social life beginning in the 1500s. Thus a study of a specific historical moment evolved into an investigation of the entire span of contact between Indians and settlers in Peru's central jungle region. Framed more broadly, our book became a meditation on the ambitions, anxieties, and dreams of human beings caught in a colonial maelstrom.

Colleagues sometimes asked us why we would bother to study an episode that occupies but a line or two in history books, if it is mentioned at all. Even many Peruvians regard the guerrilla struggle of the MIR as an act of romantic folly that had little impact on the history of their country. Now that the Shining Path and other leftist groups dominate events in Peru, however, the insurgency of 1965 must be seen as a first step toward the far more intractable guerrilla war of the 1980s and 1990s. Moreover, the cast of characters in the 1965 drama is not so different from that of struggles elsewhere in Latin America, suggesting that it might represent a microcosm of contending forces in neighboring countries.

Although this history encompasses peoples of diverse nationalities and backgrounds, our chief interest is in the Amazon's native peoples. In the popular imagination, Amazonian Indians are victims—casualties of nations hungry for resources and international organizations promoting capitalist development. Without denying the unequal contest between native peoples and national governments, we wish to underscore the ways Indians have responded dynamically, often with great success, to the challenge of colonialism. The Asháninka are a proud people who, when circumstances demand, are capable of fighting for their land and for their way of life. Their story is not one of passive victimization but of active engagement with the colonizer, a passionate search for meaning in the harsh realities of Western power, and the anticipation of a final day of reckoning. Above all, Ashánin-kas hold tenaciously to a dream of spiritual deliverance.

A word on the specifics of the collaboration that informs every page of this book. The Asháninka accounts presented here draw on oral histories that Eduardo Fernández collected in Satipo Province, some of which have previously appeared in his book *Para que nuestra historia no se pierda* (So That Our History Is Not Lost), published in Lima in 1986. In 1988, Fernández traveled to France and Spain to track down people with important stories to tell about the guerrilla war. Research on documentary sources in the United States was conducted by Michael Brown, who also interviewed key informants in Huancayo, Pucallpa, and Lima. A growing guerrilla threat and the government's intensifying counterinsurgency campaign prevented us from doing joint fieldwork in Satipo Province, but we collaborated on interviews and archival work in 1987 and 1989 in Lima. We are together responsible for the substantive assertions of the pages that follow. The task of shaping the book in its present form fell to Michael Brown, the English-speaking coauthor, and he is solely answerable for any infelicities of expression.

The most difficult question we faced in preparing this book concerned possible harm that might befall our informants should their accounts reach the wrong hands. The Indians who shared their stories with us wanted the world to know their names and villages. Yet when many of these accounts were recorded, our interlocutors could not have known how savage the violence in rural Peru would become, how quickly it would change the contours of daily life in even the most remote Amazonian settlements. In 1970, the Peruvian government pardoned all survivors of the guerrilla war of 1965, but official clemency counts for little amid the bloodshed that has been visited upon the Indians of Peru's central Amazon since the late 1980s. The dangers of the current situation revealed themselves in December of 1989, when leftist guerrillas belonging to the Túpac Amaru Revolutionary Movement (MRTA) kidnapped and executed Alejandro Calderón Espinoza, an Asháninka leader whom the MRTA alleged had assisted government counterinsurgency forces in 1965. As we completed this manuscript, we learned that at least one man whose story we tell had been murdered by elements of the

MRTA intent upon destroying Asháninka leadership. We therefore use pseudonyms for those Indians who spoke to us about the events of 1965 and whom we know to be still alive; the names of long-deceased individuals have not been changed. In view of the small scale of village society, we follow a strategy of deliberate vagueness with respect to the names of certain Asháninka and Nomatsiguenga settlements. The identities of other people mentioned in the text have not been altered unless they requested anonymity or provided us with information that we judge to be especially sensitive.

This research drew on the assistance—in some cases, the exceptional generosity—of far too many people to name here. In the acknowledgments we recognize the help of colleagues and informants whom we can identify publicly. The Wenner-Gren Foundation for Anthropological Research, Inc., and President Francis C. Oakley of Williams College both contributed funds that put our project in motion. A National Endowment for the Humanities Fellowship allowed Michael Brown to write for a year at the School of American Research in Santa Fe, New Mexico, where he was one of several resident scholars to benefit from the encouragement of Douglas W. Schwartz, the school's president, and Jonathan Haas, then Director of Academic Programs. In 1989, we shared a research grant from the Harry Frank Guggenheim Foundation that allowed us to collaborate more closely in the final stages of writing than might otherwise have been the case. Obviously, none of our work would have been possible without the help of many Asháninka and Nomatsiguenga people, whom the vicissitudes of war prevent us from thanking.

M. F. B. and E. F.

Santa Fe/Lima/Pucallpa
1988–1990

Introduction

Pedro Kintaro sits at home in Boca Kiatari, a small Indian village in the tropical forest of eastern Peru. His voice barely rises above the sounds of the Amazonian night. It is 1986, but Kintaro's thoughts are fixed on events that took place more than twenty years before. He shudders, remembering the sight of fighter planes screaming over the hilltop toward his settlement:

> *Bombs began to fall. Airplanes! Bombs! The planes were black. They sounded like whistles. They came low and dropped bombs. We'd dug holes to hide in, and we got in them. The bombs blew up, fire . . . This is what the shamans had predicted: "A Powerful One will arrive, a tasórentsi. Fire will come." That's what they said.*[1]

In 1965, the year shamans prophesied the arrival of a Powerful One, Peru waged war against Amazonian tribesmen and the Marxist guerrillas hiding among them. As wars go, it was small. Probably no more than two hundred people died in the jungle, though casualties related to guerrilla actions elsewhere in Peru brought the total losses significantly higher.

This encounter has virtually disappeared from history. The *Area Handbook for Peru*, published by the U.S. Government Printing Office, reduces it to one sentence. "Armed attacks against police posts took place in several areas of the Andes in 1965," it says, "and these guerrilla operations were promptly suppressed by units of the armed forces."[2]

In the following pages, we tell some of the stories abridged by that sentence. Our aim is to bring out of the shadows the Indians who played an important part in the revolt of 1965, to let their voices reshape the history of a violent confrontation. Their words compel us to acknowledge their past and to rethink our own.

The native people who figured most prominently in these events call themselves Asháninka, though they are better known in Peru and abroad as "Campa."[3] They inhabit an area of perhaps 40,000 square miles, mostly Amazon rain forest, east of Lima in Peru's geographic center. Asháninkas came into contact with Europeans in the late 1500s. Since then, missionaries of every imaginable Christian sect have tried to convert them. Until quite recently, whites routinely trafficked in Asháninka children, who served as laborers and unpaid domestics. For the last 150 years, Asháninkas have fought a holding action against settlers who see the Amazon as a source of farmland and export goods, or as a haven for the lawless.

When guerrillas of the Movement of the Revolutionary Left (*Movimiento de Izquierda Revolucionaria*, or MIR) pushed down from the Andean highlands into Asháninka territory in mid-1965, scores of Asháninkas threw in their lot with the rebels. The guerrillas saw their insurgency as part of a maturing international conflict between workers and capitalists. These concepts meant little to the Asháninkas. Their interest in the revolutionaries was kindled by the prophecy of a shaman, who saw in the leader of the local MIR column the same spiritual authority that eighteenth-century Asháninkas recognized in a charismatic rebel named Juan Santos Atahualpa. To the extent that guerrillas and Indians shared aspirations, it was to end the reign of local landlords. But Asháninka hopes went beyond land reform. Those who collaborated with the MIR perceived the guerrillas as helpful spirits who would upend the relationship between servants and masters. Indians would assume their rightful place as rulers of the forest. They would again enjoy the prosperity wrested from them centuries earlier by the Spanish. The rebellion would be an end and a beginning.

The spiritual undercurrents that surfaced in the Indians' response to the MIR had welled up at least three times before, beginning in 1742. On each occasion, a charismatic outsider crossed formidable cultural barriers to awaken Ashaninka yearnings for deliverance.

A recurrent human experience that brings myth up against the flinty surface of events is the millennial dream—the hope that the present world of scarcity and suffering will give way to a glittering plenitude. As long as peoples have faced profound challenge, they have from time to time razed social orders, turned received arrangements upside down, in search of a new start. When these episodes are marked by strong religious currents, anthropologists call them millennial movements, revitalization movements, or crisis cults.[4]

Academic interest in crisis cults peaked during the early 1970s. Millennial currents in the American counterculture of the late 1960s focused attention on crisis cults, as did growing interest in all forms of social protest. Most scholars saw millennial movements as a spontaneous reply to the questions that vex tribal people when confronted with the injustices of colonialism. Why can't we live as we once did? Why are so many of our people dying from new diseases? Why do the whites have so many material goods and we so few? Why do our traditional institutions fail us when confronted by these powerful strangers? Even the most sympathetic commentators, however, thought of crisis cults as a passing phase in a society's development, to be eventually replaced by more rational responses, such as political mobilization.[5]

Today we are less confident in the inevitability of a tectonic shift to secular rationalism. Religious fundamentalists have redefined political discourse in places as different as the United States and Iran. Despite Frantz Fanon's prediction that the emerging Third World revolutionary would "discover reality" and "pour scorn upon the zombies of his ancestors," the Marxist guerrilla movement that gave birth to Zimbabwe found a way to reconcile theories of national liberation with traditional religious practices, including spirit mediumship.[6] And in Peru, insurgents belonging to an extremist group called the Shining Path have, according to some observers, spliced together elements of traditional Andean millennialism and Maoist theory to justify their war against the state.

Reflecting on the growth of the Shining Path movement, the Peruvian writer and politician Mario Vargas Llosa recently observed that a search for utopia permeates Peruvian history and indeed much of the history of Latin America.[7] This certainly holds true for the Amazon. For the first Christian missionaries as well as for today's Maoist guerrillas, the Amazon has been a potentially utopian space. As we pondered similarities between millennial currents in Asháninka history and those of the European peoples with whom they came into contact, we began to doubt that Asháninkas were alone in bringing a "mythical" perspective to their reading of the region's future. Revolutionaries, bureaucrats, missionaries, counterinsurgency experts, and entrepreneurs also hold deep-seated myths—notions of destiny, of world order, of being and becoming—that help to determine their actions. The Amazon, which from first contact has challenged Western ways of dealing with nature, invites utopian fantasies as well as their opposite, dystopian visions of exploitation and terror.[8]

In probing the persistence of millennial dreams in the Peruvian jungle, then, one of our aims is to analyze the traffic of ideas across ethnic boundaries. The discourses of natives and strangers sometimes overlap, sometimes miss each other entirely. As people fully engaged with history, Asháninkas actively respond to the thoughts and acts of the outsiders who have hurled themselves into their midst, with good intentions and bad, since the sixteenth century. The Asháninkas' story is forever entwined with the story of these strangers.

To piece together this history, we found ourselves practicing an uncommon anthropology, one for which we were not prepared by our professional training and previous field research in different parts of the Peruvian Amazon.

Both of us had engaged in conventional fieldwork among Amazonian Indians. We lived in native settlements for long periods of time, puzzling over the intricacies of language, kinship, religious life, and world view. We watched people struggle to sustain a unique, reasonably coherent society in a setting that, for observers raised in Kansas City and Buenos Aires, seemed exceptionally challenging.

History in the orthodox sense scarcely existed where we worked. There were, of course, chronicles that commented on the Indians, most often written by missionaries who saw them as unkempt idolaters of erratic temperament. Native peoples have their own versions of history, but like most anthropologists we found ourselves drawn to the deep-history of myth, which promises access to the free play of the primordial imagination, in preference to the contingent stories of more recent events. A tale accounting for the transfer of root crops from the Earth Mother to ancestral human beings somehow seemed more important than the story of how a particular settlement obtained its land title.

This kind of village fieldwork, where it is still possible, is a valuable apprenticeship and a profoundly humanizing experience. Yet its limitations became apparent as, years later, we each immersed ourselves in practical matters related to the future of Amazonian Indians—land rights, health care, agricultural credit, and forest protection. Engagement with the practical leads one inexorably toward the political, especially in a country such as Peru, where Indians wrestle with a rigid class system and the legacy of conquest. The romance of the pristine village eventually gave way to a more sober view of the shifting power relations between native peoples and the outsiders who so often influence their fate. We began to seek stories of near-history to account for current realities. In Asháninka communities affected by the MIR insurgency of 1965, narratives of the guerrilla war helped to decode the village and intervillage politics of today.

Ironically, the more we looked at the insurgency, the more we saw that its roots lay in historical events dating from the early contact period and, beyond that, to the deep-history of myth.[9] Asháninka accounts of the events of 1965 interweave recorded events and traditional ideas of prophetic revelation, ordinary people and spirits, and contradictory thoughts about the dangerous outlanders who now control so much of Asháninka life. In other words, the rebellion was an instance of what Marshall Sahlins has called "mythopraxis"—that is, the invocation of a mythic vision to frame responses to current events.[10]

We have relied upon several kinds of resources to write this book. Chapters summarizing the early history of the Asháninka draw on Spanish chronicles and the work of scholars who have mined them for information. Asháninka voices are difficult to find in these accounts, but with careful study their faint echoes can still be heard. When appropriate, we have tried to reconstruct the native outlook on events through the strategic use of contemporary oral histories.

Twentieth-century history offers richer prospects. Aside from the work of professional historians and anthropologists, we make use of newspaper accounts, government documents, and interviews with those who witnessed the events about which we write. Under the terms of the Freedom of Information Act, we obtained U.S. government records from the Departments of State and Defense, the National Archives, and the Federal Bureau of Investigation. The deteriorating security situation in Peru, a country now lacerated by political and criminal violence as intense as at any time in its history, created significant obstacles to the realization of our goals. Two vignettes from our research may convey a sense of what it was like to probe the history of the 1965 conflict amid today's unrest:

■ *September 1987.* Eduardo Fernández searches for Antonio Meza, a possible contact in the Movement of the Revolutionary Left. Meza is one of the few guerrillas to have survived the MIR-led insurgency of 1965. Fernández has been told that Meza now works for a small leftist party called the People's Democratic Union (UDP), which has an office on Lima's Plaza Dos de Mayo. In front of the plaza's decrepit buildings, street vendors press their wares on weary travelers who hope for nothing more than a seat on a bus. The several leftist political parties with offices on the plaza use loudspeakers to launch an auditory assault on passersby.

Fernández enters the building identified as the UDP's, but the drab lobby has no directory of offices. Ringing the bells on each floor, he meets families crowded into squalid rooms, small-time lawyers down on their luck, and women who invite him in for a massage. He finds an office that seems to be his destination, for when he mentions Meza's name, the occupants shift uneasily in their chairs and hide their faces behind newspapers. He is directed to an address in La Colmena's labyrinth of alleys. The place is abandoned, a forgotten world of battered desks, dust, and rat droppings. He returns to the neighborhood several times until all trails run cold. A few days later the Lima dailies explain the vanishing act: after more than twenty years of somnolence, the MIR has resumed the armed struggle by raiding the Miraflores office of Citibank and covering its walls with propaganda. Prospects for an interview pass from remote to nonexistent: Meza has reentered the clandestine world of revolutionaries. Two years later, the MIR announces that comrade Antonio Meza has fallen in combat.

■ *July 1989.* Michael Brown navigates Lima's Jirón Moquegua, one block past the area known as Ocoña, where scores of moneychangers shout exchange rates to passing drivers. Each moneychanger, or *cambista*, is equipped with an electronic calculator and a waist pouch stuffed with currency. Buyers lift banknotes to the gray light of the Lima sky, checking watermarks. The action on Ocoña is brisk. The weekly supply of cocaine dollars, rumored to average around 60 million, will soon arrive by jet from Tocache.

Brown has been directed to a heavily armored storefront under a Honda sign, where he hopes to interview the widow of an American who disappeared during the guerrilla war of 1965. A man with a four-day stubble takes Brown to a back room. There he's introduced to his interviewee, a cheerful and adipose woman of about forty-five. Another man enters the room. His guayabera shirt is size XL, and he fills it easily. He grips a nickel-plated revolver, probably a .44. Although the gun is angled toward the floor, the anthropologist begins to perspire.

Revolver is not friendly. He declines to identify himself and inspects Brown's passport with a hand lens. Still holding the pistol in his lap, Revolver grunts permission for the interview. As the conversation develops, the man's attention shifts to the three telephones on his desk, which have begun to ring. Two other men in business suits load a valise with thick bundles of Peruvian banknotes. In reply to Brown's puzzled look, Revolver slaps a brick of hundred-dollar bills on the desk, each packet of nine bills neatly clasped by a tenth. He is a high-stakes moneychanger—or so he claims. When Brown finishes interviewing the woman, who is now married to this man, he is ushered through the barred entryway to the street. "At first I thought you might be police," the man says by way of apology. "Take care," he adds, "there are some nasty characters out there."

Under the circumstances, it is remarkable that people talked to us at all. When they did consent to an interview, the sensitive nature of the information we sought invited outright lies as well as more subtle forms of misrepresentation. Official sources proved scarcely more reliable: communiqués of the Peruvian armed forces, as well as official documents released to us by agencies of the United States government, gave new meaning to the term "magical realism."

In view of what in many cases turned out to be the irreconcilable contradictions in our sources, we don't claim to have written a definitive account of "what really happened." There are significant gaps in our knowledge, just as there are in the knowledge of any one participant.[11] Rather, we attempt to distill the forms of discourse that various groups have used to talk about, and to interpret, the actions of others. We then weave these voices together to trace the misunderstandings and miscommunications that produced a distinctive series of events. The facts of the events we describe are sometimes contested; their *significance* always is. We have tried to remain as alert as possible to this struggle of alternative meanings while learning to live with a degree of indeterminacy.

One of the challenges of historical anthropology, or anthropological history, is to sketch the culture of a tribal people without commingling past and present. The Asháninkas of today are not the same as their ancestors of the sixteenth century. Yet there are persistent qualities that mark Asháninka culture through time, providing reasonably fixed points of reference for a study of their history.

A first impression that hasn't changed in four hundred years of contact with Asháninkas: they strike visitors as tall people. Their physical bearing, the stout palm-wood bows carried by men, and their characteristic garment—a long cotton robe called a *cushma* that is worn by both sexes—create the appearance of height, though they are small people by North American standards.

A male visitor's first encounter with Asháninkas is an exercise in formality. A proper guest stops on the trail about fifty yards from a house and whistles through his hands to advise the residents of his imminent arrival. The senior man of the house rarely hastens to respond. He lingers, thinking things over, finishing the task at hand. The visitor, meanwhile, places his belongings, including his weapons, on the ground. Eventually the host comes forward. If the visitor is a stranger, the host may circle around him to verify that he has a back, establishing that he is not a demon merely impersonating a human being. Humanity certified, the visitor is invited inside to drink tart manioc beer, the most palpable expression of hospitality in the Upper Amazon. Members of the household go through the visitor's personal belongings; by exploring the private things of the guest, they bring him into the family's own world. As the minutes pass, host and guest edge from formality to relaxed conversation. The host's family has probed, tested, and finally assimilated the visitor into the life of the household.

The language in which these preliminaries take place belongs to the linguistic family called Arawak, which reaches across South America like a bandolier running from the continent's right shoulder to its left waist. The Asháninka are one of several Arawakan peoples in the central Amazon of Peru, including the Yanesha (Amuesha), Machiguenga, Piro, and Nomatsiguenga. Today, Asháninkas populate a region defined by the Perené, Pachitea, Ene, Tambo, and Apurímac rivers, and by the upper reaches of the Ucayali. Estimates of their current population range from 34,000 to more than 45,000.[12] Regardless of the accuracy of these figures, there is no question that they are now, and have been since the sixteenth century, one of the largest native groups of the Peruvian Amazon.[13]

Today most Asháninkas live in small settlements—perhaps a dozen houses clustered around a primary school. Where adequate land is available, small fields of rice, root crops, and coffee bushes surround the village.[14]

The family garden provides the staples of Asháninka diet, including tubers (especially manioc and sweet potatoes), bananas, plantains, various fruits, and maize. Women rule the garden. When possible, men hunt and fish as their forefathers did, though polluted rivers and diminished forests make the search for game a disappointing enterprise today. Out of necessity, Asháninkas have turned their attention to the production of cash crops, especially coffee.

Before outsiders appropriated so much of the forest, Asháninkas preferred to live in large, independent households scattered in the forest. The male head of the household was called *itínkami*, a term also applied to the principal support beam of the house. The itínkami oversaw the activities of his wives, children, and the husbands of married daughters. His central preoccupations included the provision of food for his family, forging links of hospitality and mutual aid with neighbors, and protecting his family from harm.

Gerald Weiss, an anthropologist who studied Asháninka communities along the Río Tambo in the 1960s, observes that Asháninka culture has a "strong masculine bias." Based on field research among Asháninkas of the Río Pichis, another anthropologist, John Elick, reports that the ideal Asháninka woman is "submissive, faithful, and hard-working."[15] Regrettably, we still lack field accounts that can build on these general observations to provide a more nuanced view of relations between the sexes in Asháninka society.

Political leadership is an elusive thing in Asháninka communities. In the colonial period, Asháninka "chiefs" were mostly a figment of the Spanish imagination—or a form of wishful thinking, since the absence of formal political institutions was a constant headache for colonial administrators and missionaries. Local leaders (called *pinkatsári* or, beginning in the colonial period, *caciques* or *curacas*) have always based their authority on persuasive rhetoric, the strength of their kinship ties, and proven skill in diplomacy and warfare. Nevertheless, pinkatsári have only a limited ability to coerce other household heads to act against their own wishes. Since the 1960s, new leadership roles have emerged in Asháninka communities to complement older traditions of authority. Native schoolteachers, catechists, and health workers now vie with headmen for the power to influence community decisions.

A common motif in Asháninka contact history is the explosive temperament of Asháninka men. In his reflections on the disheartening results of centuries of Franciscan missionary labor in the central Amazon, Padre Alberto Gridilla describes the Asháninka as "enamored and jealous of his liberty" and "reluctant to embrace Christianity, a religion that imposes duties on him and which curbs his disordered passions." "He does not," Gridilla concludes, "want impositions from anyone."[16] As we will see, much of the violence that has shaken the Upper Amazon follows from the unsettling effects of colonization; the advance of "civilization" has been, in Peru as in so many places, a murderous process. But there is no reason to think that Asháninkas were unfamiliar with violence before the Spanish Conquest. Since their first contact with outsiders they have demonstrated their willingness to use force on scores of occasions.

Where Asháninkas have proved reticent is in the disclosure of their religious life. In the words of Isidoro Llano, a Catholic missionary, the "savage . . . conceals the finer convolutions of his inner being."[17] Such concealment is relatively easy, for Asháninka religion lacks obvious physical symbols. Asháninkas build no shrines or altars, nor do they perform large-scale rituals. Their cosmology is defined not by the four cardinal directions but by the movement of rivers. Of special significance is River's End, Otsitiríko, home to kindly spirits.

For an Amazonian people, the Asháninka spiritual universe is remarkably dualistic, almost Manichaean. Spirits are either benevolent or demonic. Benevolent spirits (*tasórentsi* or *amachénga*) have special powers over the elements, over plants and animals, and over life itself. Chief among them is the Sun (Pavá, Tasórentsi, or sometimes Diós, after the Spanish word for God). Pavá is the Father, the creator, the one who watches over all. The Moon (Kashíri) is an ambivalent figure, the giver of agriculture but also a hungry presence that swallows the dead. Sun, Moon, and other powerful beings may send spirits to help the Asháninka people. Demons (*kamári*), on the other hand, appear in myriad forms to confound and kill. One must always be alert for their subterfuges.

Standing between the world of ordinary people and that of powerful beings is the shaman or *sheripiári*. Asháninka shamans use tobacco and a powerful hallucinogen called *ayahuasca* to enter healing trances.[18] In trance, they dance with spirits, travel to distant places, and search the spirit world for prophetic messages.

The message that emerges most persistently is that the present world is about to make way for another. Asháninkas, Gerald Weiss writes, "anticipate a time when Tasórentsi will destroy the world or, rather, transform it into a new world." "When that occurs," he adds, "sky and earth will again be close together, the earth will speak once again, and its inhabitants will be a new race of humanity knowing nothing of sickness, death, or toil."[19] John Elick found a similar belief among the Asháninkas he knew. "This world, tainted and contaminated by the intrusion of evil forces and beings," they told him, "will also pass away."[20] This persistent, apocalyptic vision links the Asháninkas of today with those who received the first Spanish visitors at the end of the sixteenth century.

ONE

To Fill the Granaries of Heaven

Late in 1595, a man named Juan Vélez guided two Jesuit priests, Juan Font and Nicolás Mastrillo, to a settlement of jungle Indians east of the highland village of Andamarca. "We walked through dense forests," Padre Font later wrote to another Jesuit, "at times ascending—in other words, climbing over the roots of trees; at other times we descended, more often sitting than standing, always through marshes."[1] Eventually the foot-weary priests reached a group of Indians they referred to as Andes, who were led by a headman named Veliunti or Veluinti. Veliunti and his followers were, according to Font, "taller and livelier than those of Piru; their dress is only a large, red shirt; their faces are well formed and would look better if they were not smeared and painted red."[2]

The Jesuits spent their first hours trying to assure the Indians of their good intentions, until they won over their hosts with the humblest of gestures: they ate the food the Indians offered them. Font and Mastrillo soon found themselves overwhelmed by native hospitality. Veliunti enthusiastically agreed to build a chapel of wood and palm leaves.

The encounter so captivated Padre Font that he made four more journeys to the region between 1596 and 1601 with the hope of gaining exclusive Jesuit control over missionary activities there. In Spain Font obtained royal permission to embark on a campaign of conversion. His plea to the king was sweetened by the promise that his missionary efforts would include the allocation of four hundred Indians to a mine under the direction of a Spanish captain named Manuel Zurita. But on his return to Peru he was drawn into the vortex of political intrigue within the Jesuit order and between the Jesuits and other missionary orders interested in the region. Under fierce pressure from Jesuit superiors opposed to the venture, Font delivered a sworn statement to the effect that a mission to the central jungle was not in the best interests of the Society of Jesus.[3]

Like most sixteenth- and seventeenth-century explorers, Font found it difficult to identify the native groups he encountered on his travels. Amazonian natives were a bewildering mass of "nations," speaking incomprehensible languages and distinguishable mainly by their outward appearance and by the location of their settlements. Font's linguistic observations, for example, are limited to the remark that "all these valleys speak a single language, which is not difficult to pronounce but more difficult to learn, because our interpreter doesn't know it well."[4] Depending on circumstance or personal predilection, Spaniards were prone to excessive under-specificity or its opposite. The native peoples living east of Tarma, for instance, may be referred to generically as *chunchos*, a capacious and often pejorative term for jungle Indians, or by the inevitable labels "infidel" and "savage." Yet during the same period and in the same general region, travelers alluded to contacts with Andes, Autes, Amages, Amajes, Majes, Pilcozones, Simirinchis, Canparites, Anapatis, Pangoas, Menearos, Satipos, Copiris, Coba-

ros, Conivos, Sepivos, Mochobos, Pirros, Pisiatiris, Cuy-
entimaris, Sangirenis, Sonomoros, Pautiques, Comarosquis,
Saviroquis, Chichirenis, Zagorenis, and Quintimiris—to
provide only a partial list. Why such a thicket of tribal names?

Establishing the identity and scale of native groups has always been a problem for colonial powers. By the seventeenth
century the Spanish had come to realize that Indian peoples
were not always organized into kingdoms with clearly defined chains of command. (In one of his last statements about
the prospects of converting Veliunti and his followers, Padre
Font complained that "one cannot make much progress with
them, principally for being so few and so scattered, without
authority or leader.")[5] Yet although they ceased to look for
native kings wherever they traveled, the Spaniards had only
the dimmest notion of the actual political structure of the
Amazonian societies they encountered. The brevity of initial
contacts usually hampered assessment of the linguistic similarities and differences that are central to tribal identity. Without knowledge of the local language, it was difficult to ask
newly contacted people for their own understanding of the
boundaries that defined their social world.

Hence the tendency to fall back on generic terms such as
"chuncho" or to link social groups to specific places. The
Poyenisatis, for example, were people who lived along the
Río Poyeni. The Momoris lived near a stretch of river harboring large numbers of a fish called *momori*.[6] Sometimes
groups were given the name of a local leader known to Spanish authorities. Still another solution was to use names provided by neighboring Indians whose languages the Spaniards
already spoke. Peruvian anthropologist Stefano Varese, for
instance, argues that some of the place names and "tribes"
noted by the great Franciscan explorer Biedma in the 1680s
were assigned by his Conibo scout Cayampay. The term
Campa likewise may have its origin in one of the languages
spoken by the Franciscans' Indian guides. It certainly bears
no resemblance to the word the Campa use to identify them-

selves: *Asháninka*. Whatever its source, by the mid-1680s the term *Campa* came into general use as a replacement for the numerous tribal names that litter earlier chronicles.[7]

The first sustained missionary effort among Ashánikas is generally held to be that of Fray Jerónimo Jiménez, a Franciscan who in 1635 founded a mission at Quimirí, now the site of the substantial town of La Merced. The Quimirí mission was close to Cerro de la Sal, or Salt Mountain, a site of strategic importance. Located just north of the junction of the Chanchamayo and Perené rivers, Salt Mountain is veined with lenses of mineral salt lying near the surface of the ground, where they can be mined with simple wood and stone tools.

An inexpensive condiment that modern shoppers take for granted, salt exerts an irresistible attraction to Amazonian Indians. It is the quintessential flavoring in a native cuisine that, whatever its nutritional virtues, is notably impoverished in spices. Salting and smoking are the only means that Amazonian people have of preserving food against the tropical heat. In some parts of Amazonia, people make crude salt by burning saltgrass or leaves of the water hyacinth. But if veins of mineral salt are known, Indians are willing to travel hundreds of miles, risking privation and enemy attack, to unearth the precious substance in large quantities.

Several different Amazonian peoples, as well as Indians from the eastern Andes, traveled annually to Salt Mountain to mine salt, cutting it into transportable blocks that were shipped downriver on balsawood rafts or carried out in baskets. The Asháninka, Yanesha, Conibo, and Piro were involved in the salt trade, which ramified, as indigenous trading systems often do, into a regional network that included commerce in cotton cloth, vanilla pods, feathers, pelts, and bronze tools from the Andes. Observing this system in action at Salt Mountain, the Franciscans concluded that the site offered them access to a captive audience drawn from all the heathen tribes of the region. A letter written in the eighteenth century by Fray José de San Antonio exemplifies Franciscan strategic thought dating back to the early 1600s:

> *The supplicant makes known to Your Majesty that, being numerous the gentile nations that come up and down the rivers each year to remove from Salt Mountain considerable quantities of this product, the supplicant judges it very convenient and necessary to defend the entrance to this mountain with fifty or more soldiers. . . . And this, Lord, is the easiest means of achieving the end of the Apostolic Ministers, who as loyal vassals of Your Majesty seek to give God innumerable souls with which to fill the granaries of Heaven, and to Your Majesty a new empire for the extension of your dominion; to which said gentile nations will not be opposed, for fear that by means of catholic arms they might be prohibited from extracting the salt for which they have such a craving.*[8]

Little is known about the early months of the Quimirí mission, but Franciscan chronicles record that in early December of 1637 Fray Jiménez and a priest named Larios or Larríos were martyred by the Asháninkas on the Río Perené—evidence, according to the Franciscan historian Izaguirre, of what the Indians' "barbarous breasts could conceive and their inhuman arms could undertake."[9] The issue leading to the martyrdom was one that became a persistent sore spot in relations between Franciscans and Asháninkas: the church's opposition to the practice of polygyny—that is, having multiple wives—that was commonly followed by Asháninka caciques or headmen. The headman in question was Andrés Zampati, who "believed that once the missionaries were dead, he would enjoy great liberty, coupled with the authority of being cacique."[10]

Given the risks of establishing settlements in jungle areas at the farthest margins of Spain's zone of control, the motives of secular and religious pioneers are difficult to comprehend. What had missionaries like the martyred Fray Jiménez to gain by launching themselves into a situation of known dangers and unknown rewards? The question has to be pondered on two fronts, a large-scale political one and a human one.

The forces that drove Spanish colonization efforts in the New World arose in the Old, when a united Spain emerged successful from its long crusade to expel the Moors in the late fifteenth century. Christian Spain was a military power afflicted with an unhealthy economy: the tiny landowning minority imposed what Eric Wolf has called a "tributary mode of production" that supported an increasingly bloated royal bureaucracy. At the same time, people of common birth and even minor nobles had few opportunities for advancement.[11] The New World presented welcome vistas of pillage for Spaniards who saw in their own country an already crowded horizon. Ironically, the wealth that eventually began to flow in the sixteenth century from Spain's new possessions further diminished prospects at home by fueling inflation and tempting the Crown to indulge in deficit spending supported by loans from foreign banks.

The smoldering financial crisis of Spain manifested itself in the New World through official inconsistency regarding the goals of colonization. The Crown naturally wanted to establish efficient and humane dominion over its new lands. Nevertheless, the possibility that undiscovered riches might lie beyond the current frontier made royal officials receptive to proposals from entrepreneurial soldiers—often of questionable reputation—who sought permission to probe the wilderness in search of mines or mythical native kingdoms.

The singular career of Pedro Bohórquez Girón provides an example of how these abstract forces played themselves out in an individual human life. Around 1620, the eighteen-year-old Bohórquez left the poverty of Andalucía to seek his fortune in Peru. He lived in relative obscurity until his arrival in Lima in 1637 with a group of highland Indians who claimed to know the location of the fabulously wealthy kingdom of Paitití. The viceroy authorized an expedition in search of the city but excluded Bohórquez from the expedition's ranks. The venture met with disaster and Bohórquez was held responsible. Lying low in La Plata and Potosí for a time, he plotted a new search for the fabled Paitití, now in the area of Salt Mountain, which he believed might bear rich mineral deposits.[12]

At this point Bohórquez's deeds are clouded by the contradictions of colonial documents. Using information from a newly discovered manuscript, the anthropologist Fernando Santos argues that Pedro Bohórquez is the same Bohórquez whom Franciscan chroniclers identify as the cause of so much mischief in the Salt Mountain area between 1645 and 1651.[13] Bohórquez apparently exploited the competition between the Franciscan and Dominican orders to obtain Dominican support for his expedition to Salt Mountain. During the months he and his band of freebooters controlled the settlement of Quimirí, they rustled cattle from nearby highland communities, murdered a native headman, abused the wives of Asháninka converts, and abducted Indian children for use as servants. Eventually Bohórquez's men soured on their fruitless search for gold and came within a hair's-breadth of killing their leader. He was taken to Valdivia and imprisoned, but it was too late for the Dominicans: the Bohórquez reign of terror had undone four years of Dominican missionary work among the Asháninka, all of whom fled Quimirí.

Although Bohórquez's contacts with Asháninkas ended around 1651, he had one last adventure. Escaping from prison yet again in 1656, he crossed the Andes to the Calchaquí Valley, where he persuaded 25,000 Indians that he had come to restore the Inca Empire. His tenure as the Son of the Sun lasted until 1659, when the Spanish arrested him because of their unhappiness with the rebellious behavior of his Calchaquí vassals. Bohórquez languished in prison until January 3, 1667, when the authorities garroted him in his cell at midnight.

In a cynical age it is easy to dismiss the expansion of Franciscan or Dominican missions into frontier areas as simply a more refined form of the exploitation practiced by Bohórquez and other Spanish soldiers of fortune. Viceregal authorities were often happy to let missionaries pave the way for secular colonization in remote regions. Leaders of the Franciscan, Dominican, and Jesuit orders bickered over mission territories like small-time litigants in a county court, often for reasons that had little to do with saving souls. But the front-line missionary who braved the thorns of the jungle and the arrows of Indians such as Asháninkas had poor prospects of personal gain. One must conclude that most went into the wilderness for the greater glory of God, moved by the challenge of bringing heathens into the Christian fold. Many Spanish priests and monks were driven by what Eric Wolf calls a "transcendental simplicity." "Upon the ruins of pagan shrines and idols in a new continent filled with souls hungry for salvation, yet uncorrupted by the age-old vices of the Old World," Wolf writes, "they would erect their own utopia."[14]

The year 1671 saw the Franciscans make another concerted attempt to establish a stable mission system in the central jungle region. "Although at first they had great difficulty in scattering the seeds of the divine world," writes the eighteenth-century Franciscan chronicler José Amich, "with patience and tolerance they succeeded in softening those tough but rational people, who attracted by the good treatment and kindness of the fathers, came to receive the light of the Holy Gospel."[15] Franciscan sources claim that during this period Asháninka delegations made the arduous journey to the highland community of Andamarca to petition for religious instruction.

This missionary thrust led in 1673 to the first expedition of Padre Manuel Biedma, whose exploration of the central

Peruvian Amazon continues to excite the admiration of historians. Biedma and his companions traveled from Comas to Pangoa, a most difficult journey, where they were welcomed by an Asháninka headman named Tonté. Tonté interceded on their behalf with other Indian leaders who advocated killing or expelling the clerics from the region. A mission was founded near Tonté's community and given the name Santa Cruz de Sonomoro.

Despite the promising start at Sonomoro and the founding of another mission at Pichana in 1674, Franciscan efforts in the region soon suffered another setback. A headman named Mangoré persisted in the sin of polygyny despite the entreaties of Padre Francisco Izquierdo. "Mangoré was of irascible temperament, high spirited, an arrogant heart, of violent resolutions; he sheltered neither fear of God nor fear of men, nor respect for the incipient society of Pichana," writes Izaguirre.[16] Amich concurs: "Little effect was made on that hard heart by the loving admonitions [of Padre Izquierdo] because, in the grip of his lasciviousness, he listened not to divine inspiration."[17] With the encouragement of the cacique of Salt Mountain, Siquincho, Mangoré convinced his followers to kill Izquierdo and two other missionaries. "Such was the rain of arrows unleashed on them by the sacrilegious Indians," adds Amich, "that in a brief moment the three looked like a hedgehog, so sewn together and pierced by darts were they."[18]

By the end of the seventeenth century, the mission system was again on the verge of collapse. "The frequent deaths of so many missionaries at the hands of the infidels in such a short space of time inspired so much terror in the rest of the religious and secular authorities that no one dared begin a new conquest among the Andes [Asháninkas]," writes Amich.[19]

One should not discount the demoralizing effect of the landscape on the progress of the mission system. Travelers' impressions of the upland forest of Peru are remarkably consistent from the seventeenth through the twentieth century:

they all stress the inhospitable quality of the terrain to human feet, hands, and spirits. Amich describes the country as

a place of many large ravines . . . and in these ravines rockfalls are frequent and the cliffs formidable. The continual rains that one experiences in the jungle cause the poor walker to go most of the time with wet clothing, and as the soil is always damp and covered with rotting leaves, one frequently slips . . . The continual fatigue and sweat that afflict the wayfarer who travels through such a hot climate, carrying with him the few victuals that he will eat, sometimes oblige him to lean against a tree, and just when he imagines he has obtained relief he finds himself attacked by fierce ants.[20]

Seeking similar release from the tedium of the jungle, the nineteenth-century French traveler Olivier Ordinaire took his rest on the first grassy spot he saw, only to find himself beset by spider-mites called *isango*, which carry the descriptive scientific name *Tetranicus molestissimus*.[21]

Here one finds neither the striking flatness of the Amazon basin nor its parklike forests and stately rivers, but instead a fusion of mountainous terrain with the climatic hardships of the tropics. Watercourses such as the Perené and Ene can be navigated, but they tax the boatman's nerve with rapids, hidden logs, and mercurial changes in water level.

Ashaninkas moved through this refractory world with an ease that seemed miraculous, and at the same time diabolical, to the Spanish missionaries. With a knowledge of the forest's food resources, the Indians could travel relatively unencumbered by the "victuals" mentioned by Padre Amich. Their toes splayed like the fingers of a hand, and their feet moving in rapid cadence, Ashaninkas followed narrow trails invisible to the Franciscans. Where the Ashaninkas and their neighbors differ from other native peoples of the western Amazon is in their use of the *cushma*, a long, poncho-like cotton garment that from the Spanish perspective became a key symbol of native identity. The cushma seems an incongruous garment for a tribe of fierce bowmen, yet Asháninka men manage to flow forward inside the enfolding cotton without snagging it on the thorns that tormented the wandering Franciscans and which even today cause the otherwise agnostic traveler to reconsider his or her doubts about the existence of Purgatory.

Languishing missionary efforts were revitalized in 1709 by the creation of the Apostolic Institute, a unified Franciscan missionary society with a high degree of autonomy from the viceroy and Franciscan authorities in Lima. The Apostolic Institute trained its own missionaries and sought funding directly from the Crown. Eventually the Institute acquired the monastery called Santa Rosa de Ocopa, located twenty-five kilometers from the highland city of Huancayo—an ideal location from which to administer a network of mission stations in the central jungle.[22]

Franciscan missions were expensive to run. Aside from the costs of transportation, livestock, and the importation of foodstuffs that could not be locally produced, even the most modest mission stations had a large inventory of religious articles considered necessary for celebration of the Mass and for the religious instruction of unlettered natives—among them, chalices, chrismatories, missals, crosses, altar bells, candelabras, surplices, paintings, and reliquaries. Although the church at San Antonio de Eneno, one of the most important Franciscan missions, was constructed of logs and roofed with palm leaves, it housed an altar made of carved Huamanga alabaster. On the altar were paintings depicting the fate of souls in heaven and in hell. The mission's small school for the religious education of Indian boys contained twenty-four books, mostly bibles and works of history and theology.[23]

The missions also warehoused considerable quantities of manufactured goods. Indeed, this seems to have been one of their principal attractions from the Indian point of view. Inventories of goods stored in six missions functioning in the 1720s include formidable quantities of axes, machetes, fishhooks, and hoes. Early nineteenth-century Franciscan missions annually distributed thousands of steel knives and hundreds of thousands of fishhooks.[24] The strategy of attracting Indians with trade goods was regarded with misgivings by those friars perceptive enough to realize that the motives of converts often had more to do with a desire for tools than with a fervent interest in Christian salvation.[25]

Beginning in 1709, mission centers were either reestablished or founded at Quimirí in the Chanchamayo valley, Salt Mountain, and then progressively down the Río Perené at Metraro, Eneno, Epillo, Pichana, and San Judas Tadeo de los Autes. By the 1720s there were stations on the Río Mazamari and at a place called Chavini, not far from present-day Satipo. Some of these primary settlements had smaller satellite stations that rose and disappeared according to the vicissitudes of conversion and the productivity of local soils.[26]

The most ambitious demarche of the missionary campaign was the entry of Franciscans into the Gran Pajonál in the early 1720s.[27] The Pajonál, a plateau of rolling grassland surrounded by unforgiving mountain ranges, excited the imagination of the friars. Its inaccessibility held out the promise of countless souls waiting to be saved. The Asháninka population of the region seemed large to the Spanish, with early estimates running as high as ten thousand Indians. The terrain itself, which two royal officials described as "a land that is vast and of a temperate climate"[28] exerted a special fascination for Spaniards jaded by the heat and the relentless verdure of the tropical forest.

Several expeditions prior to the 1740s established small Christian communities in the Pajonál, though the difficulties of maintaining communication with such remote settlements prevented these sites from consolidating themselves into stable mission stations. In some cases the missionary foothold in the Pajonál communities was limited to a Christianized

Indian or a few black settlers. Headmen from the Pajonál paid occasional visits to missions along the Perené, and there is evidence of trade goods circulating into remote Pajonál communities. Even these infrequent contacts were too much for some Pajonalinos: the missionary Juan de la Marca discovered, while conducting a census in Sabirochqui, that women were hiding their children because they feared that the Franciscans intended to remove them to the mission at San Tadeo.[29]

A serious threat to the early eighteenth-century mission campaign arose in the form of a rebellion organized by the headman Ignacio Torote in 1737. The spark that ignited this uprising may have come from Torote's father, Fernando Torote, whom the historian Izaguirre implicates in the 1724 martyrdom of Padre Fernando de San José. "From that year of 1724 when Torote stopped being a good Christian, newly thinking of his ancient liberties and the prospect of having more than one wife . . . he propagandized against the missionary fathers among his kin, trying to sow discord in the field of their teachings."[30]

His lessons took root in his son Ignacio. First he organized the killing of a novice monk and several Indian converts in Catalipango, then he attacked the mission at Sonomoro, killing three priests, a novice, and some Indian converts. When asked by the dying Fray Manuel Bajo why he felt compelled to engage in such treachery, Ignacio is said to have responded: "Because you and yours are killing us every day with your sermons and catechisms, taking away our liberty."[31]

The Spanish carried out reprisals with vigor. Although Ignacio Torote never fell into their hands, three Indians were executed at Eneno and their severed heads and hands placed on forest trails where they would be seen by other Asháninkas.[32] Amich reports that when the accused rebels were interrogated, they declared that Torote and his supporters killed the priests because "they continually admonished them to live as good Christians, they ordered them to attend catechism classes and kneel during Mass, and finally, because they prohibited them from marrying many women and from stealing the tools in the convent."[33]

Why did the Asháninka resist the missions so resolutely? After all, the actual area controlled by the missions of the late seventeenth and early eighteenth centuries was small—so small, in fact, that the historian Jay Lehnertz observes a process of "progressive encystment" among the Franciscan settlements of the 1720s and 1730s.[34] The number of Indians who lived for extended periods of time in the missions was equally modest. Lehnertz reports that the largest number of residents for the nine missions of the *conversión* of Tarma occurred in 1718, when there were 1,287 resident Indians. (This figure apparently includes significant numbers of Quechua Indian residents brought from the highlands to provide military security and expertise in essential crafts.) Figures for later years are considerably lower, reaching as few as 605 in 1730.[35] Mission records suggest that within this population there was considerable turnover. Many more Indians may have had direct contact with stations, at least for brief periods, than the census would imply, but few were thoroughly integrated into the mission world.

The incessant admonitions of the Franciscans about polygyny were, as we have mentioned, a recurrent source of conflict, especially since the men most likely to have several wives were local caciques. Presumably the priests attempted to interfere with the activities of shamans and other practitioners of traditional religion, which also would have nettled the Indians.

Probably more significant, however, was the association of mission outposts with disease. The Indian population of the Eneno mission, for instance, fell from 800 to 220 as the result of a major epidemic in 1722–1723, though it is unclear how much of this rapid decline is attributable to defections rather than disease-related deaths.[36] Franciscan chroniclers record the absolute terror of Asháninkas in the face of epidemics—a terror that seemed incomprehensible to the Spaniards, who themselves were relatively immune to the illnesses. Speaking of a smallpox epidemic that seized the Santa Cruz de Sonomoro mission in 1673, Izaguirre writes:

> *This event always repeats itself in cases of epidemics among the natives: they have no resistance to the horror that comes upon them with death's siege. On these occasions they forget their Christian obligations, they leave charity aside, they forsake the infirm, and they take care only to avoid the plague.[37]*

The Indians who overcame their well-founded fear of plagues to live in the mission stations, even for short periods, discovered themselves subject to an alien discipline. For the Franciscans, a rigid division of time and labor was spiritually liberating; for Asháninkas, it negated the essence of Amazonian life—which, if it did not allow for material plenty, did provide a fluid, constantly changing panorama of activities underwritten by a high degree of personal liberty. One has only to look at the guidelines for the "politico-religious organization of the conversions" to sense the collision of cultures:

> *20. At five-thirty and six in the morning the bell will be rung and at the sound everyone will go to the door of their house or some other visible point to sing the Ave Marias.*
>
> *21. Then everyone, men and women, will put on their church clothes and meet in the temple. The Father will have them pray the compendium of Christian doctrine in their langauge, and on Thursdays and Sundays in Spanish . . .*
>
> *24. The following custom will be promoted: that the Indians will pay an evening visit to the priest, who will join them in sitting in the fresh air for awhile. After they have retired, the priest will walk around the plaza and through the streets, accompanied by his native assistants; then the bell for silence will be*

sounded in an opportune manner, Sundays and feast days at 10 pm.[38]

Small wonder that the rate of "apostasy," as measured by the number of Indians fleeing the missions, was so high. In reply to queries about the motives behind his flight, an Indian told Fray Simón de Jesús in 1737 that he ran away "so as not to endure many things such as asking permission all the time for every little thing . . . and not to suffer my children being taken away by the priests such as you, so that I have no company when I walk in the forest because my children are in the convent."[39]

This assertion of control over children and, indeed, over entire families, who were sometimes moved from one settlement to another for the Franciscans' purposes, may well have been the most oppressive aspect of the mission experience from the Asháninka point of view. The records of the eighteenth-century missions of the central jungle are remarkably silent about excesses of corporal punishment such as Franciscans are known to have imposed on Indians in California and Mexico, but one must assume that such cases occurred and that they contributed to Asháninka unrest. Although Asháninkas hardly qualify as pacifists, systematic corporal punishment, especially accompanied by public humiliation, is not known to have existed in their society. Jay Lehnertz mentions the case of the cacique Mateo de Assia, who was ordered by a Franciscan to whip an Asháninka guilty of maintaining more than one wife. De Assia refused and was then subjected to a flogging himself. That experience, and the loss of five of his children in the epidemic of 1737, turned the cacique against the missionaries. In 1742 he was one of the first to join the major uprising that began in the Gran Pajonál.[40]

Another factor that is only touched upon in the early mission records is the Franciscans' use of other Indian groups as guides during *entradas* into Asháninka country. The warlike Conibos, whose territory during the seventeenth century was apparently the upper reaches of the Río Ucayali, supported Franciscans on their explorations of the Ríos Perené, Tambo, and Ene. Father Huerta, for instance, notes in his description of an 1686 expedition: "On the second day of the *entrada* into the Ene, we came ashore to shelter ourselves from the sun; following some human footprints for a short stretch, the [Conibos] came upon some Campa houses and, after surrounding them, they sacked the settlement, kidnapping women and children and taking whatever else was there." Stefano Varese argues that some Franciscans favored the use of Conibo mercenaries in an aggressive campaign of missionary conquest until their plans were dashed by a Conibo revolt in the 1690s.[41]

Finally, one should not discount the hostility generated by Spanish freebooters, such as Pedro Bohórquez, who used missionary outposts for ends that had little to do with the conversion of infidels. Alluding to this problem, Padre Amich complains that "the frequent stories that Salt Mountain was filled with gold deposits awoke at this time the greed of some Spaniards, instigated by the common enemy [presumably Satan] to destroy the work of those who labored in the vineyard of the Lord."[42] Here Amich plaintively echoes the charge, brought by Catholic missionaries throughout the New World, that the fealty the Church hoped to gain through Christian love was lost to the greed of impious settlers.

One disruptive influence rarely explored in studies of the social milieu of the central jungle is the presence of escaped Indians from the highlands of Huánuco, Tarma, Jauja, and Huanta, widely known as *retirados*. In 1691, several highland Indians testified that two substantial towns of *retirados* existed in the jungle. Indeed, a community called Pucutuguaru was rumored to be populated by more than six thousand highland Indians. In 1738, Franciscan travelers encountered a community of two score highland apostates in the jungle—"very lazy people, and as ugly of appearance as of deed."[43] Even if colonial documents exaggerate the numerical significance of these communities of runaways, the contact between jungle

Indians and highlanders who had direct experience of Spanish cruelty may have contributed to Asháninka restiveness.

After putting down the rebellion of Ignacio Torote in 1737, the Franciscans had reason to hope for a period of peace in which they could win Indian souls. In late May of 1742, however, the Asháninka residents of missions along the Río Perené suddenly gathered their things and walked away. When asked by the friars why they were leaving, the Indians replied that they were traveling to the Gran Pajonál to see a Lord Inca who had come to a place called Quisopango, near the Río Simaqui. Under the protection of the local cacique, Mateo Santabangori, this Inca was holding court and promising to lead the Indians in the creation of a new world order.

The first written reports of the messiah's message came in early June of 1742. A friar from the mission of San Tadeo, Santiago Vázquez de Caicedo, traveled to Quisopango to meet this mysterious Inca, whom the Indians called Juan Santos Atahualpa Apu-Inca Huayna Capac:[44]

When I entered the village . . . I found myself among a multitude of Indians standing in a semicircle. I said, "Ave Maria," and they replied, "Conceived without sin." At the moment when I asked, "Where is the Inca?" in the Ande tongue, they closed the circle about me. Then they grabbed me, took from me my baculum and the crucifix of chonta wood that I carried in my hand. Then the Inca arrived . . . He greeted me and I him, and the first question he asked me was this: "How long has it been since our Redemptor died?" I answered him. I asked him his name, which he gave me, then I asked if he were a Christian and he responded that he was . . . I told him to recite the Creed, and he responded: "Creo inunum Deum, etc." After all this he told me to be seated, gave me something to eat, and then said that since 1740 he had been ready to come but that God had not given him license and that this year God had given him such license and that he comes to organize his kingdom.[45]

The messiah explained to the astonished priest that "the viceroy had best let him take possession of his kingdoms, because if he refused he and his son would have their necks broken like pullets."[46] Furthermore, he intended to secure his empire with the assistance of "his kinsmen," the English, who would attack by sea. His desire was to see the friars sent back to Spain where they belonged, after which the sons of Incas would be ordained as priests; the only Spaniards allowed to proselytize in the new kingdom would be Jesuits.

The audience ended, Padre Vázquez hastened back to his mission to write a report for his superiors. Close at the heels of this account came the testimony of two blacks, El Congo and Francisco, who staggered into the Pichana mission with a tale of their own encounter with the Quisopango messiah. Among the information revealed to them was that Juan Santos hailed from Cuzco, that he had traveled to "Angola and the Congos," and that his goal was not to replace Christianity but to give control of it to the Indians. He chewed coca leaf, which he insisted was an "herb of God and not one of sorcerers as the whites said."[47]

The testimony of these witnesses convinced the Spanish authorities that a serious threat to their tenuous control had arisen in the Pajonál. This challenge had to be confronted, presumably by means of military force, before the hundreds of Indians converging on Quisopango in canoes and on foot could coalesce into an organized fighting force. Events soon revealed the situation to be far more perilous to Spanish rule than even the most pessimistic observers had feared.

Return of Lord Inca

His body is about the size of Manuel Grande (this being a corpulent Negro who was given as an offering by a benefactor in Lima, to accompany the missionary fathers as a slave on our missions to the infidels); said Indian is much loved; he has hair on his arms, but only a slight moustache, which appears closely trimmed: his beard is about three fingers long: he has an attractive face . . . [H]is skin is a light brown color: his hair is cut off in front above his eyebrows, while the hair in back is tied; dressed in a painted cushma or cotton tunic, he has at his side and at his command the following nations: the cañibos, setibos, jitipos, simirinchis, pautiques, comarosquis, saviroquis: all the people of these missions and those of Huancabamba.[1]

This passage, taken from the report of Fray Santiago Vázquez de Caicedo to his superior, Fray Joseph Gil Muñoz, is the most detailed physical description we have of a man who came to be known to the Spanish world as Juan Santos Atahualpa, Lord Inca—or more bluntly, "the Indian Rebel."

Juan Santos, a wanderer from the Andes, proclaimed a spiritual message that in short order led Asháninkas and neighboring peoples to abandon Franciscan missions and begin active resistance to Spanish control. Juan Santos's message, to the extent that we know it, was nativistic in emphasis. He sought the removal of Spaniards from Peru and the reestablishment of an Indian civilization, over which he was to reign as monarch. As we have seen, a vigorous tradition of Asháninka rebellion had taken root long before Juan Santos's appearance. What remains mysterious about his movement is why this new gospel—which in its allusions to the Inca empire was as alien to Asháninka political practice as the teachings of the Franciscans—appealed to Asháninkas at all. Did Juan Santos somehow mobilize a preexisting belief in world renewal? Or did he himself lay the foundation for what was to become a robust millennial tradition? Whatever the answer to these questions, we know that the events he set in motion vexed several viceroys and the Franciscan hierarchy for more than half a century. More important, this explosive reaction to colonization became the symbolic template for recurrent outbreaks of millennial enthusiasm among Asháninkas in the nineteenth and twentieth centuries.

The Marqués de Villa García, Viceroy of Peru, was disturbed by reports of the appearance of a new Lord Inca in Quisopango. The disruption of Franciscan missions among the jungle tribes was trouble enough, but the message of Juan Santos was also directed to millions of highland Indians. The prosperity of Spanish settlers and the stability of the colony depended on the labor of Indians in fields and mines. A general uprising would leave the Spanish outnumbered and vulnerable in their frontier outposts.

Writing to the king, Villa García explained that "there has introduced himself into the forests of the Andes an Indian who, calling himself Inca, intends to crown himself King, saying that he would restore his ancient Empire . . . and with this purpose he has obtained the allegiance of some barbarians and caused a commotion among Indians now converted to the faith."[2] The viceroy appropriated six thousand pesos and authorized the distribution of firearms and powder from the royal armory in Lima. Don Benito Troncoso and don Pedro Francisco Arostegui, both holding the title of frontier governor, were charged with the task of employing "the most rapid and opportune means to bring peace to this movement through the apprehension of said Indian."[3] At the same time, the viceroy authorized the creation of a rearguard force to prevent the spread of any "spark of restlessness" from jungle to sierra.

Troncoso led his expeditionary force to Sonomoro in September of 1742. The first serious Spanish casualties had already occurred when Indian bowmen killed some Franciscans repairing a bridge on the Perené. Rather than wait for a second force under the leadership of Pedro Milla, which was to arrive through Quimirí, Troncoso pushed directly on toward Quisopango, where Juan Santos was said to have constructed a small fortress. In Sonomoro, Troncoso found local Indian support: a converted cacique named Bartolomé Quintimari provided a party of Asháninka fighters. The Spanish took Quisopango, killing Santabangori, the headman who had welcomed Juan Santos to the Pajonál. Juan Santos himself was nowhere to be found.

Meanwhile, the fate of Milla's party set the pattern for subsequent campaigns against the new Lord Inca. There were frustrating delays in organizing the expedition. Once the troops arrived at Salt Mountain, they were winnowed by sickness, dulled by sinking morale, and harassed by stealthy Indians who never seemed to engage the Spanish in a fair fight on open ground. Milla decided to move toward his rendezvous with Troncoso in Sonomoro. But the Indians were now organized: at every step of the trail there was a new ambush. Milla's retreat was cut off. By the time the men fought their way back to Salt Mountain and Quimirí, almost all had been wounded.

The rainy season of late 1742–early 1743 belonged to the rebels. In August of 1743, the dry season, Juan Santos took control of the Quimirí mission after letting the resident Franciscan evacuate to Chanchamayo. Amich reports that the Inca arrived with "two thousand Indians of various nations," a number which, if accurate, represents an astonishing fighting force for peoples whose traditional aggregations rarely numbered in the hundreds. A message arrived in Chanchamayo to the effect that Juan Santos meant no harm to his highland children. With this news, the highlanders "held great feasts, dances, and drinking bouts, celebrating like the *chunchos* the arrival of their Inca."[4]

The viceroy and his advisors decided that Quimirí should be retaken and fortified as a staging area for a final assault on the infidels. They also hoped that the fort would check the movement of spies and agitators into the highlands. The Corregidor of Tarma, General Alfonso Santa y Ortega, was made commander of the expedition. Frontier Governor Benito Troncoso, veteran of the first foray into rebel territory, was also dispatched to the region.

The disastrous second campaign that began in October 1743 is documented in a diary apparently kept by Benito Troncoso's secretary. En route from Acobamba to Oxapampa, Troncoso's small army is deserted by the Huarochirí Indians who handle baggage transport. The troops toil down the difficult trail on foot, complaining of inadequate rations and suffering under torrential rains. A soldier seriously injures his leg in a fall, "and everyone is moved to pity by such cries of pain, all for wanting to remain mounted on his mule in the dangerous parts of the trail."[5] Morale is bad, discipline increasingly frayed. Above a place called Naranjuyo they find the corpse of a settler named Suárez who has evidently been killed by Indians. The priest administers the sacrament of final absolution to the gathered troops.

Troncoso's secretary records the interrogation of Indians

whom the soldiers capture as they near rebel territory. One is a chuncho from Quimirí named Simonga Baquero, who refuses to talk "either because he is a great brute or a great dog." A highland captive, Pedro Pulipunche, proves more garrulous. He describes the rebel's resources, which now include firearms taken during the pillage of Suárez's hacienda. Plans are afoot for the fortification of Quimirí against Spanish attack. The rebels have contacts with highland Indians in Jauja and a network of spies everywhere. Juan Santos's followers include a group of fifty-two highland wives and widows led by a black woman, the former slave of doña Ana of Tarma. The Inca wants the Franciscans to be replaced by Jesuits, with whom he is prepared to sue for peace. The Simirinchis who killed Suárez adorn their necklaces with his teeth. When the Rebel is convulsed by anger, "they say that the earth shakes from fear."

More suspects fall into Spanish hands. A black named Simón tries to convince General Santa that a large force of rebel Indians awaits the Spanish in Quimirí. But the Spanish speculate that this is part of a campaign of disinformation undertaken by Juan Santos's spies. Two Indians report that Juan Santos has a "minister," a 130-year-old Indian from Huamanga, whom the Lord Inca treats with deference. Juan Santos wears the insignia of the Inca royal family, calls himself don Juan Santos Huaynacapac Apu-Inca, and lives the life of an ascetic: eating little, chewing only modest amounts of coca, and avoiding contact with women. He tells his followers that success is inevitable thanks to the support of "my Lord Jesus Christ and his Most Holy Mother, because now is the time that the Empire of our Inca will be restored to us."[6]

On the twelfth day of the expedition the troops make contact with rebel forces. A mixed group of highland and jungle Indians appears. The Spaniards charge. Indians melt into the forest as the Spanish explode grenades and shout "Long live the King of Spain!" The Spanish enter Quimirí without opposition. It appears that the expedition will be a stunning success.

The Spanish begin to fortify Quimirí and to lure back the residents of the community with offers of food and promises of amnesty. Sundry bits of intelligence about the rebels sift into the camp from soldiers out sweeping the forest for Indians. But discipline continues to deteriorate: one soldier kills another with a saber. Worse still, the news arrives that a rebel force under the command of Antonio Gatica and others has taken the settlement of Huancabamba with a force of 150 chunchos and highland Indians. Gatica and his men see to it that Juan Santos enters the village with all the pomp of an Inca lord. It is said that the rebel force numbers as many as 500.

On November 8, General Santa departs for Tarma, leaving Captain Fabricio Bartoli in command of a force of ninety-six men. Troncoso and his secretary leave shortly thereafter. The Quimirí fort is provisioned with four small and four large cannons, 3,464 lead bullets for rifles and cannon shot, various containers of gunpowder, three full boxes of grenades plus one already opened, and instructions to send a message to Tarma if reinforcements are needed.

Here the useful information in the diary of Troncoso's secretary ends, save for his notation, approximately a week after his departure from Quimirí, of the "funereal and horrible news" of a new series of rebel attacks.

The Indians had delivered the Spanish a devastating setback. A mule train bringing supplies to the Quimirí fort was seized by the rebels, leaving seventeen dead. The Indians then laid siege to Bartoli's troops in the fortress. Descriptions of the siege vary in significant details, but most agree that Juan Santos offered Bartoli and his men a truce so that they could retreat from Quimirí to Tarma.[7] Expecting Troncoso to deliver on his promise of reinforcements at any moment, Bartoli stood firm.

Sometime between November 24, when Padre Lorenzo

Núñez arrived in Tarma with news of the attack, and January 3, 1744, when the rescue expedition of Benito Troncoso found itself blocked at the Río Chanchamayo by constant fire from Indians and blacks wearing armor and clothing that could only have come from the troops in Quimirí, Bartoli and his men were overrun and killed. Troncoso's secretary concludes his lugubrious diary with the news that the Quimirí corpses lack heads "because the chunchos cook them and eat them."[8] The news of the massacre caused panic in Tarma, as settlers feared that an assault on the highlands was now imminent.

Stung by the appalling failure of the Spanish campaigns and weakened by advancing age, the viceroy fell back on a dilatory policy of cutting off supplies to the rebels. The government prohibited traffic in axes and knives but undertook no new punitive expeditions. "I would consider that to repeat these forays into the jungle would be to consume men, arms, and wealth without utility," Villa García wrote to the king on August 16, 1744. The problem, he explained, was the elusiveness of the Spaniards' adversary:

In that jungle reside the Indians, more like wild beasts than rational beings; there they maintain themselves by fishing and hunting, without joining together in civil company, here scattered in low dwellings that they make from trees on a site that seems right to them, and they move at their fancy; they mock great force through their flight, because there isn't a river, no matter how swift, that they can't swim across like fishes, nor jungle, no matter how great or tangled, that they can't penetrate like wild animals; and they themselves find the most pleasurable foods in the vermin, vipers, and filthy animals that abound there; and all they plant, by clearing a little of the forest, is the seed of maize and other roots that there are called yucas, which serve as their bread; there they have weapons in the very trees, from which they fashion their arrows and clubs or spears that they make from chonta, which is a hard and heavy wood, capable of considerable sharpness, that they use with agility and dexterity; they dress in no other clothes than a spreading garment that they call cushma, which covers their entire body and which they make from the great quantities of cotton produced there . . . [I]nvading the barbarians in the jungle would be the same as wanting to punish or capture the beasts of the forest, where nature itself has given them unconquerable protection. . . .

In this same letter the viceroy went on to describe the rebel leader:

The Indian introduced with the title of Inca, according to the news obtained from those who spoke with and saw him in Quimirí, is an imposter who persuades the barbarians that he can dominate the elements; that those who pursue him invariably perish; that he can transform stones into gold and precious metals; that the earth trembles before his Empire because he was sent from the Heavens to establish the reign of the Incas and expel the Spaniards; and he has acquired their obeisance through these falsehoods.[9]

The viceroy authorized a diplomatic mission by the Jesuits to see whether Juan Santos would make good on his promise to allow the Society of Jesus to catechize in the area formerly controlled by Franciscans. Two Jesuits apparently entered the jungle in 1745 to talk with rebel leaders, but the details of the negotiations are shrouded in mystery. All that is known is that the priests returned to Lima without wringing any concessions from Juan Santos. Persistent attempts to persuade Asháninka caciques to betray Juan Santos—to which there are repeated, if veiled, allusions in colonial correspondence—proved equally fruitless.

In July of 1745, the octogenarian Villa García was replaced as viceroy by José Antonio Manso de Velasco, Count of Superunda, one of whose mandates was to put down the jungle rebellion as swiftly as possible. But ambition occluded his tactical judgment: early in 1746, forces totaling more than eight hundred men, led by General José de Llamas and the indefatigable Benito Troncoso, attempted a rainy-season march on rebel territory. Mud, rain, disease, and hunger staged a frontal assault on the expedition, to which occasional skirmishes with hostile Indians added only a demoralizing undercurrent. The campaign ended in total failure.

Meanwhile, Juan Santos mounted an audacious daylight attack on the settlement of Monobamba, located in the province of Jauja, in which at least thirty-two people were killed. Whatever reaction Viceroy Manso may have had to the disastrous direction of the struggle against the rebels is lost in the flurry of correspondence surrounding a major earthquake that ripped Lima apart in late October of 1746. Following the earthquake, the sea rose and swept away much of the port of Callao and its inhabitants. The tidal wave destroyed or tossed ashore the ships anchored in Callao harbor.

The next four years passed without major gains by either side. The Franciscans attempted a peaceful reconquest by dispatching groups of friars to the rebel-held zone. One group, entering through Huanta, was massacred near the Río Mantaro; a second commission, which succeeded in establishing direct contact with Juan Santos, returned safely but without effecting any change in the situation. In 1750, highland rebellions in Huarochirí, Lambayeque, and Canta, as well as a conspiracy in Lima, lent credence to Juan Santos's claims of an approaching pan-Indian revolt against the Spanish. Yet unlike the tenacious rebellion in the jungle, these uprisings were put down with brutal efficiency.

Studies of Juan Santos Atahualpa have been frustrated by the small number of documents containing firsthand information about him and the social movement he engendered. After hostilities began in earnest, of course, communication between the forces of the Indian Rebel and the Spanish was necessarily limited. Although there was a lively traffic in stories about Juan Santos among Spanish colonial officials, few of these tales are reliable. Documents suggest that the Rebel sent letters or communiqués to colonial authorities, but their whereabouts are unknown. Twentieth-century Peruvian scholarship has tended to portray him as a nationalist hero who struck one of the first major blows for Peruvian independence. Historians with a populist bent see him as an early practitioner of *fidelismo*, Fidel Castro's guerrilla war against colonial oppression. Thus while eighteenth-century sources depict him as a heretic and imposter, twentieth-century hagiography makes Juan Santos out to be "a superior man, endowed with great intelligence and verbal facility; in addition to Quechua, Spanish, and Latin, which he already spoke, he rapidly assimilated French and English, which permitted him to undertake conversations with the English, then at war with Spain."[10] But Juan Santos's goals, both political and religious, shared little in common with the vision of republican Peru or with the radical left of the twentieth century.

Such evidence as exists tells us the following. Juan Santos, who most likely came from the imperial city of Cuzco, arrived in the Gran Pajonál accompanied by a Simirinchi (Piro) cacique named Bisabequí. What brought him to this remote site is unclear, but the anthropologist Stefano Varcsc argues that Quisopango was appropriate for his purposes, first, because it was distant from Spanish military control, and second, because there lived in this community several Asháninka families who had been forcibly relocated there by the Franciscans and who therefore harbored rebellious thoughts.[11]

There is little doubt that Juan Santos was formally educated, probably in a Jesuit seminary in Cuzco. Most scholars believe he was attached to a Jesuit priest as a servant or novice. He may well have traveled to Europe, and his revolutionary ideas seem to have been inspired by a visit to Catholic missions in Africa, where black priests had to some extent been integrated into missionary activities.

It is said that his arrival in the jungle was the result of flight from criminal prosecution in Cuzco, perhaps for the murder of his Jesuit master, a theory that receives no support from written records. Juan Santos claimed to be working in concert with the English. An attack by English Vice Admiral George Anson on the coastal city of Paita late in 1741 lent credence to his assertions, yet no historian has shown that the English were co-conspirators in the jungle rebellion.[12] One less than credible account finds the awakening of Juan Santos's rebellious impulses in a conversation he overheard between two Jesuits. The priests passed him as he dozed on a bench, when one cleric remarked to the other: "Look here at who owns the kingdom of Peru, since there are no others closer in line to the Inca; this one will rise up with his kingdom some day." Juan Santos is said to have thought, "Then I shall have my kingdom, we'll see, we'll see."[13] Finally, there circulated stories that he had been traveling throughout the highlands since 1729 or 1730 to plot his rebellion with local caciques. As Varese points out, this would imply that he began to lay plans for a revolt at about the age of eighteen, even before his trip to Europe and Africa.[14]

What did Juan Santos himself set forth as his goals? He aimed foremost to expel the Spaniards and their black slaves from Peru. Then he would restore the Inca kingship, with himself as its head by right of inheritance and divine will. The Indians would propagate their own Christianity. The empire would unify Peru's Indian peoples and put an end to the abuses of Spanish overlords.

Most Peruvian historians have assumed that the messiah's vision of the movement was shared completely by his tribal followers. Yet there are hints that the jungle peoples who rallied to Juan Santos's cause were less enthusiastic about the prospects for Christian renewal than was the messiah himself. The testimony of the two blacks, El Congo and Francisco, includes the observation that the "Amajes, Andes, Conibos, Sepibos, and Simirinchis" who rendered obedience to Juan Santos shouted that "they wanted no priests, that they did not want to be Christians," all the while trying to persuade Juan Santos that the captive blacks should be killed. But we are told that "the Inca opposed all this and spoke to them in reprimands; the Indians, both Christians and infidels, do much dancing and they are quite content with their new king."[15]

One of the ironies of modern Peruvian historiography about Juan Santos is that although he is celebrated as a nationalist hero, commentators go to great lengths to portray him as respectful of the Catholic faith. Francisco Loayza, for instance, seeds his useful compendium of colonial documents related to the rebellion with terse footnotes casting doubt on any assertion that Juan Santos held to heretical beliefs or, worse still, that he participated in the desecration of churches or chapels, as the Franciscans alleged upon occasion.[16] Acknowledging that the Rebel may have deviated from Catholic orthodoxy at times, historian Mario Castro Arenas rationalizes his excesses: "There is the possibility that Juan Santos, in his zeal to spread the social-religious content of his message, departs from orthodoxy, perhaps more in the interests of popularization than in order to pervert the sacred texts."[17]

Yet from an anthropological perspective it is hard to imagine that such a movement would not deviate substantially from Catholic orthodoxy. Few of the values of the Franciscans would have been reconcilable with those of Juan Santos's Asháninka or Piro followers. Juan Santos tried to curb the anticlerical enthusiasm of the Indian rebels, but to make his message meaningful to them he would have had to adapt it to the prevailing world view. In any event, what the Indians heard Juan Santos saying may have been quite different from the views of the messiah himself. Given the cultural gulf between the highland leader and his Amazonian followers, it could hardly have been otherwise.

Did Juan Santos's persuasive power depend on his familiarity with Amazonian shamanism, as some have suggested?[18] Although Juan Santos came to be identified with culture heroes or even with deities in Indian thought, it seems unlikely that he could have acquired the appropriate shamanistic skills as soon as he arrived in the Gran Pajonál. Reports circulating during the rebellion state that Juan Santos spoke Asháninka and possibly Piro, but it is inconceivable that in his first encounters he could marshal the sophisticated linguistic abilities and esoteric knowledge demonstrated by all Asháninka shamans.

Ethnographic research among modern-day Asháninkas reveals that Inca—a figure presumably derived from the society of the same name—is held to be a powerful, revitalizing personage, though we cannot know whether such a belief existed in the eighteenth century and allowed Juan Santos to establish his ascendancy. We are left with the likelihood that Asháninkas imposed their own meaning on the message of Juan Santos, a meaning that overlapped sufficiently with that of the messiah for them to make common cause against the Spanish.

When searching for sources of the messianic and millennial ideology behind Asháninka support for Juan Santos, we should not ignore the contribution of Franciscan missionaries. The historian John Leddy Phelan has demonstrated that there were strong millennial tendencies—which Phelan calls a form of "apocalyptical mysticism"—within the Franciscan order, especially in the New World. These currents came from the twelfth-century abbot Joachim de Fiore, whose prophecies underwent a revival among Franciscans in the sixteenth and seventeenth centuries, among them the influential Franciscan historian Gerónimo de Mendieta (1525–1604).[19] Some Franciscans of an apocalyptic inclination proposed that human history could be divided into three ages: the Age of the Father, corresponding to the Old Testament world; the Age of the Son, that is, the Christian era; and the Age of the Holy Spirit, which would arrive with a universal spiritual cleansing. In the Age of the Holy Spirit, the just would assume a spiritual existence in which all their needs were satisfied.[20]

Debates about the moral significance of the New World and its peoples turned on the question of the special nature of Indians. For some commentators, the nakedness that characterized Indians in tropical regions was evidence of the Indians' essential innocence. The discovery of humans who seemed to lack the European obsession with power and property fueled utopian dreams among Old World philosophers such as Thomas More. Spaniards of a utopian persuasion saw the importation of Old World vices as the corruption of a pure realm, a belief that propelled them into conflicts with Spain's secular authorities.

The saint who best represented the utopian strain of Franciscan thought in the New World was Francisco Solano (1549–1610), canonized in 1726. A portrait of San Francisco Solano in the Franciscan monastery of Los Descalzos in Lima depicts the monk stepping on a Spanish soldier while receiving the Inca crown from one of the cherubim. The saint was noted both for his prodigious ability to convert Indians and for his public denunciation of the moral depravity of Spanish society in Peru.[21] In the pose of crushing Spanish decadence with his foot, San Francisco Solano inverts common depictions of Santiago Mataindios ("Saint James Indian-killer"), conventionally shown on horseback crushing Incas.[22]

Although it seems likely that some of the Franciscans who catechized among the Ashaninkas would have seen their missions as an opportunity to create an other-worldly spirituality that would survive the divine destruction of Spanish society, we know little about the content of early Franciscan teaching in the Perené missions. Nevertheless, it is hard to imagine that elements of Franciscan apocalyptic mysticism would have failed to cross the cultural barrier between Spanish priest and Ashaninka flock. Ashaninkas then reshaped this millennial principle to meet the needs of their own situation.

One curious feature of Juan Santos Atahualpa's movement is the shifting place of blacks in the rebellion's ideology and tactics. All initial reports of the Rebel's message stress the strong antiblack sentiment of Juan Santos and his Indian followers. Francisco and El Congo were terrorized by Asháninkas and escaped only through the direct intervention of Juan Santos. The messiah himself expressed disdain for blacks: "He calls all the Indians to him, as we said, but not negroes or Spaniards, all of whom are thieves who have taken his crown away."[23] The reasons for the hostility are obvious: black slaves were used by the Franciscans as enforcers of order in the mission frontier. In some cases, armed blacks served as the first line of defense in case of Indian attack. A black named Antonio Gatica, for example, entered the Pajonál with the cacique Mateo de Assia in 1729 in order to establish missionary contact with groups there; Gatica is praised in later documents for rounding up thirty-six relatives of Ignacio Torote after the 1737 massacre at Sonomoro.[24] He had earlier survived a 1719 ambush by Indian bowmen at a place called Caco, near Metraro.[25]

Soon after Juan Santos began to hold forth in Quisopango, however, Gatica turned up as one of the messiah's right-hand men, perhaps the most effective military leader of the rebel movement but only one of several blacks who played an important part in the struggle. At least some blacks were able to persuade Juan Santos and the Indians that it was in their interest to allow renegade slaves to join the rebellion. To some extent they had already become part of Asháninka society: by the 1740s, many blacks had married Asháninka women, thus forging family links with mission Indians. The Franciscan historian Antonine Tibesar reports that Antonio Gatica, for instance, was married to Margarita Appiñur, the sister of the cacique Mateo de Assia. Gatica was one of five blacks at the Eneno mission who had married into Indian families by 1735.[26]

In view of his negative opinion of slaves, it is ironic that Juan Santos's exposure to Catholic missions in black Africa may have been the catalyst for his vision of Indian autonomy. "He says that he was in and comes from Angola and from the Congos . . . and he has seen among the blacks some black priests, with long beards, saying the Mass, and although they aren't whites like the Spaniards they can just as well be fathers and priests."[27] Although Juan Santos saw blacks as an oppressed people who had taken charge of Christian worship in their native land, he also had to contend with their role as occasional killers of Indians. It was probably the tactical skills of blacks such as Antonio Gatica that convinced Juan Santos to put aside his prejudices and welcome them to the rebellion. He could ill afford to spurn their knowledge of Spanish weapons and fighting techniques.

The forces of Juan Santos began to move again in 1751, directing their attacks up the Río Sonomoro. By 1752, according to anthropologist Stefano Varese, all of the traditional territory of the Asháninka, Piro, and Yanesha peoples had been returned to native control.[28]

Shadowing soldiers who had evacuated the Sonomoro fortress for the highland community of Andamarca, the rebel army moved at a steady pace into the mountains in August of 1752. The small settlements of Ata and Runatullo fell into the hands of Juan Santos. Officers of the local militia dispatched hasty messages pleading for reinforcements to the Corregidor of Jauja, the Marqués of Cassatorres, but the Spanish made only feeble efforts to mount a credible defense.

Gathered in the outskirts of Andamarca, the rebels sent a messenger named Domingo Guatay to offer the town's defenders terms of a peaceful surrender. The offer was rejected and, some witnesses reported, Domingo Guatay avoided being shot at close range only by skillfully dodging the musket blast at the last instant. The army of chunchos—again estimated by witnesses as ranging in size from 700 to 2,000—advanced on the town. But then, possibly through the intervention of a rebel spy named Juan Campos, a leader among the defense forces, the people of Andamarca threw down their arms and joined the ranks of the insurgents. "They kissed the hands and feet of the Rebel, who was distinguished by the two cushmas that he wore, a black one underneath and a red one on top, by a band encircling his head, and by the sandals on his feet," reported a witness named Juan Bautista Coronado in later testimony.[29] "It is our Inca," the highlanders were said to have shouted.[30]

The occupation of Andamarca lasted only three days. The rebels imprisoned the two resident priests; sources disagree about whether the rebels were responsible for the burning of a chapel. The disgruntled clerics described the teachings of Juan Santos as including the blasphemous declaration that "he is the Holy Spirit, that only he has power in America, over which he is the absolute God." Even worse, he claimed that whereas Jesus was a sinner, "the God Inca, although a man, has not sinned. He denies the Most Holy Mary and says that he is the son of the Virgin Zapa Coya."[31] The rebels took what supplies they could from the town and made their way back to the jungle. The Spanish rescue mission arrived in time to capture two alleged spies, who were taken to Jauja and summarily hanged.[32]

One of the great mysteries of the rebellion is why the 1752 incursion into the highlands of Andamarca—perhaps the boldest campaign of the entire uprising—proved to be the last military encounter between Juan Santos and Spanish colonial authorities. Exhausted by the failure of the expensive *entradas* into the jungle, the Spanish resigned themselves to a purely defensive strategy of restricting communication between the jungle and restive highland areas. They seem not to have realized that the rebellion had lost its momentum until 1756, when a small expeditionary force met no opposition on a brief foray to Quimirí.[33] It eventually became clear to the Spanish that the new Lord Inca had disappeared as inexplicably as he had arrived.

What became of Juan Santos? Predictably, there are con-
testing versions of his death. In 1766, a Franciscan heard from
Conibo Indians that Juan Santos had died in Metraro: "Before
them his body disappeared discharging smoke." The Franciscan took this as evidence that Juan Santos was cast into hell
and was therefore horrified when the Conibos insisted that
they were "quite satisfied with the instructions and errors
given to them by their master."[34] Stories circulated that Juan
Santos had become disheartened by his failure to conquer
Peru; suspicious of his subordinate, Antonio Gatica, he had
him poisoned. Juan Santos, the story continues, was later
poisoned himself. A late nineteenth-century expedition reports that Juan Santos died during a drunken Ashaninka feast:
"An Indian vying with Santos, who took part in the fiesta,
in order to ascertain whether he was really the son of the
Divinity, and as a consequence invulnerable, aimed a stone,
hurled with a sling, that wounded him gravely and from
which wound he died."[35]

Slightly more credible are reports of ritual observances
honoring Juan Santos long after his death. During his exploration of the Perené and Tambo rivers in 1876–1877, the engineer Arturo Wertheman was told by Piro informants that
"each year at a fixed time the Campas unite in a village in the
Pajonál with the object of celebrating the military glories of
Santos Atahualpa; with great ceremony they take his sword
out on procession and finish the event with great feasts."[36]
An expedition undertaken in 1891 claimed to have located the
Inca's sepulchre in Metraro, where the natives "celebrate
feasts in homage to the memory of the valiant leader and each
year place a new tunic on the grave."[37]

The legacy of the nativistic passion of Juan Santos was
both practical and symbolic. Although the military threat
posed by the rebels had evaporated by the mid-1750s, the

stinging losses suffered by the Spanish over the previous decade made them reluctant to shift from a defensive posture to an aggressive reconquest of the central jungle. The Franciscan missionary effort had lost its momentum, and requests for increased royal support fell on unsympathetic ears. The Indians remained sullenly unwilling to cooperate with the reestablishment of the lost mission communities. A new rebellion that broke out among the Panoan Indians of the Ucayali in 1766, and which cast its influence as far upriver as the Asháninkas of the Río Tambo, dashed hopes that the power of Juan Santos's teachings was on the wane.[38] "The damages caused by Juan Santos Atahualpa with his rebellion were innumerable," laments the Franciscan friar Dionisio Ortiz. "One of the worst was that the native returned again to his primitive state of fierceness and savagery." Ironically, Fray Ortiz blames the success of the rebellion on the exemplary education that the Franciscans provided the Indian caciques, "who had left the state of savagery and taken advantage of the elements formed by the emissaries of God."[39] The Franciscans were not able to reestablish a stable mission among the Asháninka until the mid-nineteenth century, and in some remote areas such as the Gran Pajonál the mission renaissance did not take place until several decades after this.

The ideological impact of the rebellion is more elusive. Twentieth-century observers of Asháninka life have found few stories about Juan Santos, though there are many versions of a myth about a culture hero named Inca. Most have assumed that these tales are a recent introduction to the vast corpus of Asháninka myth, but when or how they might have arrived is uncertain.

Could Asháninka notions of Inca date from some contact they sustained with the last Inca rulers, who had sought refuge in the eastern jungle after their defeat by the Spanish in the sixteenth century? Writing in 1665, the Franciscan Biedma reported interviewing an Asháninka who told him of a great jungle ruler named Gabeinca or Enim. This Enim recognized as his vassals the Asháninka, Conibo, and many other nations, who paid him tribute in the form of rare feathers and other jungle products.[40] Although there are many reasons to be skeptical of the account's accuracy, it does suggest that Asháninkas had extensive knowledge of Inca pomp and circumstance at a very early point in the history of their contact with Europeans.

Asháninka stories explain that Inca once controlled the creation of all important trade goods: cloth, metal tools, firearms, machinery, and metal cooking pots. According to the stories, through the sinful behavior of the Inca's son, the *viracocha*—Europeans in general, though in this context specifically the Spaniards—emerge from a jungle lake and begin a campaign of extermination against the Asháninka people. The Spanish capture Inca and, in some versions of the story, decapitate him. An Asháninka man from the Río Ene spoke in 1982 of Inca's death: "He was Itomi Pavá, the Son of the Sun. Why did they cut his throat? The *viracochas* grabbed his crown, his clay pots, and his body and took them away."[41] Most versions of the myth conclude by explaining that whites now own Inca's head, which still lives on, providing them with all the valuable goods that Asháninkas lack. The Indians will be rich once again when they regain control of Inca's head, or when a resurrected Inca returns to them.[42]

The Asháninka story of Inca is one refraction of the myth of Inkarrí—"the Inca King"—that is widely distributed throughout the Peruvian Andes and the adjacent jungle regions.[43] It is a myth of loss and return, destruction and renewal. As we shall see, it is woven into the history of Asháninka responses to the ever-increasing power of Europeans. Although Juan Santos is now specifically remembered by few Asháninkas, his uprising was instrumental in bringing the myth of Inkarrí to life and tethering it to concrete acts of resistance.

THREE

Amachénga

The Indian lives without shame, dies
without fear, and eats without repugnance.
H. A. Guillaume, *The Amazon Provinces of
Peru as a Field for European Emigration*,
1888

However bitter the lessons of its history, the Amazon moves
men to dream. By the early nineteenth century, colonists
again began to seek their fortunes in the promising soils of
the Chanchamayo and Perené valleys. Their arrival was eventually to reawaken dreams of spiritual deliverance among
Asháninkas who suffered the brunt of frontier expansion.

To secure a new road between Palca and Chanchamayo and
to protect settlers from Asháninka raids, the Peruvian government built a fort at the junction of the Chanchamayo and
Tulumayo rivers in 1847. The American explorers William
Herndon and Lardner Gibbon, sent by the Department of the
Navy to survey the Amazon, described the fort as a "stock-
ade, embracing about six acres, armed with four brass four-
pounders, and garrisoned with forty-eight men."[1] The site
was called San Ramón.

Asháninkas abandoned the immediate area of San Ramón,
but hostilities simmered at the edges of the settlement's small
zone of control. Herndon and Gibbon observed that the
Indians

*are determined to dispute the passage of the rivers and any attempt
at further conquest. They never show themselves now in person,
but make their presence evident by occasionally setting fire to
the woods and grass on the hill-sides, and discharging their arrows
at any incautious person who may wander too near the banks of
the rivers.*[2]

And dispute the passage of rivers the Asháninkas did, with
extraordinary fcrocity. Nineteenth-century travelers navigat-
ing the Perené's treacherous currents often found themselves
the target of Asháninka arrows en route. Arturo Wertheman
led an expedition down the Perené to the Tambo and Ucayali
in late 1876. Following several preliminary skirmishes with
the Indians, Wertheman faced a fierce assault on the Río
Tambo:

*At the first bend in the river, formed by a tall hill of a conical
shape, various canoes and small rafts approached us, filled with
chunchos, who asked us for axes and knives with an insolence that
soon degenerated to threats. Unfortunately we now had nothing
to give them, and I tried to make them understand that we had lost
everything in the rapids but that on our return we would bring
them what they asked for. They retired for a moment to enter into
consultation. In a little while they returned to follow us, and when
least expected they attacked the raft "Pichincha" and then the
"Prado" with a shower of arrows. The rowers entered into the
panacaris [wooden fortifications on the rafts] before anyone was
wounded. The first wave of arrows was poorly aimed because
of the haste with which it had been launched, but one of them shot
at Captain Tirado from a distance of only four meters; he would
have been run through but for a quick movement that saved him;
the arrow penetrated twelve centimeters in a pine crate made of
two-centimeter-thick boards.*

Despite the withering gunfire laid down by the company's
riflemen, the Asháninkas pressed their attack until they succeeded in boarding one of the group's fortified rafts, whose

occupants repelled them in hand-to-hand combat. Wertheman's expedition finally battled its way out of arrow range. From this distance Wertheman could see his Asháninka adversaries "engaged in savage demonstrations of anger and desperation, throwing their weapons to the ground and hurling cries of despair."[3]

Stalwart Asháninka resistance to travelers such as Wertheman failed to stem the large-scale forces undermining the Indians' isolation and autonomy. Conquest of the jungle was no longer in the hands of missionaries supported in a desultory fashion by detachments of poorly trained soldiers. Now it was driven by powerful economic interests, backed by a state scouring the region for exportable goods and pledged to territorial control. Even the humblest farmer could afford a repeating rifle that gave him a generous advantage in firepower over Indians still equipped with bows and arrows.

In 1891, the Peruvian government placed its hopes of establishing a vigorous agricultural colony along the Perené in the hands of English venture capitalists. The country faced a serious foreign debt problem, for it had financed expensive development projects such as the Lima–La Oroya railway through the sale of bonds to European and North American investors. Peru sought to cancel the debt by ceding 500,000 hectares of land along the Río Perené to the Peruvian Corporation, Ltd., an enterprise formed in London in 1890. The Perené tract encompassed a "zone of twenty kilometers wide on each side of the Río Perené, from its confluence with the Paucartambo up to its navigable point, and another zone equivalent to twenty kilometers on both banks of the Río Ene from its mouth to some twenty kilometers upriver."[4] The British concession, commonly known as the Perené Colony, spearheaded resettlement of the entire valley.

The Perené Colony began to develop its lands in earnest in 1893. The colony's major product was coffee, then fetching a high price on the world market. By 1913 five hundred Asháninkas worked on the plantation. In 1938 the figure was closer to two thousand, if one counted temporary Indian laborers hired for the harvest season.[5] These numbers tell little about the plight of Indians who pushed into more remote areas of the Perené basin rather than endure contact with white settlers.[6] For their part, local officials saw the recruitment of Asháninkas into the plantation labor system as a means of civilizing the natives and curbing their warlike nature.[7]

The Perené Colony was the most orderly effort to settle the region, but piecemeal appropriation of Indian lands quickened elsewhere as well: in the Chanchamayo Valley (where by 1907 there reportedly were 14,000 colonists), along the Apurímac, in the valley of the Pichis, and later near Satipo.[8] Yet the relentless advance of the agricultural frontier was far less dramatic than the explosive growth of rubber tapping that began in the 1870s.

Rubber, a material summoned from plant latex, seems an unlikely candidate for a substance that could transfigure a vast, remote region of the world. The chemist knows it as a polymer of isoprene with unusually large molecules. From the late 1700s, it was used to waterproof clothing, including the familiar Mackintosh. But the discovery of the vulcanization process by Charles Goodyear in 1839, which multiplied the industrial applications of rubber, led to a sharp increase in the price of raw latex, commonly called *caucho* in Spanish. The Brazilian rubber tree, *Hevea brasiliensis*, is the most important latex-bearing species of the South American tropics. Regions endowed with *Hevea* became battlegrounds for hard men determined to make themselves rich by shaping a system of production to meet intense world demand.

For caucho was fragrant with the scent of staggering profits. Latex brought between fifty cents and a dollar a pound on the late-nineteenth-century world market; rubber merchants routinely paid producers less than 10 percent of that.[9]

In a publication designed to induce Englishmen to settle in the Peruvian Amazon, H. A. Guillaume argues that the system of paying workers only a tiny fraction of the market value of their product is "suitable to the Indian, who fears neither hunger nor cold, who does not know what the words *wealth* and *misery* mean, and who only works in order to obtain the object which he has seen," here referring to baubles or household wares.[10]

Despite Guillaume's cheerful belief in the willingness of natives to work as tappers, rubber barons wrestled with chronic labor scarcity. Rubber trees were scattered throughout the forest. Tapping the trees was an arduous and repetitive task, though less unpleasant than the tedious work of curing the latex into transportable bales. Tappers needed hard-won survival skills and a thorough knowledge of the forest. In Peru, the largest pool of potential workers with these qualifications was the Indian population. Yet the nature of the work was irreconcilable with Indian values. Rather than living in settlements enlivened by community rituals and group labor, rubber workers were deployed across the countryside in tapping territories, one per territory. The tapper's life was lonely, repetitive, geared toward production for exchange rather than for use. Why would Indians become citizens of this pitiless empire of labor?

They were rarely given the choice: the rubber barons won their services through a combination of debt servitude and force of arms. Coveted trade goods—firearms, ammunition, coarse cotton cloth, metal pots, decorative trifles—were advanced to the Indians against future caucho production. Merchants fixed the value of the goods and of the latex. Indians never produced enough to cancel the debt. Flight was futile: traders watched the rivers for tappers attempting escape. Punishment for attempted desertion was harsh, sometimes unspeakably brutal.

From a vantage in the late twentieth century, it is hard to understand the savagery of the Amazonian Rubber Boom. Not that brutality is in short supply in our time, of course.

But we maintain the fiction that people enter the rough-and-tumble of commerce through their own free will, not by force. To some extent, this was true of the Rubber Boom. Traders went to great lengths to maintain the illusion that Indian tappers worked voluntarily, though everyone knew there was no escape from the labyrinth of debt servitude. Undermining this charade was the rubber barons' liberal use of terror, the extravagant excesses of which attracted the attention of European and North American intellectuals from the early years of the twentieth century. Roger Casement was among the first, but by no means the last, to express his horror at the "deliberate murder by bullet, fire, beheading, or flogging to death, and accompanied by a variety of atrocious tortures" administered by rubber merchants in the management of their territories.[11]

Although the Rubber Boom of Peru's central jungle was less violent than its counterpart on the Río Putumayo to the northeast, it was just as likely to include commerce in human beings. On his expedition to the Gran Pajonál in 1896, the Franciscan priest Gabriel Sala found that even whites of modest means commonly bought and sold Asháninka children: "[F]rom the highest authority to the lowest farm hand or merchant, all want to have a chuncho boy or girl in service; and if they don't have one, they ask somebody to go among the chunchos or to stage a raid; and once they've obtained their chuncho, they thank [the slaver] very much and then pay him."[12] And Sala heard that things were worse elsewhere: on the Río Abujao merchants raffled off young girls or used them to cancel debts to their creditors.[13] A Franciscan traveling on the Ucayali in 1874 was moved to remark that "on these rivers all is fright, shock, dread, and panic-terror; no one on them thinks himself secure and not even life is guaranteed here."[14] Another traveler in the region reported that "a boy of ten or twelve years is normally worth five hundred soles, and if it's a Campa quite a bit more. . . . The children come to forget their savage customs, learn Spanish, and prove useful to their patrons—that is, if they live."[15]

The precise shape of traffic in Asháninka children is unclear. Stefano Varese contends that the rubber barons played one native group against another by exploiting traditional rivalries. "The method was simple," he writes. "Winchesters were delivered to the Conibo, to be paid off with Campa slaves, after which Winchesters were delivered to the Campa to be paid off with Conibo or Amuesha slaves."[16] Nevertheless, raids took place within tribes as well as between them, implying a political complexity lost in Varese's simple formulation.[17]

Asháninka headmen, acting as intermediaries between merchants and the general Indian population, often carried out forced "recruitment" of rubber workers and the outright capture of slaves. Padre Sala provides a portrait of one such headman, a man named Venancio. "[T]here suddenly appeared four canoes with twenty-five men (chunchos) well armed with rifles and led by the headman Venancio. He entered in a routine way, with a black parasol, a hat, and a scarf at his neck." Venancio and his men came to apprehend a Chinese trader wanted by Venancio's boss for unpaid debts. As the prisoner was taken away, he mournfully confessed to Sala his fear that he would never again be seen alive. On two other occasions Sala met Asháninkas sent by Venancio to conscript Indians from the Pajonál for rubber tapping on the Río Manú. "The merchant who knows how to play with his headmen grows like the foam on a whirlpool of dirty water," the priest observes.[18]

Out of this sanguinary period of Asháninka history, stories of a new messiah emerged. The most believable report comes from Padre Sala's diary of his expedition to Gran Pajonál. In the entry dated March 10, 1897, Sala records his meeting with an Asháninka named Rocas or Lucas, who told him that "in Chanchamayo the Campas and the whites are fighting, and that there has appeared again the Amachegua, descended from heaven, to help us in the combat."[19] Sala's response was to tell Rocas that the only true Amachegua is Jesus, the Son of God.

Amachegua—more properly, *amachénga* or *amachénka*—is an Asháninka word for a class of mythical saviors. These good spirits, normally invisible, present themselves to ordinary people as lightning bolts or as brilliantly plumed birds. The amachénga spirits, an Asháninka man told anthropologist Gerald Weiss in the 1960s, "flash, they all flash, that is, they are the Hidden Ones."[20] Shamans see the amachénga's true form during their healing journeys to the spirit world. And sometimes the amachénga "take on resplendent human corporeality if they so wish."[21]

Sala again picks up the trail of this amachénga eleven days later:

> *Soon we descended to a group of five households of Campas, who received us with much coldness and suspicion. Also taking refuge there was López of Metraro and other Amueshas seduced by the false god or Amachegua who calls people to the Río Pangoa and provokes them to fight against the whites. This god or brother of god, according to them, is a great rogue who mocks the sacred and the profane, with the object of uniting people to work the caucho on the Río Manú and other places: thus he has pretended to be God and a friend of the Campas, calling to his countrymen with promises and threats so that they would meet in a fixed place. . . . Once there, meeting to admire and adore this divinity with or without a moustache, Venancio and Romano come with fifty guardian angels, all with Winchester rifles, and they tell these unfortunate Campa fanatics to get into the canoes waiting on the great river, because God wants to be seen at a stream found farther downriver. Then, once they have embarked, they are taken to the Ucayali . . . to be converted into slaves.*[22]

The Venancio in question is the swaggering cacique described earlier in Sala's account—who, it turns out, is a henchman of the region's principal rubber baron, Carlos Fermín Fitzcarrald. Curiously, Sala never denounces the rubber baron by name. His discretion makes sense when we recall that Fitzcarrald was at the time the most powerful man in the region and someone who had assisted Sala in various ways during his expedition.

Writing nearly fifty years after Sala, Ernesto Reyna does not hesitate to identify Fitzcarrald as a messiah to the Indians:

Certain colonists speak of a "white Indian" from the headwaters of the Ucayali, who appeared before the Campas as the Son of the Sun. . . . In the year 1888 the Campas were notified that an Amachengua [sic] had appeared on the Pampas de Sacramento, a reincarnation of the Inca Juan Santos Atahualpa. The tribes undertook a long march and met at the indicated site, where they found a "white chuncho" dressed in the customary way of the savages, but with greater sumptuousness, carrying in his hand a carbine of the latest model and bandoliers of cartridges like necklaces. He spoke the Campa language and told them that "Father Sun had sent him with a message, that the errant tribes should live like civilized men, forming villages each with its own church. And that the man whom they were required to obey on earth, as the Sun's representative, was Carlos Fitzcarrald."[23]

The son of an Irish-American sea captain and a Peruvian woman born to the landed gentry of Ancash, Fitzcarrald or Fiscarrald (hispanicized versions of Fitzgerald) made his way to the Upper Ucayali River around 1879 and resurfaced in 1888 as the region's undisputed lord. Although his territory never attained the immense scale of other rubber fiefdoms—most notably, that of the infamous Julio César Arana of Iquitos—the circumstances of his life and early death imbue him with a mystery unique among Amazonian rubber barons.

Photographs of Fitzcarrald disclose a powerfully built man with dark hair and beard, far more Peruvian than Irish in appearance. As pitiless as his contemporaries when circumstances required, Fitzcarrald was driven by quixotic passions that ultimately proved his undoing. His most celebrated achievement was the discovery of a sliver of land separating the valleys of two great river systems, the Urubamba and the Madre de Dios. In 1894 he hauled a motor launch, the *Contamana*, across the isthmus from the headwaters of the Urubamba (hence from the Ucayali) to the headwaters of the Manú (hence to the Madre de Dios and the Madeira River, which empties into the Amazon in Brazil). Moving the launch required the labor of as many as a thousand Piros and Asháninkas and nearly a hundred whites. Their efforts lasted more than two months.[24]

The feat's commercial implications were profound: Fitzcarrald now controlled a route that gave the merchants and rubber traders of the Madre de Dios, Beni, and Madeira rivers access to markets in Iquitos at greatly reduced transportation costs and lower customs duties. Fitzcarrald and his business partners quickly placed orders in Europe for several custom-made river craft and planned the construction of a railroad to move goods across what came to be called the Isthmus of Fitzcarrald.

Meanwhile, Fitzcarrald's native army combed the jungle for Asháninkas and Piros who could be induced—at the point of a gun, if necessary—to work rubber concessions along the Urubamba, Manú, and Mishagua rivers. This intrusion led to bloody conflicts. The worst were with the Mashco (a term that includes tribes now known as Amarakaeri and Toyoeri), who doggedly resisted the efforts of rubber traders to dominate their territory. But though Mashco raids took a toll among small groups of tappers or traders, the Indians were no match for the force of four hundred heavily armed whites and Indians that Fitzcarrald assembled to put down the revolt. "The Manú was covered in corpses," writes Fitzcarrald's biographer Ernesto Reyna.[25] Zacarías Valdez Lozano, who participated in the war of extermination against the Mashco, recalls in his memoirs that when Fitzcarrald's Piro fighters "ended the combat and pursued the [Mashco] attackers to their houses, they found nothing but dead and wounded, among whom was a young man so ferociously savage that when offered food he tried to bite them."[26]

Valdez Lozano's account traces the alliances between Indians and traders that came to define Asháninka political realities during the height of the rubber frenzy. On the left bank of the Urubamba, for example, Fitzcarrald had in his employ four Piro headmen: a Supreme Chief named Curaca Agustín, and three lesser chiefs named Francisco, Jacinto, and Ronquino, who answered to Agustín. The Asháninkas of the Ucayali and Tambo were balkanized into groups under the control of traders of Peruvian, Spanish, and Chinese origin, all of whom eventually came to work for Fitzcarrald.[27]

Valdez Lozano himself traveled frequently with an Asháninka cacique named Hohuate, who in 1905 journeyed to Ayacucho to be baptized under the sponsorship of Andrés Avelino Cáceres, a former president of Peru. In honor of the occasion, Hohuate took the name Andrés Avelino Cáceres y Ruiz. But Hohuate's veneer of Christian civility remained thin. On a trip down the Tambo in 1906, Valdez Lozano found it "curious to see the Curaca Hohuate take off the boots and clothing of a civilized person, cover himself with a cushma, and paint his face with the red achiote signalling that he was alert to possible combat." Soon they made contact with Asháninkas involved in a long-standing feud with Hohuate. Fighting broke out. During the most intense moment of the battle, Valdez recalls, Hohuate "mocked his adversaries by dancing at the front of the canoe, dodging arrows with his body and shouting that they should come out on the shore so that he could see them."[28]

Fitzcarrald's empire fell in 1897. In July of that year, Fitzcarrald traveled up the Urubamba aboard the steam launch *Adolfito* with don Alberto Perla at the helm. The craft entered some rapids at a place called Mapalja and through the captain's poor navigation was hit by the full force of the current, which broke the rudder linkage. Spinning out of control, the launch entered a whirlpool, capsized, and sank. A search party found Fitzcarrald's body two days later. He was buried at the mouth of the Río Inuya.

The rubber baron's former associate, Zacarías Valdez Lozano, denies that Fitzcarrald needed to assume the mantle of a god to dominate the Asháninkas. "In the life of Fitzcarrald," he writes, "there was nothing of fantasy or legend." Valdez Lozano maintains that Fitzcarrald's ascendancy over both whites and Indians came from his own abilities, as well as the application of methods that "were perhaps a bit rough, but justifiable in those times."[29] Yet Valdez Lozano provides no alternative explanation to account for the amachénga stories collected by Padre Sala in the 1880s.

Whether Fitzcarrald, perhaps at the prodding of Venancio, was familiar enough with Asháninka religious beliefs to exploit the concept of the amachénga will never be known for certain. Does this story confirm the persistence of an Asháninka belief in salvation through the appearance of a warlike messiah? Or is it instead a feverish projection of white dreams, a fantasy of dominion over childlike and credulous savages? Might both currents be at work simultaneously? In any case, one must conclude that tales of an amachénga were circulating at the time among the Asháninkas, though their true significance may only have been dimly understood by Padre Sala.

The cacique Venancio managed to sustain his power base even after Fitzcarrald's death. In an expedition in 1900, Colonel Pedro Portillo visited Venancio's village on the Río Tambo, a place called Washington. "Washington is like a military plaza or an impregnable fortress . . . of five hundred inhabitants, subject to Venancio," Portillo reported. "From the months of June to November they are in continuous journeys to extract caucho and *sheringa* [another type of latex] from the region of Sepahua, Cuja, and Purús. . . . All are Campas, in close contact with civilized people."[30]

Western rhetoric about jungle Indians had undergone a subtle shift by the end of the nineteenth century. Prior to 1900, Western observers spoke of the need to civilize the heathens, to bring them into the fold of Christianity and respect for king and viceroy. But the Rubber Boom, the expansion of plantation agriculture, and the industrialization of Peru changed the agenda. Now native peoples had to assimilate, move, or die, because the progress of Peru could no longer be stemmed. "Happily now," muses Colonel Portillo in a report of his expedition to the central jungle in 1900, "the Huantino and Iquichano Indians will not be reactionary elements, nor obstacles to order and labor, nor will they oppose the currents of immigration and progress, because they have received very opportune and necessary lessons from the military expedition of Colonel Parra in 1896."[31]

In fact, the discourse of progress oscillates between two poles: an assertion that the Amazon territory is nearly empty—hence free of the dangerous and atavistic influence of Indian peoples—and the claim that there are indeed Indians, but tractable ones. H. A. Guillaume, for example, quotes the geographer James Orton to the effect that the Amazon "is probably the most sparsely populated region on the globe." It is only the untutored imagination, he alleges, "that peoples this pathless wilderness with uncounted swarms of savages." At the same time, Guillaume wants to counter fears about the known violence of the Asháninkas. In a section headed "Progress of Civilization Amongst the Campas Indians," he notes reassuringly that "these Campas, who have been considered for a long time to be dangerous and rebels to all civilisation, are as capable of work as the others."[32]

At least some observers express a grudging admiration for the Asháninkas' apparent willingness to remain outside of history as envisioned by Europeans. Arturo Wertheman, who elsewhere in his expedition diary shows little sympathy for Asháninkas, describes almost poetically the depth of native resistance to the white invasion:

A Campa man getting along in years, a prisoner in the camp,
feeling that he neared his end, called all his companions together to
give them his last words. The old man got up on a bench and
with tremulous voice and expressive gestures spoke to his audience.
. . . . While his fellows wept in a state of desperation, the mori-
bund old man sat down and breathed his last breath. There was
nobody to translate his sentences, but he seemed to be recommending
to his companions in misfortune that they maintain resignation
and patience as well as unity so that they could recover their
liberty and maintain untouched the rights that had been theirs since
time immemorial . . . rights that they judge sacred, but that
civilization does not grant to those unfortunates who want to live
outside of the community of nations, as if they were not part of the
world.[33]

But however much people of republican sensibilities may
admire this love of liberty, there is no question that the forward march of civilization must continue. For Portillo, Guillaume, Wertheman, and others like them, the resistance of
Indians to inclusion in "the world" is evidence of their historical inconsequence.

The shift in attitude evident in Franciscan sources is more
shocking than that of secular observers. Padre Sala's expedition report is awash in strong statements about the fate of
Indians in his vision of progress. For Sala, the word *chuncho*
is synonymous with "liar, traitor, ingrate, idler, glutton, a
vengeful and inconstant person." He continues:

And what will we do with beings such as this? What is done the
world over: supposing that they don't want to live as men, but
instead as animals, one treats them like animals and puts a bullet
in them when they unjustly oppose the lives and well-being of the
rest of us.[34]

So Asháninkas stand in the way of lives and well-being,
of progress and history. "Peru dreams a dream and antici-

pates her destiny," writes Guillaume, "a dream of welcoming multitudes of an active and industrious race of people; a dream of her uncultivated lands returning abundant harvests . . . and throughout the length and breadth of the land the light of peace and prosperity shining, never to be extinguished."[35]

In little more than half a century these dreams had reshaped the Asháninka world. Rudely thrust into what Wertheman calls the "community of nations," the Asháninkas' rivers and best agricultural lands were now controlled by immigrants from China, Italy, Spain, England, Germany, Austria, Portugal, Brazil, Bolivia, France, and North America, as well as by colonists from Andean and coastal Peru. Native headmen had become virtual warloads, armed by rubber traders and thoroughly integrated into a system of debt-slavery. In those parts of the forest where latex-bearing trees could be found, rubber tappers swarmed over the land. "At present 5,000 men from Tarapoto, machete in hand, are occupied in felling the caoutchouc [caucho] trees on the hills overlooking the Pichis," writes Guillaume.[36] The church had just begun to reestablish itself in Asháninka territory. The work of Sala and others was laying the groundwork for a return of the Franciscans, now backed by hundreds of white settlers who would help the missions secure a firm grip on the jungle and its resources. The shining dream of progress was for the Asháninka people a cruel vision of their own dissolution.

The tenacity Wertheman observed in the dying Asháninka orator continued to assert itself in local uprisings through the late nineteenth and early twentieth centuries. "It was the twelfth of May, 1896, the siesta hour," writes Dionisio Ortiz in his history of the Pangoa mission, which was reestablished in 1895.[37] "Padre Hormaeche was crushing a little sugar cane to sweeten his coffee. Padre Navarro was in bed with a high fever. . . . Meanwhile Campa enemies had approached the outskirts of the mission with warlike intent, determined to wipe out the missionaries and colonists." The child of an Asháninka family friendly to the missionaries roused the men in time for them to repel the first wave of attackers. Arrows rained down on the mission, "one of them passing through the palm-leaf roof and driving itself into the very pillow where minutes before Padre Navarro was resting." The encounter left two dead and six wounded among the colonists and friendly Indians, twelve dead among the attackers.[38] The next day the priests buried the mission's sacred articles and joined the settlers in flight. During the difficult escape to the highlands, tensions between colonists and the friendly Asháninkas who accompanied them, led by a man named Zeroti, ran high. When the priests were absent, the highlanders seized the trade goods earlier presented to the Indians as gifts. Zeroti and his family decided they had had enough of the settlers and turned back to the territory of their enemies. The fate of these Indians, "so loyal and good to the missionaries," was never known, reports Dionisio Ortiz.

A much larger uprising in the Río Pichis area claimed national attention in 1913. The world market for latex was in collapse, prompting Pichis rubber traders to sharpen their already abusive treatment of Indians. Beginning in December of 1913, Asháninka warriors raided white settlements, cut telegraph wires, and closed the Pichis Trail linking the region to the Perené Valley and the Peruvian coast. Based on a review of contemporary press reports, John Bodley estimates that 150 settlers died during the Pichis raids.[39]

Franciscans who established the mission at Obenteni in the Gran Pajonál found themselves the object of Asháninka fury in 1936. A settler named Torpuco, fooling with a gun he thought unloaded, killed an Asháninka man. The enraged Indians made short work of Torpuco and then sacked the mission. The following day, under cover of fog, the missionary and the remaining settlers escaped to a safer part of the Pajonál. Monsignor Irazola, the Franciscan who led the resettlement of the Pajonál, saw this as only a momentary set-back in colonization of a region that he described as "immense plains that through the work of men could easily become an inexhaustible source of wealth."[40]

Only a few years before Irazola was writing of the economic potential of the Asháninka homeland, a Chilean author argued that the ancestors of present-day Asháninkas had used their territory's economic potential to create a prehistoric Amazonian kingdom. The writer, identified only as "Reynolds" on the title page of this curious book, claims that the Río Tambo was once the site of a great commercial city with a population of 300,000. This jungle metropolis, which in the book's illustrations resembles an Amazonian version of Kathmandu, was part of a "Campa empire" that enjoyed cordial trading relations with Europe. We know nothing of the experiences that led the idiosyncratic Reynolds to fix on Asháninkas as the prehistoric rulers of South America, but he was certainly not alone in seeing this part of the upper Amazon as an area of vast economic promise.[41]

The agricultural frontier moved steadily from the Chanchamayo valley to Pangoa, Satipo, and the Apurímac through the 1920s and 1930s. Construction crews carved a serviceable road out of the mountains between Tarma and San Ramón so that farmers could transport their crops to markets in Lima. Beginning in 1935, the languishing agricultural colony at Satipo had an unexpected windfall: sudden foreign demand for a crop called *barbasco*, a traditional Amazonian fish poison. The active ingredient in barbasco is rotenone, an ingredient used in insecticides. The barbasco boom was followed by a sharp rise in world coffee prices in the early 1950s.[42]

There were setbacks. A violent earthquake in 1947 effaced miles of the regional road system. Export busts shadowed each boom, turning economic titans into overnight paupers. The government's interest in the region wavered according to political tides incomprehensible to most settlers. But the movement of peasants into the jungle—at the expense of Asháninka control of their traditional lands—continued inexorably. By 1947, for example, Satipo counted 5,000 settlers among approximately 3,500 Asháninkas, and the ratio of colonists to Indians in the more densely settled Chanchamayo and Perené valleys was presumably higher.[43] Alberto Yorini, an Asháninka leader, bitterly recalls the arrival of settlers to Satipo:

Yes, the colonists came from Huancayo, from Concepción; only from those areas did they come then. They also came from Andamarca. Asháninkas lived where Satipo is now until the colonists came. There Asháninkas shared their houses with the colonists. As time passed, the colonists told the Asháninkas, "These lands are not yours. Get out of here!" Well, my people left. That's why all the people have gone far, far, far away.[44]

Local labor shortages contributed to the persistence of kidnappings well into the 1950s. Manuel Ashivanti, a Nomatsiguenga man who lives in Pangoa, remembers the raids of Shora, someone recognized as a "chief" by Spanish-speaking authorities until his death in 1949:

Shora was made chief by a colonist named Antenor. He was named because he was Antenor's compadre. Just as boys and girls were traded before, this Antenor traded them for cotton cloth. He asked Shora to bring him girls and boys so that he could raise them, so that they would work for him without pay. They were only given food, sometimes clothes—but only old clothes, the poor children! He had plenty of them! Antenor also asked for children to be sent to his mother in Lima.

You delivered a child and they gave you a piece of cloth. "Bring me a child," they said to Shora, and they gave him cloth. So Shora, since he was a warrior, was able to take them from over

there, from the Río Ene. He killed the parents and took the
children. They arrived here and they were given to the one who
had paid him with cloth.[45]

Even the Franciscans found themselves in the business of
buying children. Monsignor Irazola, who established the
twentieth-century mission in Satipo, found it "prudent," as
he put it, to acquire kidnapped children from Asháninka
slave-raiders who came to the mission. He saw these children
"as a gift of the Providence that perhaps in this way seeks to
instill and propagate the faith among these infidels."[46] Other
children were entrusted to the missions when they became
the objects of sorcery accusations. For reasons that baffle anthropologists, Asháninka shamans consistently blame children, especially young girls, when life-threatening illnesses
strike adults. In the past, these sorcerer-children (called *mátsi*
or *máchi*) were attacked with what an observer otherwise
sympathetic to Asháninkas calls "merciless fury."[47] Rather
than see their child killed, parents preferred to hand over the
accused sorcerer to missionaries or white settlers. Most of
these children ended up as unpaid domestic servants.

Slavery was gradually replaced by less absolute but equally
effective forms of exploitation. Landowners wanted Asháninka families to live nearby in order to provide needed hands
at planting or harvest time—so much so that they sometimes
ceded the Indians small plots of land for houses and kitchen
gardens, though never enough that Indians could live inde-
pendently of their patrons. An Asháninka man interviewed
by Robin Shoemaker in the early 1970s recalled that his father, a shaman, chose to live among the settlers after he saw
in a vision that "the Campas would receive in airplanes vast
shipments of machetes, hoes, shotguns, metal pots and pans,
and other material goods possessed by colonist society."
Therefore, he argued, the Indians "should adopt the ways of
civilization and wait for the cargo to arrive."[48]

To keep their Indian laborers close to home, landowners
were sometimes instrumental in helping Asháninkas secure

land titles. Indians with the temerity to seek legal titles on their own faced a hostile and byzantine bureaucracy. Alberto Yorini recalls his own futile efforts to obtain a title:

I demanded that they give me a certificate of possession. Nothing.
They just had me buy papers. Mr. Horacio Merino said to me:
"Buy official paper with a seal, thirty sheets." I bought them.
And I demanded: "Handle it so that I too have my certificate of
possession and title." "Fine, fine," he said to me. I returned
on such-and-such a date: "Come back on this month, that month,
this month," he told me. I got nothing. Then Horacio Merino
said to me: "Listen, Yorini, why don't you shut up, man? You're
just a native, you don't have any reason to have a paper. Only
colonists have papers!"

When Asháninka communities managed to secure land titles, their parcels usually proved inadequate either for traditional subsistence agriculture or for the production of cash crops. Many native households in the Perené valley had fewer than five hectares of farmland, far too little to coax a living from fragile tropical soils.

As pressure on the best agricultural lands mounted, settlers began to covet the vast landholdings of the Perené Colony. Beginning in 1946, the Colony transferred parcels to smallholders while at the same time using every means at its disposal to prevent independent settlers from marketing their coffee. Nevertheless, spontaneous appropriation of Colony lands by smallholders on the south bank of the Perené intensified in the 1950s. The Peruvian Corporation maneuvered to defend itself: in 1958 it was reorganized as two separate companies incorporated within Peru, thereby appearing to cut its ties to foreign capital. But the die was cast. A growing peasant movement, led by leftist organizers from Huancayo and Lima, used increasingly militant tactics to promote an agrarian reform that would turn over the plantation's lands to farm families. Asháninkas were only peripherally involved in peasant mobilization, however, for their interests scarcely coincided with those of smallholder colonists who in other parts of the valley were seizing Indian land.[49] Indeed, the Peruvian Corporation ceded land to Asháninkas with the stipulation that it could not be passed on to non-Indians, in the hope that the Indians would protect the plantation from further invasion by peasants.[50]

From the 1920s onward, hundreds of Asháninkas chose to escape the threat of raids or the burdensome demands of white landowners by moving to the mission communities that sprang up throughout the region. When John H. Bodley studied the Asháninkas in the 1960s, he found thirty-eight mission settlements functioning in their territory, mostly under the aegis of Protestant denominations.[51]

Despite the dedication of the missionaries, among whom were Americans or Europeans who devoted their lives to saving Indian souls, Asháninka converts proved as wayward in the twentieth century as their ancestors had in the eighteenth. Commenting on the negligible impact of twenty years of Protestant missionary work at the Cahuapanas mission, John Elick, an anthropologist and missionary who lived with Asháninkas for seven years, notes that many exhibited "a gradual rejection of what apparently comes to be an unsatisfying way of life and a return to the old Campa ways."[52] His remarks echo the complaint of Padre Luis Sabaté, who during an expedition into Asháninka country in 1874 decided to spend an extra day in a community called Sinquiventini to catechize among "these brutalized people, who more than once offered to become Christians, but when the chance arose mocked the zeal of the missionary fathers."[53]

However inconstant the Asháninkas' devotion to Christianity, the missions offered undeniable attractions: a degree of protection from outsiders, medical care and education, trade goods, livestock, and the drama of radio communications and airplane landings. More significant, the material plenty of the missions gave rise to new utopian dreams.

A widespread outburst of millennial enthusiasm linked to missionary work occurred in the 1920s, when F. A. Stahl, a Seventh-Day Adventist from the United States, established a mission on Peruvian Corporation land along the Río Perené. Stahl's efforts yielded little progress at first, but by the mid-1920s Asháninkas began to show glimmerings of interest. Writing of this change of attitude, Stahl comments: "Now there was a great increase in the attendance at all our meetings. People began to come from away in the interior, calling for someone to come down and teach them about the true God."[54] Stahl's visits to villages along the Perené attracted large groups of Indians waiting to be baptized: "Suddenly we came in view of an open valley, and as we entered the valley we were met by hundreds of Campa Indians, who greeted us warmly."[55] The photographs that accompany Stahl's account of his work show scores of Asháninkas standing stiffly beside the missionary.

In his research on Stahl's mission, John Bodley found that Asháninka interest in Stahl's message had achieved a life of its own, in many cases even before the missionary entered into direct contact with specific communities. Stahl preached of the imminent return of Christ, who would destroy those who failed to respect the Word of God. According to Bodley, Asháninkas elaborated their own interpretation of these preachings:

They expected Christ to appear today or tomorrow, not ten or twenty years in the future. The coming was to be an extremely cataclysmic event. One informant said the dead would arise, all evil would be destroyed, and the believers and risen dead would be taken to the house of God in the sky where there would be no more sickness, death, or growing old . . . Some confused Stahl with the promised messiah, however, and there were reports that God had already descended to earth at Metraro [Stahl's mission station].[56]

Hundreds of Asháninkas—indeed, perhaps as many as two thousand—assembled spontaneously along the Perené to await the predicted cataclysm. In areas where the movement took hold, landowners were enraged by the sudden disappearance of Asháninka workers. They organized reprisals against native catechists, including the murder of one on the Río Shahuaya. Most of the Asháninkas dispersed when Christ failed to appear, but two hundred or more adherents remained in communities organized by native leaders at La Cascada and Tambo.[57]

Another millennial outburst occurred in the late 1950s or early 1960s, when a Protestant missionary named Bulner attracted a significant Asháninka following at a site called Puerto Rico on the Río Ene.[58] Marta, a Nomatsiguenga woman, recalls that people spoke of this gringo as a messiah.

At that time we were living there in my village, and I heard people speaking this way: "Upcountry there is a gringo, a little gringo who is a brother, who is a god. He is white." He was white. The people said: "You ought to believe it! He's Sun, our god!" Since he was a gringo, everyone believed him, every last person believed him. People from everywhere came to see this gringo. The people believed that he was Itomi Pavá [Son of the Sun]. That's the way it was!

He was an evangelist. I don't remember his name, but I got a good look at him. My people believed that he was Itomi Pavá. Yes! They said: "Our god comes from Lima in an airplane." "Let's go to the Río Ene," said the gringo. "Let's go to the Ene," they answered him. . . . Before leaving for the Ene all of my people began to drink manioc beer. They partied all day. They sang, too. They said: "Itomi Pavá has come." That's the song they sang. Grabbing each other by the hand, they danced together. At sunrise, they all left. Nobody remained behind. All of them went with the gringo. . . .

All of my people who went with the gringo died of malaria. All of them died, nobody survived. And when some people tried to cross the river on a raft, it turned over and they perished. Only

one saved himself and returned to his home to tell what happened.
A while later, another person returned, explaining: "Lies, lies.
He wasn't the Son of God! We believed he was Itomi Pavá, but it
was a lie. He finished off all of our people."[59]

By 1960, the Asháninka homeland had become an intricate social mosaic in which Indians no longer had a dominant place. The native peoples of Chanchamayo and Satipo were outnumbered by highland peasants who arrived with machetes and a few rags, leaving their played-out farms in the mountains to chase a dream of crimson coffee berries. Asháninkas taught the newcomers how to meet the stringent demands of jungle life, then found themselves pushed aside when land rights were committed to paper.

Paper was a powerful presence in this New World. Before the arrival of white settlers, one was simply the son of Mishari, daughter of Mencoina, husband of Ompíquiri. The self was defined by bonds of kinship and human association. Now Indians were expected to carry identity cards, passports in the kingdom of paper. The masters of this domain were schoolteachers, functionaries, policemen, judges. They lived by rules whose contours Asháninkas could barely discern.

Missionaries were another piece of the mosaic. Franciscans, usually Spaniards, ran their communities with a stern hand. Stocking their missions with cattle and other tokens of wealth, they celebrated poverty while living well, at least by local standards. Priests "rescued" children from the slave-trade, then consigned them to the more mysterious servitude of convent school, producing adults who looked like Indians but lacked the skills needed to contribute to traditional Asháninka life.

American missionaries with hair like the pale fiber of the *chambira* palm arrived in airplanes, offloading apparently limitless quantities of trade goods. The emissaries of Protestant teaching were more inclined than Franciscans to advance an apocalyptic image of the end of the world: Indians must bathe in the waters of Christ to save themselves from God's purifying fire. The stations established by the Protestants afforded some protection from slavers and predatory merchants while offering hints that the secrets of the foreigners' wealth might be revealed in due time.

Asháninkas responded to these circumstances by adopting a protean flexibility. Moved by the urge to be rid of all disturbance and confusion, some lost themselves in the jungle refuge areas along the Tambo or Ene rivers to hunt, fish, and farm in peace. Eventually the lure of trade goods—the machetes, cloth, iron pots, and firearms that had become necessities—drew them back into the dangerous orbit of white merchants and landowners. Nor can one discount the attracting force of the sheer spectacle of life in mestizo villages or mission stations.

After a time, the burden of wage work, the unfairness and brutality of it, drove people back to the forest. Asháninkas grew tired of living as shadows in the blinding light of the white world, needed for their labor but despised for their way of life. Beneath the false veneer of reciprocity in their relationships with whites, they saw only menace.

As the Indians moved between these different points of reference—sampling mission discipline for awhile, working as peons in coffee plantations, traveling upcountry for a time to capture a more traditional life—they nurtured two impulses that had been sustained throughout their recorded history: an inclination to resist forcibly the intrusion of whites, to respond to the whites' ferocity in kind; and the belief that a redeeming spirit would restore the prosperity and freedom so roughly torn from their grasp.

FOUR

Toward Armed Struggle

Peru's capital, Lima, is a city that defies idealism. The rich live in singular comfort, but outside the wealthy, protected districts—now known in Lima slang as "zoos" because of the proliferation of barred doors and windows—the sidewalks are ruled by an army of peddlers, shoeshine boys, pickpockets, and paupers. By day, people traffic in stories of disenchantment. Guerrilla strikes on distant electrical towers darken the city's nights.

The Lima of the early 1960s was a brighter place. The magazines and newspapers of the period shimmer with an innocence now lost. When the press dealt with the predicament of Amazonian Indians, it was as if these unfortunate natives lived on another planet. News of rural unrest or national politics was often subordinated to coverage of spectacular misdeeds among Lima's upper classes.

An especially memorable diversion was the case of Ingrid Schwend. The German-Peruvian wife of an engineer named Oliveira, she was alleged to have killed José Manuel Sartorius, a Spanish count, by perforating his thorax with four rounds from a .38 caliber revolver. The press speculated that "La Ingrid," as she came to be known, was protecting her husband, who had arranged for her to have affairs with other men in order to satisfy his voyeuristic appetite. The enterprising Sartorius was not on the list of authorized lovers. When Oliveira discovered his young wife's infidelity, rumor had it, he murdered the Spanish playboy and persuaded his wife to confess to the killing, claiming self-defense against attempted rape. The case contained elements guaranteed to titillate the Lima middle classes, who frankly emulated the Kennedy-era Camelot to the north: an attractive woman portrayed as a nymphomaniac, furtive assignations in elegant houses or expensive cars, jealousy, betrayal, and high-life corruption.[1]

Such a setting seems an unlikely place for the rise of a new current of utopian thought. But by 1960, hundreds of young intellectuals in Lima had come under the spell of revolutionary Marxism—a movement that would eventually touch Asháninka communities many miles to the east. This was the direct result of events in Cuba.

It is easy to forget the electrifying effect the Cuban Revolution had on the Latin American left in 1959. A group of poorly armed guerrillas, striking from bases in the mountains, routed the army of a dictator favored by the United States. When, two years later, the powerful presence to the north unleashed its forces against the people's army, the people's army prevailed. Cuba proved that a Marxist revolution could take place in what was then coming to be called the Third World. It showed that young Latin Americans could transform societies whose modern history, it seemed, had previously been little more than melodramas written and directed by United Fruit or the U.S. Department of State. The face of Castro's Cuba had yet to be blemished by the Mariel boatlift, a foreign adventure in Angola, and the sovietization of the economy.

Many leftists believed that Peru needed only a nudge to

release its own revolutionary avalanche. Although Peru's economy was relatively diversified and stable, the distribution of agricultural land was as skewed as that of any country in the region.[2] According to one source, 0.1 percent of the population controlled over 60 percent of the arable land.[3] In the Andean Departments of Junín and Pasco, 90 percent of the agricultural land was held by seventy-two families.[4] As if the land tenure situation were not bad enough, landlords insisted on conserving practices more appropriate to medieval manors than to twentieth-century estates. As part of their obligations to hacienda owners, Andean peasants routinely worked as grooms, shepherds, housekeepers, and, at times, as bearers of the owner himself, when he preferred to be carried on a litter rather than walk.[5]

Prior to the Cuban Revolution, the middle-class intellectuals who made up the Peruvian left contented themselves with passionate doctrinal disputation and ruthless purges of apostate party members. The legacy of such formidable socialist thinkers as José Carlos Mariátegui, whose influential book *Seven Interpretive Essays on Peruvian Reality* was published in 1928, was not enough to prevent the left from dividing into increasingly querulous factions in the 1950s and 1960s—a process that produced a phylogenetic thicket of first-, second-, and third-order splinter groups, including Stalinists, Leninists, Socialists, Maoists, Progressive Socialists, several Trotskyite parties, and even a pro-Albania faction.[6] By the early 1960s, the left had gained ascendancy in Peru's universities to the point that professors who taught in ways deemed politically incorrect could be dismissed by their students.[7] But outside of the universities, the influence of mainstream Marxism in the country's politics was negligible. This was principally due to the power of a home-grown populist party, the American Popular Revolutionary Alliance (APRA).

When it was founded by Victor Raúl Haya de la Torre in 1924, APRA's program was avowedly socialist, anti-imperialist, and anticlerical. With a strong labor following and a robust party structure, APRA attracted many young intellectuals who might otherwise have been drawn into the orbit of the Communist party. Because APRA controlled the Peruvian Workers Confederation, an organization that included almost 90 percent of trade union membership, it presented a formidable threat to the conservative Peruvian elite.[8] The party was subjected to persistent repression, with occasional brief periods of rapprochement with the government, until 1956. In that year APRA leaders reached an understanding, usually referred to as the *convivencia* ("coexistence"), with President Manuel Prado. Prado legalized APRA in exchange for its support of his presidency and a softening of the party's socialist goals.

The convivencia sparked dissatisfaction among APRA's younger, left-leaning members, who cast their eyes toward the frankly revolutionary aims of orthodox Marxism. In Cuba they saw radical thought turned to action. "Cuban socialism established the problems of revolution as the issues for today, not for a more or less distant tomorrow," wrote the Peruvian guerrilla Hector Béjar in 1969.[9] The principal theoretician of the Cuban socialism that so enchanted them was an Argentine physician named Che Guevara.

Despite the waning fortunes of communism in Europe, the hold of Ernesto Guevara de la Serna on the Latin American popular imagination continues to be remarkably strong. The iconography of Che—with the obligatory beard, red-starred beret, and military fatigues—is everywhere in Peru, from the walls of universities to the spattered mudflaps of trucks on the Central Highway. But in the early 1960s Che was not yet a martyr to the revolution: he was an active warrior in the people's struggle. By dint of experience, he spoke with an authority unmatched by most Latin American Marxists, for whom armed struggle was still a vague dream.

"Che," Eduardo Galeano has written recently, "was not a man of the desk, he was a creator of revolutions."[10]

Guevara first expounded his ideas of revolutionary strategy in the book *Guerrilla Warfare*, published in 1960. Central to his scheme is the revolutionary *foco* or focal point, a place where the revolution is made. "The foco," Raúl Castro is reported to have said, "is the little motor that sets in motion the great motor of the revolution."[11]

For Guevara and Fidel Castro, the problem with making a revolution in Latin America was that social conditions failed to meet the classic Marxist prerequisites. The hemisphere's nations lacked the level of industrialization that Marx saw as necessary for the creation of revolutionary masses. Revolutionaries could either "wait patiently in the doorway for the corpse of imperialism to pass by," or they could alter the conditions themselves until a general insurrection became possible.

The foco, Che argued, is a way to jump-start the revolution. A foco consists of a small, mobile revolutionary vanguard trained in Marxist ideology and guerrilla tactics. By establishing themselves in isolated parts of the countryside, the revolutionaries enjoy some protection from the police while they educate the rural masses in the realities of their situation. The revolutionary teaches by example, living a life that is part warrior, part teacher, part saint.[12] Once peasants join the ranks of the guerrillas and the regions around each foco liberate themselves from official control, the government will resort to iron-fisted tactics to reestablish order. Official savagery, the theory continues, unmasks the true nature of "pseudodemocracies" such as Peru. The increasingly intolerable repression propels urban workers and intellectuals to the barricades, leading to a general uprising that overwhelms the military. The key phrase taken up by Peruvian followers of Che was "revolutionary audacity"—the willingness to risk everything to serve as a catalyst for radical change.

Che's blueprint had obvious attractions. It had already

worked in Cuba; it was not just another bloodless theory. It advocated *action* rather than the interminable wait of orthodox Leninists for the perfect window of revolutionary opportunity. And it suited the political anatomy of Peru, where there were few signs of insurrection in the complacent, APRA-dominated labor movement but almost daily signals of unrest among the peasantry.

Historical connections between Che and Peru added to the theory's mystique for Peruvian leftists. Che's first wife, Hilda Gadea, was Peruvian, an exiled member of APRA whom Che had met in Guatemala. Che visited Peru twice during his peregrinations through Latin America in the 1950s. On the 1952 trip he worked in the Peruvian government's leprosarium at San Pablo, on the Amazon, before floating down the river to Colombia on a balsawood raft that he and a traveling companion christened "Tangomambo."

But the links between Che and Peru were more than sentimental. In 1960, Peru broke off diplomatic relations with Cuba when the government discovered that the Cubans were financing radical groups in Lima and elsewhere in the country. (Years later, Philip Agee alleged that Cuban embassy documents showing cash payments to Peruvian leftists were in fact forgeries made by CIA technicians at the agency's Lima station.)[13] In a 1987 interview, ex-president Fernando Belaúnde told a journalist that he met Che in 1962 in the remote town of Puerto Bermúdez during Belaúnde's presidential campaign. "He had a light Argentine accent," recalls Belaúnde, "and he wore a beret even in a place as hot as this."[14] There has since been considerable speculation that Che made a clandestine trip to Peru to assess prospects for the establishment of a revolutionary foco there. Whether or not Che actually plotted revolutionary action in Peru in the 1960s is less interesting than the widespread belief that he was there working in the shadows—an elusive agent of utopian transformation in the minds of Peru's hopeful revolutionaries.

By the early 1960s, Cuba was providing guerrilla training

to as many as 1,500 Latin Americans a year.[15] A generation of Peruvian revolutionaries—among them Héctor Béjar, Luis de la Puente, Guillermo Lobatón, Javier Heraud, Edgardo Tello, Máximo Velando, and Ricardo Gadea—learned basic guerrilla tactics there. They relished the occasional attention of Che himself, usually during his famous all-night office hours, to which he might summon foreign comrades for discussion and debate. "He listened to us," recalls Hector Béjar, "because he listened a lot—as compared to Fidel, who spoke to us a lot."[16] Twenty-five years later, Béjar remembers the preparation for armed struggle as a charmed period of his life:

> *The fact is that we spent the sixties in military training camps under truly tough conditions that tested the firmness of our resolve. Traveling with false passports in Europe and Latin America, hidden in safe houses in Bolivia, crossing the Bolivian jungle on foot or by other means, making secret contacts and fooling the police. . . . And, finally, fighting in the sierra of Peru.[17]*

Before these young insurrectionists could put their Cuban training to use, a rural uprising in the Department of Cuzco claimed national attention. The focus of this unrest was the valley of La Convención, about ninety miles north of Cuzco, a semitropical region controlled by a few landowners presiding over a large population of Indian sharecroppers. Changing economic conditions in the 1950s, including a sharp increase in the market value of the coffee produced in the valley, prompted landowners to replace sharecropping with a plantation system. They thought it unnecessary to provide compensation for the tenants' improvements to the land. Reaction from farmers was spirited. They organized themselves into local unions and linked the unions together as regional federations. Into this volatile situation stepped a young Trotskyite organizer named Hugo Blanco.

Blanco, a native of Cuzco educated at the University of La Plata in Argentina, was the first Peruvian leftist to overcome the cultural barrier between urban, Spanish-speaking professional and Quechua-speaking Indian. In 1958, Blanco took up residence in the Convención Valley as a subtenant farmer and immediately immersed himself in peasant politics. Climbing through the ranks of local and regional peasant unions, he urged more militant action against landowners, including strikes and hacienda takeovers.[18] "We are reaching victory," he wrote in 1962, "by means of stoppages, strikes, meetings, division of land contrary to bourgeois law, and the confiscation of haciendas that is also contrary to bourgeois law."[19] The rallying cry of the movement was "Land or Death." Between 1958 and 1962, the peasants of La Convención acquired the former and paid for it with the latter.

Blanco's community of Chaupimayo set up its own system of governance, popular justice, defense, and education—grass-roots institutions that, in opposition to the government, created what Blanco referred to as a pattern of "dual power." For the first time in modern Peruvian history, the masses rose to achieve a program of socialist change. The swift radicalization of the region excited the interest of Blanco's superiors in the Revolutionary Workers Party (POR) and its continental umbrella organization, the Latin American Secretariat of Orthodox Trotskyism (SLATO).[20] SLATO pledged funds in support of an armed guerrilla insurrection—money that it tried to obtain through the "revolutionary expropriation" of Peruvian banks. With the help of two Argentine *pistoleros*, Che Pereyra and Juan Kreus, and a Spaniard named Juan Martorell, Trotskyite militants staged two bank robberies in Lima, including a daylight raid on the Miraflores branch of the Banco de Crédito that netted them the equivalent of $120,000. The *troskos* had an aptitude for stick-ups but not for escape, and they were soon captured by the police. Only about 10 percent of the funds found their way to the struggle in La Convención. The rest either disappeared, presumably into private hands, or were seized by the police.[21]

The momentum of the peasant movement sparked debate about the rebellion's ultimate direction. The POR and other groups advocated a large-scale guerrilla insurrection, whereas Blanco and his fellow union members favored land seizures and the creation of purely defensive peasant militias. But events got away from Blanco. In November he led a group of union followers to a police post in Pucyura with the goal of appropriating weapons. Once in possession of the arms, they planned to arrest a hacienda owner who had allegedly raped a union member's daughter. A policeman had the temerity to resist, and Blanco shot him point-blank—a killing that leftist writers, through a nimble twist of logic, classify as an act of "self-defense."[22] A report prepared four years later by the military describes the event in equally improbable terms, this time using the language of dime novels:

> *Meanwhile, the policeman Briceño . . . gave a final shout in the very face of the murderer: "You're a damned communist. One day you'll pay for this crime!" He hadn't time to say more, for a steel bar broke his skull. The scene was appalling: Hugo Blanco stood holding the bar with the smile of the sadist who enjoys pain and death, while brains spilled over the face of officer Briceño.*[23]

With Blanco fleeing from a murder charge and peasant violence escalating rapidly, police units moved to quell the unions, which had by that time shut down seventy haciendas. Confrontations with the police culminated in the massacre of as many as thirty peasants in Chaullay on Christmas Day.[24] Blanco was captured in May of 1963 and later sentenced to twenty-five years in prison.

Although short-lived, the "liberation" of La Convención made an impression on the government in Lima. A law ending personal labor services to landowners was passed in April of 1962; in March 1963, the military junta that had staged a coup d'etat after the 1962 national elections issued an Agrarian Reform Law applicable to the Convención and Lares valleys. The reforms muffled peasant militancy in Cuzco but did little to stem the rate of invasions in other parts of the Peruvian Andes. According to Hector Béjar, 300,000 peasants were mobilized for hacienda invasions by 1963. Concern about the scale and intensity of rural militancy, Béjar contends, led landowners to imagine bearded guerrillas behind every tree.[25]

In the same month that Hugo Blanco surrendered to the authorities, the landowners' worst fears were confirmed. Six members of a group that called itself the Army of National Liberation (ELN), returning from months of training in Cuba, found themselves in a shootout with the police in Puerto Maldonado, an Amazonian river town close to the Bolivian frontier. A young poet born of an upper-middle-class Lima family, Javier Heraud, died in the ensuing manhunt, and the other members of the group fell into police hands. Heraud and his companions were the advance guard of a larger group of ELN militants, who managed to retreat into Bolivia. Accounts vary as to the original aims of the ELN contingent, but it is likely that they intended to provide military assistance and expertise to Hugo Blanco and his peasant unions.[26]

Although the death toll in Puerto Maldonado was insignificant in comparison to the massacres of peasants in other parts of the country at the same time, it sent shock waves through Peru. In the provinces, peasants were rising up in the greatest wave of agrarian unrest since the eighteenth century. The hope of Peruvian society, college-educated youths such as Javier Heraud, were training as guerrillas in Cuba and filtering back into the country. The 1962 military coup had made a mockery of Peru's democratic institutions, the integrity of which was only partly restored by the junta's decision to hold prompt elections. Fernando Belaúnde, the man who emerged as president during the election of 1963, faced widespread disorder in the countryside and mounting leftist militancy in the cities. It appeared that a Cuban-style insurrection could erupt at any moment.

The ELN's 1963 debacle in Puerto Maldonado was a setback for those who harbored dreams of an armed uprising. But in Lima, another Guevarist group, directed by Luis de la Puente Uceda, had come together under the name Movement of the Revolutionary Left (*Movimiento de Izquierda Revolucionaria*, or MIR).

In photographs taken during the 1950s and early 1960s, de la Puente is soberly dressed, a man of delicate build, thick glasses, a receding hairline, and sharp features often described as aristocratic. Born in 1926 to a landowning family, de la Puente joined the ranks of APRA in his teens and was exiled to Mexico after a 1948 arrest during a crackdown on APRA activities by the Odría dictatorship. Some sources assert that de la Puente befriended Fidel Castro during Castro's exile in Mexico. Returning clandestinely to Peru in 1954 or 1955, he conspired with APRA extremists to bring down the Odría regime, for which he was again arrested and imprisoned. After his release from detention in 1956, de la Puente completed a law degree at the University of Trujillo. De la Puente's trip to a 1959 agrarian reform conference in Havana proved to be a major turning point in his political development. His undisguised admiration for the Cuban Revolution was not well received by his APRA superiors when he returned from Havana, nor was his pivotal role in the formation of a radical faction within the party that eventually took the name Rebel APRA. APRA drummed de la Puente out of the party in 1959 for his fierce criticism of the convivencia.[27]

De la Puente again found himself in prison for killing an APRA goon—a "buffalo" in the parlance of the time—during an altercation in Trujillo in 1961. He emerged from jail in 1962 to assume leadership of Rebel APRA, which had by then transformed itself into the Movement of the Revolutionary Left.

The MIR was a party in the Guevarist mold, espousing a pragmatic form of Marxism with an ironclad commitment to armed struggle. In a position paper published in the United States in 1965, de la Puente argued that

> *the only element lacking in our country is a revolutionary vanguard capable of channeling the burning demands of our people, capable of giving form and organization to the masses, and of leading them along the right path. . . . We have emphasized the need to face up to the problem starting from armed struggle in the countryside by means of guerrilla strategy and tactics . . . that is, a people's war pushing outward from the Andes to the Coast, from the countryside to the cities, from the provinces to the capital.*[28]

De la Puente counted on peasant support for the MIR's *foquista* program of guerrilla struggle. In 1964 the party began to proselytize among peasants in the three fronts from which it planned to launch armed insurrection: in the northern department of Piura, near the Ecuadorian frontier; in the central highlands near Huancayo; and in the valley of La Convención, Department of Cuzco, where the MIR hoped to take advantage of the rural unrest stirred up by Hugo Blanco.[29]

De la Puente orchestrated the best-advertised guerrilla struggle in the history of Latin America. He announced the MIR's intention to take up arms during his most important public speech, given in Lima's Plaza San Martín in February of 1964. Later that year, he went underground to begin final preparations for war, but not before holding an informal press conference to announce his plans. Albert Brun, a reporter for the news agency France-Presse and perhaps the most prominent foreign correspondent in Peru, recalls the occasion well:

> *They called me one Sunday on behalf of de la Puente, who wasn't yet involved in guerrilla fighting or anything like that. It*

*was a farewell cocktail party on the Avenida Arequipa. So we got
together and had a pisco sour. Then de la Puente called together
the six or seven foreign correspondents who were there and said, in
the dramatic tone of voice that one uses on such occasions, that the
party was to say farewell before he went to begin the guerrilla
war. The announcement was taken as a joke by the reporters, but
not by the Intelligence Service.*[30]

Brun remembers de la Puente as a romantic totally unsuited
for combat: "The first gun de la Puente had in his hands was
one of those double-barreled shotguns used for hunting. He
learned to shoot with this so that the firing wouldn't scare
him. He just closed his eyes and fired." Brun's memories of
de la Puente contrast with the more martial impression of
Sebastián Salazar Bondy, who in 1965 described de la Puente's
violent encounter with APRA buffaloes four years earlier: "In
1961 a group of Apristas threatened him during a demonstration in Trujillo. Before they had a chance to do anything,
de la Puente whipped out a pistol and killed the ringleader
. . . His delicate appearance and his impeccable manners
give no hint of his fiery, stubborn temperament."[31]

Although MIR doctrine called for the preparation of a
peasant base before the commencement of armed struggle,
there is little evidence that the party's organizational activities
were effective. Where the party may have most successfully
established links to peasant organizations was in the central
front, the Department of Junín's highland provinces of Andamarca and Tarma and the adjacent jungle province of
Satipo.

The MIR's chief organizer in this region was Máximo Velando, a man born to a peasant family in Pampachacra, a
small community in Ayacucho. Like many in Peru's revolutionary left, he studied for a time in Argentina and there became a Communist party militant. In 1961 he went to Cuba
to see for himself what Radio Havana still calls "Free Territory in the Americas." Because the few Peruvians in Cuba
tended to stick together, Velando soon met Ricardo Gadea

and the other Peruvians who would make up the vanguard of the MIR and the ELN. During the months that Velando spent in Cuba in 1961, and later in 1962–1963, the country was under constant threat of invasion by the United States. "Bearing witness to this aggression consolidated our revolutionary project and, through this, our friendship," Ricardo Gadea remembers.[32]

In 1963 Velando returned to Peru and began work as a peasant organizer in Huancayo. His knowledge of the Quechua language and his rural background helped him gain acceptance among peasant syndicalists. His Argentine wife Carmen remembers that he spent the greatest part of his time in Andamarca, the highland community briefly held by the forces of Juan Santos Atahualpa in 1752.

In the tropical forest to the east of Máximo Velando's area of operations, a peasant activist and MIR sympathizer named Juan Paucarcaja Chávez tried to increase the militancy of the Federation of Smallholders and Colonists of Satipo (FEPCASA).[33] A surviving member of the MIR of the 1960s recalls Paucarcaja as hailing from Andamarca. He had migrated from the highlands to the eastern jungle only to find the same injustice: large landowners such as the Peruvian Corporation preventing smallholders from getting their coffee to market. Paucarcaja was a passionate advocate of hacienda invasions and of a broad agrarian reform that would include the jungle region as well as the highlands. Late in 1964, Paucarcaja and Velando were joined in Junín by Guillermo Lobatón, who had been designated leader of the MIR's operations in the area.

While organizers such as Velando and Paucarcaja forged links between the party and regional peasant organizations, de la Puente prepared the party for war. Through various clandestine connections in Peru and Bolivia, the MIR was able to assemble a ragged collection of carbines, handguns, and grenades. The origin of these arms and munitions has remained a mystery, though in 1987 Albert Brun reported that some of the rifles had been purchased in Bolivia from a mysterious German named Klaus Altmann, later unmasked as the escaped Nazi Klaus Barbie, "The Butcher of Lyons."[34] According to Brun's sources, the Bolivian intermediary used by Altmann-Barbie to deliver the arms, which were Mausers dating to World War I, replaced some of the weapons in the shipment with cheaper rifles lacking firing pins and ammunition of the proper caliber, rendering them useless. Although these and other weapons made their way to clandestine depots in the three front areas, MIR strategists counted on obtaining most of their arms from raids on police posts and army bases.

The human resources of the MIR resist easy estimation. Each party involved in the conflict—the left, the military, the press—had cause to exaggerate or underreport the number of MIR combatants. The MIR had obvious reasons to represent the guerrilla forces as substantial, their ranks swelling with peasants spontaneously moved to join the rebels. Although it was in the government's interest to portray the rebels as a tiny group of fanatics, the hamfisted repression of the armed forces, which included mass arrests of "guerrilla suspects," led to inflated estimates of the scale of the uprising to justify the numerous detentions. But it seems unlikely that the total number of MIR combatants in June 1965 was much in excess of one hundred—and these were spread out in three fronts, separated by hundreds of miles.[35]

Years of preparation and dreams had convinced the guerrillas that numbers and weaponry were less important keys to victory than determination, nerve, and the sheer weight of history. De la Puente's last public address in 1964 focused on the inevitability of capitalism's collapse. "The Revolution advances unstoppably through the world," he insisted during the speech. The time was right for a demonstration of revolutionary boldness in Peru.

By the middle of 1965, de la Puente had organized the MIR into a National Revolutionary Command and assumed the title of Supreme Commander. Breaking the cardinal rule of guerrilla warfare—mobility—he established himself in a fortified base camp at Mesa Pelada, to the east of Chaullay in the Convención valley. In case anyone had failed to notice that the MIR was determined to take up arms, the National Revolutionary Command issued a fifteen-page "Revolutionary Proclamation" announcing that the guerrilla war was under way: "We have chosen a guerrilla struggle in the sierra to begin the process, and we now have three guerrilla zones located in the northern, central, and southern parts of the country, where we will soon confront whatever kind and quantity of repressive forces that seek to subdue us."[36]

The political program enunciated by the MIR was nearly silent on the subject of the Indians expected to form the movement's base and to count themselves among the primary beneficiaries of the MIR's revolution. In part this reflects the legacy of orthodox Marxism. Marx saw native peoples as representatives of "archaic" or "Asiatic" societies that, though they may exhibit forms of primitive communism, are destined to be swept aside by the historic tide that will thunder ashore as a proletarian revolution. In any case, most Peruvian leftists were college-educated urbanites and (despite all protestations to the contrary) therefore subject to the ethnic prejudices that led city-dwellers to take for granted their intellectual ascendancy over Indians.

As early as the 1920s, José Carlos Mariátegui saw the Indian majority as a problematic issue for a truly Peruvian revolution. Like many Latin American thinkers of the time, Mariátegui wanted to incorporate the glories of pre-Columbian civilization into a vision of Peruvian socialism. He described Inca society as a "highly-developed and harmonious communistic system" that provided a model for progressive change in Peru.[37] Despite this romantic idea of the Indian past, however, Mariátegui was convinced that centuries of oppression had deadened Indians' capacity for insurrection. "The revolutionary spirit," he wrote, "always resides in the cities." The city is where man is confronted by the need for collective action, whereas the countryside only "excited his individualism."[38]

Mariátegui's views on the "Indian Problem" may be contradictory and suffer from armchair intellectualism, but at least he saw the issue as significant. His successors, however, failed to take up this theme. For the MIR, Indians were visible only as generic peasants (campesinos) or even as "rural proletarians." In the grip of his revolutionary fervor, de la Puente failed to realize that as far as Andean peasants were concerned, the leftist organizer from Lima might be as worthy of suspicion as the land-grabbing lawyer or landlord.[39]

The left is not entirely to blame for this failure of imagination. Despite the efforts of such Quechua-speaking intellectuals as José María Arguedas, Peruvian anthropology hadn't yet developed a strong tradition of field research among the country's Indian peoples. In the late 1950s and early 1960s, there was precious little information about how Andean peoples lived, thought, or worked. Clearly the land-tenure question was important to the Indians, but how they wanted to use the land once they got it was not well understood by Peruvian intellectuals. The MIR sometimes used Andean religious symbols for rhetorical effect in its communiqués—such as when it wrote that "the legendary Auquis and Apus [mountain spirits] are with us, because our cause is noble, just, patriotic"—but a deeper knowledge of the role of these mountain spirits in the peasant's life on the land is nowhere to be seen.[40]

De la Puente recognized, of course, that a wide cultural and linguistic gulf divided guerrillas and the rural population needed to sustain them. The ability of a few of the activists of the 1960s—most notably Hugo Blanco and Máximo Velando—to speak Quechua and thereby to communicate directly with peasants was frequently commented upon. But other leftist leaders lacked the skills to emulate them.

If the life of the Andean Indian was at the edge of the

intellectual map of urban leftists, the world of jungle Indians was off in the abyss. Leftist literature on prospects for jungle warfare in Peru describes eastern Peru as "unpopulated."[41] In a curious meditation on the possibility of bringing Asháninkas into the revolutionary fold, Héctor Béjar describes these "primitive men" as easily manipulated through religious proselytizing by unscrupulous landowners: "Fear of God is confused with fear of the *patrón* in the primitive imagination." Béjar continues:

If there is a visible difference in level [our emphasis] between the Quechua peasant and the creole guerrilla, the difference is even greater between the latter and the jungle Indian. For them to understand one another, there will necessarily be a long process of adaptation during which the guerrilla will learn new dialects and customs.[42]

A "difference in level"—a metaphor that reveals much about the prejudices of the revolutionaries who believed their mission was to bring the Indians face-to-face with history. Elías Murillo [a pseudonym],[43] who joined the MIR as it launched its guerrilla war, summed up his feelings about the Asháninkas' place in the revolution:

The Campas have to be shown how to live . . . They're just there with their little arrows, hunting, fishing—they're very lazy. We [of the MIR] thought that we must take their children to the schools and universities in order to educate them, so that they could return to educate their own parents, show them what work is . . . These Campas must believe in the new generation, to have the Marxist-Leninist idea of the new generation . . . to make them feel the need to change.[44]

But Asháninkas had their own view of history and of the shape of the new generation. As de la Puente and his followers prepared for armed insurrection, they had no idea how important a part this Asháninka vision would play in the coming struggle.

FIVE

Túpac Amaru

The guerrilla column making up the central front of the
MIR's three-front insurgency took the name Túpac Amaru
after the Inca rebel José Gabriel Condorcanqui, also known
as Túpac Amaru II, who challenged Spanish control of Andean Peru in the 1780s. In April of 1965 the Túpac Amaru
began field preparations for its uprising by establishing camps
at Yugurpampa, Jatunhuasi, Intihallamuy, Ajospampa, and
Pucutá in the provinces of Concepción and Satipo, all highland villages within a thirty-five kilometer radius of Andamarca. Some of these camps were little more than buried
caches of supplies. Others, such as Pucutá, were designated
"security zones" and included a network of trenches, as well
as shelters serving as factories for the production of crude
land mines and grenades. Aside from these homemade ex-
plosives, the weaponry of the Túpac Amaru consisted of re-
volvers, shotguns, carbines, and a few light automatic rifles.
    The area around Andamarca seemed to be textbook terrain
for guerrilla war. Mountainous, cold, fogbound, untracked

by roads, these valleys afforded the isolation Che Guevara identified as essential to the development of a revolutionary foco. Jungle areas were immediately accessible to the east, offering an escape route if government pressure made the highland camps too dangerous. The presence of haciendas and mines, coupled with a vigorous local tradition of agrarian rebellion, created fertile ground for revolutionary education among the local peasantry.[1]

The unfolding relations between the guerrillas of the Túpac Amaru and local peasant communities have inspired conflicting claims. Military sources are hopelessly contradictory. The army detained scores of peasants who committed no crime other than living near the guerrilla base camps; yet in the trials after the guerrilla war, the military prosecutors attempted to show that most of the peasants had been forcibly recruited by MIR guerrillas. In his postmortem of the guerrilla war, General Armando Artola claims that the guerrilla base at Yugurpampa was "surrounded by small plantations of tilled land worked by peasant families under an unhuman regime that began at dawn and didn't end until sunset. That is to say, in practice the guerrillas did the same thing as the exploiters and hacienda owners of the area."[2]

The peasants presented a different version of events when called to testify in 1969 about the guerrilla war. A young man named Guillermo Loardo explained that he had joined the guerrillas because "they spoke to me of misery and inequality and their causes. . . . I found out that there is misery and inequality because there are people with great property and the immorality of public officials favors those who have large landholdings."[3] Many of the peasants must have shared these sentiments; even if they were not willing to take up arms with the Túpac Amaru, they were ready to provide supplies or donate their labor for the construction of camps and a network of footpaths. One MIR survivor claims that scores of peasants supported the guerrillas despite their traditional suspicion of people from Peru's coastal region:

In the highlands, for example, there were thirteen of us in the Andamarca area, thirteen persons, but with the peasants we were more than sixty or seventy. . . . The peasantry helped us enthusiastically. They helped us carry provisions, arms, medicines, to take us from one site to another, to show us places and trails with great enthusiasm. Furthermore, we gave them medicine and food when they needed it.[4]

Testimonials of local support notwithstanding, some peasants harbored doubts about the guerrillas or found themselves indifferent to the MIR's message of revolutionary deliverance.

The members of the Túpac Amaru made a point of distinguishing themselves from peasants by their dress. According to Elías Murillo, this consisted of "a black jacket, Lee jeans, and boots that came halfway to the knee." The revolutionaries self-consciously avoided dressing like peasants, he adds, "because one had to let the army know that one was a guerrilla, not a peasant or a Campa."[5]

The commander of the Túpac Amaru, and the man who would inspire new utopian aspirations among Asháninkas, was Guillermo Lobatón Milla.[6] Of all the leaders of the MIR, Lobatón may have best represented the hopes and contradictions of the Peruvian left. Tall, bearded, with a high forehead and piercing eyes, Lobatón looked more like a revolutionary than did Luis de la Puente, the MIR's supreme commander. And unlike the aristocratic de la Puente, Lobatón came from a poor family in Lima, where the surname Lobatón is common among blacks of Haitian origin. He was raised in a society that, although not racist in the same way as the United States during this period, saw few blacks reach positions of political power.

Born in 1927, Lobatón went to primary school in the part of Lima known as Pueblo Libre. He attended a business school but found it distasteful, in part because of the prevailing prejudice against blacks and Indians. By 1948 he had begun to study literature, and later philosophy, at San Marcos University. His love for the high ideals of philosophy was soon tempered by the bitter experience of imprisonment for his involvement in student agitation against the Odría dictatorship. From a cell in El Frontón prison he wrote to the rector of San Marcos, his philosophy professor:

Victim of the most horrible injustice, plunged into the darkest pessimism, I ask the philosopher who gave me these most beautiful lessons in philosophy, can I still believe in the high destiny of man? Can I have faith in his praiseworthy value? Can I still hope that someone takes seriously my place in the world and will show me again that life is worth living?[7]

Exiled by the Odría government in 1954, Lobatón settled in Paris, where he read philosophy at the Sorbonne. He lived in France under difficult conditions. The war in Algeria heightened French hostility toward dark-skinned peoples. He scratched out a living by collecting scrap paper for a Spaniard on the rue San Jacques. There he met his future wife, Jacqueline Eluau, a Frenchwoman deeply committed to revolutionary change.

In 1988, Eduardo Fernández interviewed Jacqueline in her modest house located in the far suburbs of Paris. She reminded him of women shown storming the Bastille in eighteenth-century French paintings, a volatile mixture of eroticism and violence. Her commitment to revolutionary struggle remains strong despite the years that have passed since Guillermo Lobatón and the other members of the Túpac Amaru fell in combat.

Jacqueline remembers Lobatón as a voracious intellectual who found pleasure in adversity:

When I met him, he was a solitary type, a great reader. He
read the classics in those inexpensive versions, and magazines
about current politics. He was very restless. He read Mao in
German. He had tremendous curiosity. But he had a non-
intellectual side, too. He liked to cook. He pressed his eight-year-
old trousers by putting them between the mattress and the bed
frame. That's how he ironed them, his impeccable trousers! When
he took his morning bath he sang traditional waltzes from Lima.
He especially liked "The Guardian," which goes: "My lover
should not come to my tomb to weep." He told me never to cry.
That's the way Guillermo was. He didn't like fame, power,
or money. He was a humble man.

Lobatón was very religious. Look, in this letter he speaks of
Christ, of Lenin, of Vallejo. He thought that Lenin was a saint.
He had a special feeling for purity, for saintliness. He always
said he was going to make the Revolution in Peru.[8]

By 1959 his fame as an intellectual force among Paris's Peruvian expatriates led the Peruvian Communist party to provide Lobatón with a scholarship to study economics in East
Germany. His time there was unhappy. His German hosts
eventually deported him for his criticism of Stalinist bureaucracy. And he was tired of Europe, anxious to join the popular struggle in Latin America. By 1961 he was training in
Cuba with Luis de la Puente and the other Peruvians who
would make up the leadership of the MIR.[9]

Jacqueline Eluau recalls that from 1961 until the start of
the guerrilla war, Guillermo traveled a great deal—to Cuba,
Argentina, Brazil, and Chile. In Lima, he renewed his links
to the Guevarist left and helped formulate plans for the coming revolution. So much of what he saw in his colleagues and
in socialist experiments abroad disappointed him. "When he
returned from Cuba," Jacqueline remembers, "he didn't
want to say anything about it, he didn't want to speak of
Cuba. He wept over it. He had great doubts." Lobatón was
above all a humanist, not an ideologue.

He also harbored doubts about the middle-class progres-

sives who ran with the militant left, among them Sebastián
Salazar Bondy and Ricardo Letts. "Lobatón didn't mix with
them," says Jacqueline. "He kept his distance." In part this
was due to what Jacqueline sees as his sense of inferiority.
"He had something of a racial complex, a sense of being less,
as a black man, which in Peru means being even lower than
an Indian," she claims. To the extent that Lobatón socialized
with Ricardo Letts, the relationship was of "humble servant
to boss." Jacqueline remembers Letts as a "white from a good
family who played at revolution."

Twenty-two years after the MIR uprising, Ricardo Letts
recalls Lobatón with affection. Stirring his coffee in a small
Miraflores café, Letts looks a bit like Lenin: tall and slender,
a dark goatee, in a plain blue suit and white shirt buttoned at
the collar. "I remember Guillermo as serene, resolved, willing to listen but absolutely certain that the MIR would repeat
the success of the Cuban Revolution," Letts says. "He smiled
a lot, and there was a certain sparkle in his eyes. In the
strength of his conviction he was like a missionary. For him,
the revolution was about to start."[10]

Underneath Letts's warm recollections of Lobatón is a critical view of his Marxism: "Guillermo had made the leap from
the life of the intellectual to the life of action. But as he did
this, his Marxism became oversimplified. Like Mariátegui,
Lobatón had Trotskyite tendencies." Which meant, among
other things, that he was prone to forms of "adventurism"
leading to premature action.

Lobatón had his doubts about the MIR, too, but he kept
them to himself. "He said that de la Puente had a base of
support, that it was not the time for criticism," his widow
remembers. "He had to assist and develop the struggle. He
dissented only in a solitary way, always trying to prevent
disunity."

When the MIR guerrillas eventually came to be front-page
news, the Peruvian press showed a special fascination with
Lobatón's cultured background and intellectual accomplish-

ment. An article in the Huancayo newspaper *Correo* on June 26, 1965, describes Lobatón as a

strong mulatto who speaks seven languages and has traveled over half the world. . . . A cultivated man, he studied political philosophy at San Marcos University for six years. At the Sorbonne in Paris he studied political science and at the University of Leipzig in East Germany he studied political economy. . . . The fruit of those trips is his total mastery of English, French, Hebrew, Portuguese, Italian, and Spanish. His favorite sport is skiing, and in France he skied Mont Blanc, the highest peak in Europe. In Lima he was a standout forward in the soccer club "Lloque Yupanqui" of Jesús María.[11]

The discrepancy between Lobatón's Afro-American, working-class background and his cosmopolitan experience clearly made him a perplexing figure for Peruvians. Here was a black man with the best of all status symbols in Peru: a *gringa* wife invariably described in the media as a "blonde, green-eyed Frenchwoman." Perhaps it was Lobatón's romantic image that prompted compensatory excesses from the Peruvian army's propaganda machine, which described him as "astute, cold, calculating, and bloodthirsty."[12] Whatever his limitations as a guerrilla leader, Lobatón was not cold and calculating. His letters reveal a passionate man capable of fierce loyalty and love. When preparations for the guerrilla struggle were underway in May 1965, he wrote his mother from the field:

You are in my memory as you will be there always: courageous and full of concern for our welfare. I am the son of your courage and of your concern. . . . Give me your blessing, mother, and let me go forward. Your son will never forget you.[13]

As news of the MIR's insurgency reached the young writer Mario Vargas Llosa in Paris, he wrote to his friend Francisco

Moncloa that "Lobatón is an extraordinary man in whom one can have blind confidence."[14]

At dawn on June 9, the Túpac Amaru took to the field. Commandeering a truck at a place called Chapicancha, guerrillas raided the powder magazine of the Santa Rosa mine, making off with twenty-two boxes of dynamite. During their escape from the mining settlement, they blew up the bridge over the Maraniyoc River. Later that morning, the guerrillas "expropriated" carbines, ammunition, and food from the Runatullo hacienda. The insurgents made brief speeches to local peasants and presented them with some of the captured food. Meanwhile, another group from the Túpac Amaru raided the Civil Guard post in Andamarca, securing more guns and ammunition.

These operations, which involved no casualties, were followed by a series of similar actions over the next ten days. The Túpac Amaru raided the Punta, Armas, and Alegría haciendas, distributing cattle among the peasants. They damaged another bridge at Comas. Whenever possible, the guerrillas issued revolutionary proclamations to the sometimes bewildered onlookers. In his official communiqué of June 20, Guillermo Lobatón called these events "armed propaganda":

We held meetings and gave out food from the stores, all along the road, from the lorry which we captured and returned undamaged. All the next day we were masters of our zone of influence. . . . We accounted for the Alegría hacienda, which belonged to one of our worst enemies and a scourge of the poor, Raúl Ribeck. The police were already in Andamarca, one day away from the hacienda. We turned it into a commune and the goods were shared out among the peasants.[15]

The Túpac Amaru's acts of revolutionary "propaganda" soon led to a shooting war. An attempt by the guerrillas to ambush a police patrol near Andamarca went awry on June 15. The police fought their way out of the trap, and another one the following day, without casualties. Five guerrillas died in these clashes. Things turned around for the Túpac Amaru on June 27, however. A guerrilla column led by Máximo Velando trapped a twenty-nine-member detachment of the 10th Command of the Civil Guard in a narrow defile at Yahuarina. Nine civil guards, including the commanding officer, Major Horacio Patiño, died in the firefight. The rest surrendered. After attending to the wounded policemen and lecturing Lieutenant Edilberto Terry on the need to "cease serving the rich," Velando ordered the prisoners released. From the action at Yahuarina the Túpac Amaru obtained fourteen rifles, several automatic weapons, medical supplies, and other key items of materiel.[16]

The news of the battle at Yahuarina came scarcely a fortnight after government officials announced that the violence in Andamarca was the work of common cattle-rustlers. As late as June 15, President Fernando Belaúnde insisted that the guerrillas were a "fiction."[17] Nevertheless, sensationalistic articles appeared in the Lima press claiming that the rustlers were indeed communists—and well-equipped ones, with anti-aircraft weapons, clandestine radio transmitters, and airplanes. Raúl Ribeck, the hacienda owner villified by Lobatón as an enemy of the people, told a reporter that the guerrillas had two landing strips near Pucutá. A captain in the Civil Guard claimed to have seen "four hundred guerrillas transporting heavy weapons on horseback."[18]

By late June the insurgency was beyond the control of the Civil Guard. The police were poorly equipped and in questionable physical shape; on June 14, twenty-five guardsmen incapacitated by altitude sickness had to be evacuated to Runatullo. Civil Guard units still in the field suffered from such a shortage of provisions that they began to appropriate cattle belonging to local peasants—ironic behavior in view of the government's claim that the police mission was to capture rustlers. Files of the police training program of the U.S. Agency for International Development show that civil guards had received little or no training in the use of the firearms they carried. One inspection revealed that 95 percent of the radios used by the police were broken.[19]

The Peruvian congress empowered the army to take over counterinsurgency operations on July 2. The government suspended civil rights two days later, after bombs exploded at the Hotel Crillón and at a debutante ball underway at the Club Nacional de Lima.

The army placed its hopes of a quick counterinsurgency campaign in a special Ranger unit trained by the United States Army at Fort Gulick in the Panama Canal Zone. Since Castro's takeover in Cuba, the United States had stepped up direct support for antiguerrilla training in friendly Latin American countries. The goal was to create small, mobile fighting forces—patterned closely on the U.S. Army's Green Berets—that could "smash small, sometimes Red-oriented guerrilla bands before they can grab for power in Castro style," in the crisp language of the *Wall Street Journal*.[20]

The Peruvian military had misgivings about a major shift toward a counterinsurgency orientation. General Edgardo Mercado Jarrín, the leading Peruvian strategist of counterinsurgency doctrine, notes that by its very nature the military is depersonalized by the antiguerrilla struggle.[21] In part this is a security measure: the identity of officers must remain a secret to protect them and their families from reprisals. But it is also because the essentially political mission of counterinsurgency is incompatible with a classical notion of military heroism. The enemy is a fellow countryman rather than a foreigner, a poor peasant or unarmed student rather than a well-trained combatant. To the Peruvian armed forces, writes the military historian Victor Villanueva, guerrillas were "hordes with no respect for the principles of warfare, who haven't read Clausewitz, who violate tactical norms, who don't play the game by the rules, [and] who fight like rustlers while ignoring military honor."[22]

Both Peru and the United States hoped that a small-scale guerrilla threat could be met by regular police rather than by the army. Beginning in 1960, the Office of Public Safety of the U.S. Agency for International Development (OPS-AID) attempted to strengthen and professionalize Peru's police forces, while improving their public reputation. The underlying assumption was that police were the "first line of defense against subversion and insurgency."[23] The rationale for OPS assistance was couched in terms of development, or as one OPS document states, "to improve the capacity of the police to maintain internal security and encourage a climate conducive to the economic, social, and political development of Peru."[24] There was also a strategic motive at work. According to one CIA insider, the OPS program gave U.S. intelligence agents privileged access to police officials and personnel in related branches of government.[25]

OPS operations in Peru intensified as the guerrilla threat in the Andes loomed ever larger in the early 1960s. In 1964, OPS and its counterparts in the Peruvian Civil Guard began to discuss the feasibility of training an elite police parachute unit that could provide a strike force against insurgencies in remote areas. This eventually came to be known as the Special Police Emergency Unit (SPEU).

By early 1965, OPS officers were meeting on a weekly basis with the director of the Civil Guard to lay plans for the counterinsurgency unit. The urgency of these plans increased dramatically when the MIR took up arms in June, to the point that the United States agreed to pay virtually all of the expenses associated with the creation and training of the SPEU during its first year. One OPS document laments the "long guerrilla lead on public order," presumably referring to the roots put down by leftist organizations in some rural areas.[26] The developing guerrilla struggle in Junín confirmed the worst fears of the United States about the lack of police readiness in Peru. The OPS chief observed in his situation report for June 1965 that the Civil Guard had shown "minimal capability to contain rural dissident actions that are fluid and fast moving." Worse still, he concluded, "the foraging of police for food has resulted in some criticism"—a polite way of saying that peasants found the police more objectionable than the guerrillas.[27]

The number of OPS personnel in Peru went from one in 1960 to twelve in 1966, not counting a number of advisors who worked for OPS on short-term assignments. Financial support for the SPEU counterinsurgency effort amounted to $1.4 million in 1965 and 1966.

The Peruvian government constructed a training area for the SPEU at Mazamari, near the town of Satipo, close to the theater of operations of the Túpac Amaru guerrillas. Tension between the civilian and military aspects of the counterinsurgency program was inevitable. OPS personnel liked to refer to the unit as "premilitary," but it was in essence a small airborne assault team with a force level of approximately 150 men, not counting support personnel. The commodities provided for the program by the United States were mostly military: parachutes, jumpsuits, helmets, tents, automatic weapons, medical gear, as well as a C-46 aircraft and military helicopters. OPS employees collaborated with the U.S. military mission in the preparation of supply lists and in piggybacking orders on Department of Defense consignments. Police officials and cabinet ministers pressured the OPS team to "give the police the same kind of material assistance that the U.S. military mission provides the Peruvian Armed Forces."[28] When it proved difficult to find American police advisors who spoke Spanish, the embassy considered turning to the U.S. Southern Command in Panama for bilingual military officers. Eventually this was rejected on the grounds that it conflicted with the "civilian" mission of OPS.[29]

Despite accelerated training and the opening of a floodgate of U.S. support for the SPEU, the guerrilla war moved too swiftly for the Civil Guard antiguerrilla squad to play an important role. Under intense pressure from Peruvian politicians, the army overcame its reluctance and took on the responsibility of putting down the insurgency.[30]

The generals set tough conditions before committing their soldiers to the field. Although the Belaúnde regime put the army in charge of the counterinsurgency in early July, the military refrained from direct action for two weeks, by which time it had been assured of a free hand with regard to press controls and the application of repressive measures in the countryside.[31]

Central to the emerging counterinsurgency doctrine of the time was a concern with "the human element." No longer could officers confine their analysis to terrain, weather, and troop strength. If the enemy was among the ordinary people, one had to understand the ordinary people in order to find the enemy. In a lecture presented to the military intelligence service, a Peruvian general called for studies of the "population, health, housing, diet, education, religion, languages, customs, etc., duly grouped, classified, and refined."[32] This led to an interest in ethnology in the Peruvian armed forces that, in its own way, produced results as peculiar as the polemical "anthropology" of the militant left.

The Ministry of War's report on the MIR insurgency, for instance, analyzes the principal ethnic groups involved in the conflict. Most important are highland Indians, "exploited for centuries without significant opportunities to educate themselves, with a low level of life, suffering the penury of the countryside or their habitual workplace, dedicated to heavy work and constant sacrifice to assure daily sustenance."[33] In contrast, the typical coastal person is "essentially incorporated into civilization, extroverted, an excellent worker in the country or the town, permeable to social concerns, still living in precarious circumstances and searching for better conditions for himself and for his family."

The report devotes a surprising amount of space to a description of the Asháninka:

The Campa, in a constant struggle with nature, has developed qualities that make him the undisputed lord of the jungle, which he knows absolutely. Far from civilization and the development of humanity, he has been confronted for many years by the white man who comes with colonizing passion or brought by his ambition to the riches he hopes to exploit. The need to struggle constantly and then take refuge far from navigable rivers; the occasional relations with some whites; the apostolic action of the missionaries who, with affection and persuasion put [the Indian] in gradual contact with civilization; the transformation of jungle zones by the push of progress; labor within different systems from the ones that [the Indian] knows—these are, among other things, the factors that mold the psychology of the contemporary Campa: rebellious, independent, [and] extremely suspicious until he is sure of the intentions and attitudes of people who approach him.[34]

In a history of the guerrilla war published in 1976, General Armando Artola includes a section entitled "Ethnology," in which he analyzes the part Asháninkas played in the struggle:

During the operations . . . [Asháninkas] served as guides for both sides and came to have a role in missions of exploration and ambush, after payment and the presentation of transistor radios, carbines, flashlights, etc. With the exception of their principal chiefs, they really didn't understand what it was all about until very late in the campaign, which gave rise to much confusion of every sort.[35]

It would be easy to ridicule this simpleminded "anthropology," which merely reflects the ethnic stereotypes of the Peruvian middle class, if it did not so obviously emulate social research conducted elsewhere in Latin America under the aegis of the United States. The most infamous case was Project Camelot, a research project sponsored by the Department of Defense and administered by the Special Operations Research Office (SORO) of American University. Project Camelot was a study of the social causes of revolution and unrest. SORO planned to conduct pilot research in Chile, using U.S. and Chilean social scientists to analyze all sectors of Chilean society. When news of the project slipped out in 1965, it created a major diplomatic scandal in Latin America and prompted anguished soul-searching in the North American academic world, the reverberations of which can still be heard today in anthropology. Twenty-five years later, the high dudgeon of the rhetoric about Project Camelot seems out of proportion to the significance of the project itself. Yet Camelot quickly became, and continues to be, a symbol of North American "academic espionage" for Latin Americans.[36]

Peru had its own brush with Camelot. Not long after the Túpac Amaru entered into armed struggle, several Lima dailies alleged that the same U.S. organization responsible for Project Camelot was conducting a similar study in the Peruvian jungle.[37] A State Department cable released under the Freedom of Information Act describes the research as "an unclassified SORO project through American University to study colonization which is [the] subject of civic action collaboration between [the] U.S. Army Mission and [the] Peruvian Army. . . . Two U.S. researchers, Dr. Milton Jacobs and Dr. Alexander Askenasy, are active in the country." The project had the unfortunate name of Task Colony, which served as grist for the editorial mill of Lima newspapers and magazines as late as February of 1966 and doubtless contributed to the subsequent discontinuation of the research. Adding to public suspicion of Task Colony was its superficial similarity to a controversial project in Colombia called Task Simpático, an attempt to formulate "noncombat ways in which indigenous military forces make the attitudes of civilians more favorable toward their governments and military forces."[38]

Peruvian military leaders cooperated with the Task Colony project because most believed that economic development in the jungle would solve the country's political problems while strengthening military control of frontier regions. "Colonization was conceived of as a technocratic solution to rural conflicts, as well as a means of reducing the flow of migrants to the city and the consequent process of slum formation," writes the political scientist Jorge Rodríguez Beruff.[39] Although the United States received no immediate benefit from the colonization of the Peruvian Amazon, Peru's efforts to open up remote regions with military manpower did fit nicely with the emerging U.S. doctrine of civic action—that is, using military equipment and expertise for public works projects that would improve the popular image of the armed forces and link the government with social reform in the minds of the peasantry. By the mid-1960s, civic action and counterinsurgency had become two sides of the same coin in attempts to thwart communist subversion.[40]

Once the army took charge of the campaign against the MIR, it exercised total control over the dissemination of information. Few journalists were allowed into the field to cover the story, a policy that one American diplomat felt did nothing but encourage the spread of sensational rumors about the MIR's strength and military victories.[41] The army's own communiqués were infrequent, cryptic, and self-serving. Even after a quarter-century of research on the conflict, precise information on the movements of men and materiel during the campaign remains scarce.

The army's Second Military Region, which took charge of the response to the Túpac Amaru, deployed the Second Light Division and a specially trained company of the Republican

Guard (a paramilitary police branch normally assigned to border protection and prison management) to encircle the Andamarca area with the hope that the region could be turned into an isolated killing field. Army and police checkpoints blocked access roads. The navy patrolled the jungle rivers east of the guerrillas' theater of operations. The air force took over the airfield at Jauja for supply operations and constructed a small heliport at Chilifruta.

Beginning on July 20, Zorro and Loma Companies of the Second Light Division made a slow sweep toward the communities of Huancamayo and Balcón, with orders to establish advance bases from which they could commence a pincer movement on Pucutá, the Túpac Amaru's most important encampment. There was no armed contact between the army and the guerrillas until July 30, when Zorro Company found itself under fire by guerrillas using small arms and homemade grenades. The official army report claims that the attack was repulsed, leaving four guerrillas dead.[42] While Zorro moved on toward Pucutá, Guillermo Lobatón led a detachment of guerrillas toward the army's forward base at Balcón with the hope of surprising the small group of soldiers left behind to defend it. But the plan had to be abandoned when one member of a supply train overtaken by the guerrillas escaped to warn the authorities of the Túpac Amaru's presence in the area.

The army's primary objective, Pucutá, was held by Máximo Velando and a handful of guerrillas. As Zorro and Loma Companies closed in on the camp, the Peruvian air force used Canberra jets based in Piura to bomb and strafe the site, softening it up for a land assault. The weapon that the air force hoped would clear the area of guerrillas was napalm.

The origin of the napalm used by the air force is still the subject of speculation. The U.S. embassy had turned down a request for napalm from the Peruvian government, citing the difficulty of distinguishing guerrilla positions from peasant settlements.[43] Victor Villanueva, a Peruvian military historian, believes that the source of the substance was the International Petroleum Company, a subsidiary of Standard Oil of New Jersey, which hoped to stave off nationalization of its Peruvian holdings by assisting the Belaúnde government with the counterinsurgency. He alleges that the locally produced napalm was loaded into gasoline drums and pushed out of a C-46 airplane after the terrified crew lit simple fuses.[44] U.S. embassy documents state that by August 25 the Peruvian air force had dropped twelve of the sixteen napalm bombs in its possession.[45]

Despite the home-brewed quality of the napalm, its effect on the target was devastating. "The bomb fell and burned an immense stretch of ground, maybe a hundred meters around," remembers Elías Murillo, who witnessed one of the air attacks on Pucutá. "There was a huge hole, and the rest blackened. Snakes and toads were swollen up from the flames . . . it was a terrible fire."[46] According to Murillo, the bombing and strafing of Pucutá killed only peasants, who took shelter in their houses, easy targets for the attacking aircraft.

The infantry struggle for Pucutá began on August 1 and continued through August 3, when Velando led the other defenders in a retreat toward Intihallamuy. Lobatón's group made its own way east by a different route. Guerrilla dead and wounded numbered eleven; the army registered confirmed casualties of seven, including four dead. Under the pressure of hundreds of government troops, the Túpac Amaru escaped from the mountains toward the heavily forested foothills of the Río Sonomoro. The highland struggle had been lost; the jungle struggle was about to begin.

 Itomi Pavá

Pedro Kintaro is one of the senior men in a village that sits on a densely forested range of hills dividing the Pangoa and Ene valleys. When Kintaro speaks of his life before the arrival of the MIR guerrillas, his anger churns like the river heaving over the rocks near his house:

I was born in Alto Sanibeni, not here. I never knew my father well because he died in Sanibeni when I was a child. Since I didn't have a father, I went naked. There was no money for clothes, for a cook pot—nothing! We were poor. I left Sanibeni to find work, and I came to know civilization. I learned to speak some of the Spaniard's language, but not much. So I grew up like a slave of the haciendas, working on the farms of the patrones.[1]

In July of 1965, tensions between colonists and Asháninkas were near the flashpoint in the area around Kintaro's community. The land invasions that brought down the Perené Colony had lured thousands of settlers to Satipo Province; all too often, the new arrivals pushed Asháninkas aside. More specific grievances in the area of Cubantía were linked to the abuses of large landowners and policemen, who assumed they had natural rights over the bodies of Indian women and the labor of Indian men.

Kintaro's subservience abruptly ended in a most improbable place—the high forest west of Cubantía, where he and his kinsman, Ernesto Andrés, had gone to hunt spider monkeys:

> *There, walking on the old trail to Jatunhuasi, I met Juan Paucarcaja. He was from Satipo. He defended the peasants. Yes, this was why he fought in the guerrilla war. "I'm fighting against the landowners," he said. "I want you to help us. You suffer a lot. The gringos, the landowners exploit you, no?" "Yes, it's true," I told him. "All my people work for the landowners and they can't work their own fields. Their children, their wives— they have nothing to eat! We have no education. We have no schools like there are where the landowners live."*

Paucarcaja introduced Pedro and Ernesto to the leaders of the Túpac Amaru:

> *Well, the guerrillas said, "We're going to punish the ones who abuse you. We'll take away their coffee plantations. Land for the people! That's what we want. The same as in Lima and Huancayo. There are no soldiers there anymore, no policemen. We've killed them all!"*
>
> *That's how we talked in Cubantía. That's how I met Lobatón. Yes, the bearded one. After that there were Jaime Martínez [the nom de guerre of Froilán Herrera, the Túpac Amaru's third in command] and Humberto, a tall gringo, and Máximo Velando and Vallejos, and Mario—all of them. . . . Yes, Lobatón talked to me. He was black. With a beard. Black, but he spoke the Spanish language. He was the commander, the leader. He spoke a lot. But I didn't understand much. What was a revolution? What was a community? . . . Soon all my people were with the*

guerrillas—those from villages here, there, and other places. They taught all of us how to use firearms. Carbines, pistols, everything. Oh, we sure made enough noise! That's how we learned to defend ourselves, to fire weapons. Not well, but we learned something.

Yes, I spoke with Lobatón. He was older, he tired rapidly. He always said to me, "Brother, we've come to defend you."

Pedro Kintaro speaks of his first encounter with the Túpac Amaru in political terms, his recollection of these events doubtless colored by the months he subsequently spent in jail with members of the MIR and other political prisoners. Kintaro's kinsman Ernesto, a shaman (*sheripiári*), saw the meeting in a different light—one that ultimately cost him his life. Today the shaman's words are accessible only through the accounts of others. Manuel Ashivánti, a master storyteller from Pangoa, describes Ernesto's reaction to the guerrillas' request for assistance:

The shaman met the leader, who had a big beard like this . . . ssh . . . like this . . . uh! Yes, quite a beard the leader had, well! There the shaman met him, there he spoke with the leader.

He said that he was the Amachénga; the bearded one said he was the son of God. "Itomi Pavá," the Son of the Sun, thought the shaman. Then they began to speak there.

"I am a son of God, we are sons of God. I want to help you. Are there colonists on your land?"

"Yes, there are."

"Ah, OK. What does the colonist say to you? Does he pay you well when you work for him? Does he give you gifts?"

"No!"

"How do you work? Do you live with the colonist?"

"He just orders me around! He orders me to work, he tricks me! He never pays. Since we don't know much about money, he doesn't pay me. He orders me to work in his field and he doesn't pay me. He mistreats me, he tricks me."

"And what are the names of these colonists?"
The shaman gave him the names of all the colonists who made
him work.
"Ah . . . now . . . this is bad!" said the leader. "They
trick you a lot. You natives shouldn't help them; they are colonists,
they are millionaires, they are hacienda owners. You shouldn't
work for them; you should work in your own fields so that you
have what they have. Those who cheat you, those who threaten
you—we're going to eliminate them so they can't trick you again.
Because I am the true son of God!"[2]

Asháninka oral histories quickly leap from this first encounter to the distribution of weapons by the guerrillas. According to Ashivánti, Guillermo Lobatón, the bearded one,
presided over the instruction of Asháninka comrades:

The one we met first was Lobatón, but they called him Sabino
[Lobatón's nom de guerre]. He was a guerrilla, the com-
mander. . . . . Sabino took charge of teaching about weapons,
teaching about why they're going to kill, how they'll kill. Sabino
taught these things to our people. He showed them how to use a
machine gun. He gave them out to each man, saying, "This is for
you, for you, for you." Each one a machine gun. "This is how
you'll shoot." Well, my people learned, all right.

The precise sequence of events that drew Asháninkas into
the orbit of the MIR will probably never be known. The
Indians' oral histories of the encounter compress time so se-
verely that there is scarcely a gap between first contact and
full entanglement in the insurgency. The guerrillas who made
the contact are dead. Surviving members of the MIR, anxious to defend the party from the accusation of other Marxist
groups that they were "adventurers," portray the MIR-
Asháninka alliance as the result of a long period of grass-

roots organizing in Satipo Province.[3] The MIR survivor Elías Murillo claims that a local member of the party named Antonio Meza began working with Asháninkas as early as 1963.[4] Froilán Herrera had also established links with peasant communities near Satipo.[5] But while there were probably some contacts between radicals and Indians prior to 1965, there is little evidence that the MIR had laid a strong foundation among the Asháninkas. The MIR's interest in the Indians intensified when the guerrillas had to buy time, to find the food and shelter they needed after weeks of fighting in the highlands. They saw an opportunity to use a tribal people legendary for their ferocity to carry the insurgency into the lowlands.

Asháninka accounts suggest that the key liaison to the guerrillas was not Antonio Meza but the peasant activist Juan Paucarcaja. Even conservative landowners of the Satipo area remember Paucarcaja as a hard-working, honest man whose farm in Sonomoro was prosperous by local standards. Eugenio Sarove, a Spaniard who worked a farm next to Paucarcaja's, recalls: "Paucarcaja and I had friendly working relations, friendly in every sense. He lived for work. He had a Campa wife, and he lived like a Campa." Sarove insists that Paucarcaja was "used" by the guerrillas, whose Marxist ideology the peasant organizer could barely understand.[6]

Paucarcaja arranged the contact, but it was Lobatón who made the biggest impression on the Asháninkas. Lobatón spoke of a sudden social transformation and a settling of accounts with the hacienda owners. The Indians would soon have all the trade goods that eluded them in their present poverty. Lobatón's blackness and his great beard—consistently mentioned in Asháninka accounts—must have contributed to his otherness, to the sense that he was somehow part of the outside world yet different from it. Like his eighteenth-century counterpart, Antonio Gatica, Lobatón managed to inspire some Asháninkas to transcend, however briefly, their own sharply circumscribed political loyalties in favor of a larger goal of liberation.

Pedro Kintaro now denies that the guerrillas were spirits, but he remembers Ernesto's conviction that Lobatón was sent by Pavá, Father Sun:

He believed it. He always took ayahuasca *[a hallucinogen used by shamans to seek visions]. He smoked tobacco. Well, he was a shaman, a sheripiári! People said: "It's the Son of the Sun." They said it about the guerrillas. Ernesto was the first to see them. He was the first to see Lobatón.*

It is possible that Ernesto's identification of Guillermo Lobatón as a helpful spirit was a decision made in an instant, but it seems more likely that he had given prior thought to the matter as rumors of the highland struggle filtered into Cubantía. Asháninka sheripiári are expected to decipher alarming portents, to recast news into terms meaningful to their followers. The process of interpretation can be risky for the shaman if events prove him wrong. It can also be an opportunity for increased influence, especially if he can bind the agents of these events to his own vision of the world. Just as a sheripiári in the Gran Pajonál may have shaped the message of Juan Santos Atahualpa to an Asháninka mold, so Ernesto appropriated Lobatón's message for his own prophecy of apocalyptic change—one that fit the well-established pattern of Asháninka messianic dreams.

Despite the years that have passed since the guerrilla war and the bitterness that remains after so much death and destruction, people still remember the excitement of Ernesto's prophecy. Alfredo Atiri was a young man in 1965:

Around Kiatari we heard the news that Itomi Pavá had come. "He's come down," the old people said. There was a shaman in Kiatari, he was the first to say this, warning, "He's come down, Itomi Pavá, yes." The news traveled fast. Everyone talked about it. They asked: "How is this? How will we recognize him?" Since no one had seen him, they didn't know how to recognize him.

*So people were saying: "The Sun is coming. Now he's come!
He's come here! He's come to bring justice . . ." I was doubtful.
But the oldest ones, they believed, believed that it was the moment
for justice. "It will be the end of deceptions, of abuses. Now they
won't take our land. We'll have lots of things—everything that
the white people have!" That's what they said. Since there had
been so many abuses, everyone believed that Itomi Pavá was going
to finish it, that we Indians would have justice.*

*My father believed. How could he not believe it? So many
abuses. Someone arrived who promised to wipe out all the exploiters, and my people believed him.*[7]

Alberto Yorini has similar recollections:

*They worshipped the guerrilla. They said he was Itomi Pavá,
that he had come to shower us with riches, with everything. . . .
[They said] he was going to come like that, dressed as a colonist
or as one of my people. "These are Sons of the Sun," they said.
That's why they believed the guerrillas.*[8]

Even at this early stage in the relationship with the Túpac
Amaru, however, there were some who doubted. Manuel
Ashivánti, himself a shaman, remembers that he went to visit
Ernesto to question him about this Itomi Pavá. They debated
the possibility that Lobatón was not a helpful spirit but a
kamári, a demon:

*"No, he's not fooling me," said the sheripiári. "It's the truth!
He's taken me into the sky, where he lives. I've been there. It's so
good! I've been where the Sun lives. There are huge quantities
of things there. I've been there, that's why I believe."*

Ashivánti warned Ernesto that there are false spirits:

*Be careful, brother-in-law. You should live peacefully, because
one day the Sun will come to earth, and he'll kill you. Just you
wait. We'll meet before the Sun, before God, and there we'll find
the truth.*

Although Ashivánti doubted the prophecy of Ernesto, when he returned to Pangoa he reported to his kinsmen that despite his doubts he would wait to see what developed: "Will it be the Sun or not? Is it the truth or a lie? Let's wait and find out."

Even before Asháninkas were being taught how to use automatic weapons by the guerrillas, rumors of an imminent Indian uprising swept through Satipo. On June 15, *La Prensa* reported that a group of five hundred guerrillas had established a base camp on the Río Pangoa, near Mazamari. Among these subversives were Asháninkas "brought from places nearby." Two days later, the same paper quoted the prefect of the Department of Junín, Raúl Zárate Jurado, to the effect that 60 percent of the Asháninkas were prepared to assist the guerrillas.[9] An article in *Correo* reported on June 16 that "peasants described the extremists as men who look like Campas, wearing dirty clothes, with long hair and beards." These guerrillas, the newspaper continued, "run like goats in the hills."

General Artola makes the plausible claim that soon after the Túpac Amaru's June 27 ambush at Yahuarina, Guillermo Lobatón sent Froilán Herrera and Juan Paucarcaja to Cubantía to scout escape routes to the lowlands in case the guerrilla campaign in the highlands should go badly. Other comrades explored potential hideouts near Mazaronquiari and along the Chinchireni and Anapati rivers.[10] By the end of July, members of the Túpac Amaru had established themselves near Cubantía while Velando and Lobatón defended Pucutá and Intihallamuy against the army.

Froilán Herrera framed plans for a local assault that would open a new front in the jungle. The Indians were happy to suggest a target: the coffee hacienda "Cubantía," owned by an Italian named Antonio Fávaro. Alfredo Atiri, who takes Fávaro to be a Spaniard, explains it this way:

> This Fávaro threatened my people. He was a hacienda owner, a Spaniard. These men are Spaniards! He invited us to work, saying, "You should work on a road with me so that everyone will be able to carry his produce on the road." We paid him no mind, and he made his own road with wage laborers.
>
> Since we hadn't worked for him, he prohibited us from walking on his road. "Don't go there! Open your own road if you want to walk with your stuff." That's how he began to make threats, because my people didn't help him. He threatened several of them. He shouted at them: "Why have you brought your coffee by here? Why didn't you come to work on the road? . . . Why didn't you come when I called you? You can't walk here now. Get out!"
>
> But my people wanted to walk there. He threatened them: "If you walk here, I'm going to kill you!" And he took out his revolver—a big goddam revolver! Well, my people were scared. They turned around and headed the other way.

According to Atiri, the guerrillas decided to kill Fávaro one night when they were drinking.

> Everyone was drunk. Damn! And Sabino [Lobatón] wasn't there. He was far away, in Cuba. They went to Chuquibambilla with Jaime [Froilán Herrera] to kill Fávaro. . . . . My people told the guerrillas: "There's a Spaniard, he's got a revolver. I helped him a lot with the work in his fields, weeding, harvesting his coffee. He threatened me, he doesn't want me to pass on his road, he's prohibited us. He says that it's his house."
>
> They told everything. That's how the guerrillas got angry. "Right, son, tomorrow we have to kill this man!" All of my people had automatic weapons, so they went to kill Fávaro.

Lobatón was not, of course, in Cuba at the time of this discussion, as Atiri remembers. He had returned to the highlands to help stop the army's cleanup operation moving relentlessly toward Intihallamuy. For Atiri, "Cuba" represents a distant center of power, the place where Lobatón and other guerrillas were trained and armed to kill the landowners.

Anticipating trouble, the army had stationed a detachment of civil guards at Fávaro's hacienda, which boasted an airstrip and a shortwave transmitter. A smaller police unit guarded the Kiatari hacienda, twelve kilometers away, and several strategic points where large rivers were crossed by *huaros*, rustic hand-powered cable cars. The civil guard unit at Cubantía numbered twenty-five. There may have been as many as a hundred guerrillas near the hacienda, most of them Asháninkas.[11] Asháninka accounts of the assault are vague as to the numbers of people involved, speaking only of "many people," or "all of the people of thus and such a community."

On August 6, the guerrillas approached the hacienda before dawn, but their attack was thwarted by the braying of a mule, which woke the police. The insurgents tried again three days later.[12] Alfredo Atiri remembers the first act of the assault, the detonation of a grenade in Fávaro's house:

"Boom!" went the grenade. How loud would it be, eh? Well, it was strong! Then the shootout began: "Tak, tak, tak, tak!" The soldiers fired a machine gun over here: "Fuuu, fuuu, fuuu!" They fired in vain. The ones who'd thrown the grenade were safe, far away. "Ha, ha!" They laughed, watching how the soldiers fired because they were scared, even though they couldn't see anyone.

News stories published after the attack describe this initial exchange as a veritable siege, during which Antonio Fávaro sent frantic radio messages begging for reinforcements. In response to the calls for help, the reports claim, a young agronomist named Ismael Castillo, the administrator of the nearby Kiatari hacienda, offered to drive several civil guards to Cubantía in his pickup truck. On the way to Cubantía, insurgents ambushed them. Three people in the truck, including Castillo, died in the encounter. *Correo* reported that Indians played a key role in the ambush:

> *Engineer Castillo, who was much loved by the Campa Indians, got out of his truck to speak with them and avoid any incident. . . . One of the Campas shouted, "Die, you wretch!" and there were gunshots. At the same instant two machine guns opened fire from the bushes and it was a true massacre.*[13]

Antonio Fávaro's own version of events, published six days after the attack, has a matter-of-fact tone that lends it weight. He reports that the attack on his hacienda was over by dawn. The Asháninkas who lived at the hacienda had all disappeared. Calling upon the services of a pilot who landed at Cubantía later that morning, Fávaro flew over his own lands and nearby farms in Kiatari and Alto Sonomoro to assess the situation from the air. The Asháninka settlements were all deserted. He dropped a message to Ismael Castillo at Kiatari, alerting him of trouble. Returning to Cubantía, he reported the desertion of the Indians to the officer in charge of the civil guard detachment, who expressed his alarm. "However," he writes, "I can confirm that the Campas, owing to their special character, have not yielded to the communists." He does not elaborate on what their "special character" might be.

Early the next morning, Fávaro continues, employees from Cubantía found the burned-out shell of Ismael Castillo's truck and four bodies on the road not far from the hacienda. The dead included Castillo and two civil guards. The fourth body proved to be a "civilized Campa" who was badly wounded but still alive. Later reports explain that a police detective in the truck escaped harm by playing dead; the guerrillas spared a wounded Civil Guard, a woman, and a child who were also in the truck.[14] Apparently Castillo had been attempting to bring food and supplies to the hacienda before he evacuated the area.[15]

Elías Murillo, who participated in the ambush of Castillo's

truck, recalls that the guerrillas pressed the attack expecting to head off members of the police on their way to Cubantía:

When we heard the sound of the truck, we dropped tree trunks in the road to stop the vehicle. Even before it stopped, dynamite was thrown, homemade grenades. So when I got there—you can't watch everything, no? You just perform your mission—I got there and put a bullet in the guy who was [he pauses] . . . The grenade had emptied his guts and he asked please would I finish it, so I gave him the coup de grace. *Each one fulfills his mission, no?*

Alfredo Atiri's version of events is more colorful and less tinged with horror than Murillo's:

Right there they threw the grenade: "psh." The guerrilla had judged it right, throwing it in the cargo bed: "Poom, poom!" The soldiers were thrown out like something coming from a tin can. Ha, ha! But they didn't die, they were thrown out wounded. Ismael got out, looking around. "What's happening?" he asked. He recognized several of my people. All of those who said that they had found Pavá, the Sun Father.

"I haven't done anything. We're like brothers. I pay you well when you work with me. I don't cheat you, I don't fool you, we know each other well. Let me live." That's what Ismael asked.

But those who were most drunk shouted: "Damn! You are helping them! That's why those soldiers were coming to kill us." So they killed him. Who? It's not known . . .

Since the soldiers were transporting crates of beer and boxes of ammunition, half was taken and the rest burned. . . . They carried the boxes, running, running, running. They came to the camp. One of the guerrillas said: "This is what we wanted, brothers! This is what we'll do tomorrow, when we go to the store. Yes. Each one of you will take a machete, canned tuna, candy, crackers, anything that you find there. That's what we'll do—eat well. This is what we want. To eat as well as the landowners!"

Well, everyone was content, happy. "Cheers, cheers," they toasted one another. Each one with his bottle. Damn! Brandy, beer, cane liquor.

"Yes, brother. God, thanks. You who defended us, you're Itomi Pavá, Sons of the Sun!"

The guerrillas' contentment was short-lived. As soon as news of the attack reached the military command, the air force sent Canberra jets on sorties to suspected MIR positions in the Pangoa valley.[16] Eugenio Sarove, a Spanish colonist, remembers that "the fighter-bombers came directly from Lima, dropped their merchandise, and returned to Lima."
Elías Murillo was there:

First they strafed the ground, and the earth boiled. In the fields where we were—the ground boiled! . . . We even found toads and snakes killed when the strafing passed over them. We dug up the bullets after the planes had passed. Enormous slugs! . . . In these bombings peasants died, not guerrillas. The peasants were strafed. Mostly peasants died because they resisted the idea of leaving their houses. They hid around their houses or inside of them.

According to Atiri, most Asháninkas followed the advice of the guerrillas to evacuate their houses:

The planes threw here, threw there, throwing fire. My people were in Sonomoro, in safety. They were watching. "Oh, my poor house!" None of my people were there now. Everyone had escaped to the other side of the river, to Mazaronquiari. The planes dropped bombs just for the hell of it. What did they do? Nothing. My people were safe over there. They went to hide in trenches in the bush. The planes came low like this, looking for them. But there was no one. They were invisible, hidden there in the jungle. There were only houses. . . . They burned the houses. My people were so angry! "Damn it, why did they burn my house? Now I'm going." A plane came back, really close. One of my people watched it. He wanted to shoot it. Really, he was going to kill it with an arrow! But someone else told him, "Leave it alone. Don't shoot."

The officers of the United States Embassy in Lima were far from the deadly particulars of a napalm assault on arrow-wielding natives. Nevertheless, the embassy found itself in a delicate position as the insurgency intensified. Ambassador J. Wesley Jones recalls that his first goal was to keep President Belaúnde in power and maintain the stability of the government, lest Peru suffer another military coup.[17] Several contentious issues prevented the United States from enjoying completely cordial relations with the Belaúnde government. The first was the Peruvian government's threat to nationalize the International Petroleum Company (IPC), which had for decades paid Peru scandalously low commissions for its oil.[18] The United States was actually less interested in the IPC's small concession than it was in the precedent expropriation might set for Venezuela, with its much larger petroleum reserves.[19] Other dark clouds on the horizon included an escalating dispute about fishing rights in Peruvian coastal waters and Peru's opposition to American military intervention in the Dominican Republic.

When the MIR guerrillas opened their campaign in early June, the embassy staff was exasperated by what it saw as President Belaúnde's reluctance to acknowledge the reality of the communist threat. The embassy may well have had better intelligence than Belaúnde. Philip Agee claims that as a CIA employee in the Quito station he recruited an agent within the MIR code-named DUHAM-1, elsewhere identified as Enrique Amaya Quintana. DUHAM-1 provided information on bases and weapons caches of the MIR, which the CIA had previously identified as the leftist group most likely to commence the armed struggle.[20] Years after the MIR insurgency, however, MIR leader Gonzalo Fernández Gasco vo-ciferously denied that Amaya was an agent.[21]

Whether Amaya worked for the CIA or not, embassy documents imply that the United States had a source within the party. The day after the assault on the Santa Rosa mine, the embassy filed a situation report to Washington that closes by stating that the attack was the "overt guerrilla activity [name excised] reported would be launched by MIR in central area around mid-June."[22] A telegram dated June 19 notes that the names of guerrillas released by the Minister of Government were not those of MIR members known to be operating in the area, implying that the embassy already possessed information on the identities of the guerrillas.[23] The embassy pleaded its case to an unidentified, but presumably high-level, official of the Peruvian government on June 24:

[Name excised] asked DCM [Deputy Chief of Mission, Ernest V. Siracusa] for his frank, personal view of guerrilla problem. DCM said he thought these people really existed, that they were not repeat not "cattle rustlers," that they were repeat were internationally backed repeat backed activists who had long been preparing for this move and that GOP [Government of Peru] would do well to take serious view of them [Excised].[24]

Although members of the MIR and other leftist parties were filtering into the country from guerrilla training bases abroad, the embassy's political strategists saw Peru's fragile democracy as also vulnerable to subversion from within. One State Department report claimed that 30 to 60 percent of Peru's university and secondary-school students were communists. The embassy's "Internal Defense Plan for Peru" of 1965 includes allegations that the Belaúnde administration had permitted communists to find positions in government ministries, especially the Ministry of Education. The State Department estimated that Peru was home to more than 6,000 hard-core communists and 28,000 communist sympathizers.[25]

Moving beyond the recitation of Cold War mantras, some members of the embassy staff called attention to the roots of class conflict within Peruvian society. "The majority of the Peruvian people have yet to receive any substantial benefit from the wealth of their country," one document states, "and their poverty contrasts all too visibly with even the moderate prosperity of the middle classes."[26] There was an appreciation for the extent to which relentless infighting by Peru's political parties made it difficult for President Belaúnde to implement programs that would address these difficult social issues. Finally, some analysts were frank about what their intelligence sources saw as "considerable hatred of the police in rural areas."[27]

The embassy eventually settled on a policy of increased military and paramilitary assistance to Peru to contain the immediate political threat posed by the insurgency, coupled with pressure on Peru to accept the U.S. position on the IPC's oil leases and the need for social reforms of the sort favored by the Alliance for Progress.

Once the uprising gathered momentum, however, the embassy had difficulty following events in the field. Important sources of information in the Civil Guard dried up when the army took charge of the counterinsurgency. A postmortem assessment of the insurgency complains that the armed forces kept the emergency zone off limits even to military attachés. The only exception, apparently, was the U.S. air attaché, who accompanied his Peruvian counterparts on an overflight of Pucutá and Satipo in mid-August.[28] In only a few cases was the political staff able to access high-level sources that could clarify the murky and contradictory stories appearing in the Lima and provincial dailies.[29]

Despite frustration with the high level of disorganization within the Peruvian military and skepticism about the accuracy of the military's communiqués, the embassy quickly increased support for the Special Police Emergency Unit in Mazamari. By early September, the United States had eleven public safety advisors working with the SPEU and four more expected.[30] The United States also accelerated delivery of equipment under the terms of the Military Assistance Program, including helicopters, field rations, and radios.[31]

Occasionally embassy employees obtained information fresh from the field. One of the most interesting cases was an encounter between James Haahr, the embassy's first secretary, and two landowners from the Cubantía area. The men, whose names have been excised from Haahr's report, came to the embassy on August 13, only a few days after the ambush at Cubantía. Haahr remembers them as walk-ins. In view of the scarcity of accurate information coming from the combat zone, he thought it worthwhile to give them an hour of his time. One of them

expressed the view that the communist guerrillas had gained everything that they had set out to do, i.e., secured arms, created panic among the civilian population, begun the process of economic paralyzation of the area which probably would provide them with further recruits, forced the Armed Forces to kill campesinos *and generally demonstrated to the country that the Armed Forces and Police did not have the training and capability to conduct the anti-guerrilla campaign. . . . He said that a few days ago he had repeated this same story to General [excised] of the Armed Forces and that [excised] also recognized privately that the Army's anti-guerrilla battle would neither be short nor easily won . . . [B]ecause of poor training and unfamiliarity with the terrain, morale among the troops was bad and becoming worse.*

Haahr judged the informant trustworthy and essentially correct in his assessment of how the guerrillas might benefit from the chaos in Satipo Province.[32]

The absence of detailed field reports may account for the near invisibility of Asháninkas in embassy documents. The Indians living around Mazamari are mentioned as recipients of medical assistance under the SPEU's civic action program, and baffled-looking Asháninkas appear in file photos taken by an AID employee. After the raid on Cubantía in August, the OPS restricted American advisors to the SPEU base in Mazamari, noting that Asháninkas had apparently cooperated with the guerrillas who staged the attack. A memo issued on October 26 again mentions "unconfirmed reports that the guerrillas have obtained support from the jungle Campas indian tribe [sic]." "If so," the memo continues, "this could be a serious development, and its significance would have to be evaluated by on-the-spot observation and analysis."[33] The documents provide no evidence that such close observation was ever attempted.

The only American eyewitness to write about the Asháninka role in the conflict was a journalist named Norman Gall. In the MIR courtship of the Asháninkas, Gall saw a strategy resembling the U.S. recruitment of Hmong tribesmen in Vietnam. In an article in the *Wall Street Journal*, Gall wrote:

So far the Communist guerrillas have enjoyed notable success in winning the critical collaboration of marginal populations either abandoned or untouched by Western civilization. Among these are the semi-aboriginal Campa Indians of the Peruvian jungle, who since the 17th century have wiped out several waves of Spanish missionaries.[34]

The sudden appearance of guerrillas in Satipo Province— and the alliance between guerrillas and the province's large Asháninka population—provoked fears of an attack upon the town of Satipo by combined elements of communists and Indians. People who lived in Satipo at the time recall that the mood was jittery. The army declared a state of siege and imposed a curfew. The snap of gunfire could be heard sporadically after dark, though no one knew whether the din came from an actual firefight or represented an attempt by the army to scare people into remaining at home.[35]

The press, fueled by a combination of hearsay and prejudice, gamely tried to make sense of an Asháninka alliance
with the Túpac Amaru. "Officially it was announced yesterday that the communists are rousing the Campa tribes for
their struggle against the army," *El Expreso* reported on August 12. "The extremists are playing with the theme of land
to plant discontent among the peaceful tribes of the Campa
in the area of Satipo." Huancayo's *Correo*, always looking for
a sensational wrinkle in current events, announced on August
16 that the guerrillas had enlisted the support of a cannibal-
istic tribe of Indians called Choviaros:

*San Ramón de Pangoa. A group of Campa leaders yesterday
made a heart-rending and almost pathetic plea: "We want peace.
We aren't the ones aiding the guerrillas." Thay have also undertaken the evacuation of the Campa settlements near Cubantía.
Only vultures fly in the sky there now. According to official information obtained yesterday, only a small group of Campas have al-
lied with the rebels that operate in Cubantía and the Satipo
area. . . . The Campas, however, accuse the Choviaros of
being the ones to blame for the massacre at Cubantía. The Choviaros are from the Gran Pajonál. They paint their faces with yel-
low achiote and are cannibals.*

The use of the curious term "Choviaros" brings to mind
the profusion of tribal names in colonial documents. The
identity of the Choviaros remains a mystery, though the term
most likely refers to followers of the Asháninka headman
Choviante of Gloriabamba, near Puerto Ocopa. In his analysis of the guerrilla war, General Armando Artola also falls
back on tribal names more than two centuries old, such as
Sonomoros and Pilcosumis.[36] The reappearance of these ancient labels shows the limited impact of scientific knowledge
about Amazonian Indians on the popular discourse of the
1960s. Even today, non–Indian residents of the Peruvian Amazon persist in referring to native tongues as "dialects" (*di-*

alectos) rather than as "languages" (*idiomas*), subtly relegating them to second-class status.

Representations of the Asháninkas in *Correo* and other newspapers swung between exaggerated claims about the Indians' primitiveness—for example, the reference to the practice of cannibalism among Choviaros—and patronizing descriptions of their place in the local system of exploitation. "The drama of the Campa," writes *Correo*, "is the drama of the jungle person, exploited from time immemorial and secularly marginalized from civilization."[37]

In a few instances press reports fixed on specific Asháninka grievances, though the murkiness of the details defies close analysis. On August 17, *Correo* attempted to interpret the death of the police officer Lieutenant Guillermo Alcántara in the ambush at Cubantía. The paper's Asháninka informant explained that Lieutenant Alcántara failed to investigate the rape of an Asháninka girl by a mestizo colonist, enraging her father and prompting him to target the officer for assassination. This account, the accuracy of which we have been unable to verify, is an archetype of ethnic conflict, a scenario repeated scores of times in Asháninka communities when whites assumed that their natural ascendancy over Indians included a right of sexual access to Indian women. In the memory of Alberto Yorini, an Asháninka leader from the community of Teoría, the officer was not just a passive accomplice but the perpetrator of the assault:

A week before [the assault on Cubantía], a girl had gone to catch fish with fish-poison. This girl was lame. She was collecting the fish when the "Sergeant" came . . . what's his name . . . a police investigator. He offered her an orange. Then the policeman grabbed her hand, and he forced her. "Ah, now we are going to join them, we're going to make a guerrilla war so that there won't be any more abuses," the natives said.

The most common explanation for the Asháninkas' involvement in the conflict focused on the MIR's promises of material rewards. Consider the statement of the late hacienda owner Eugenio Sarove, which while perhaps more starkly racist than one might hear from other settlers in the Satipo area, captures the essence of their opinion:

> The Campas were involved in the guerrilla war through trickery. They were tricked. The Campa is a child, he has an infantile mind, an infantile mind, of which he himself is unaware. If you give them a mirror they'll clear you a hectare of forest— just for a mirror! They have no sense of relative values. Their mind is very untutored. They haven't developed enough to evaluate things, to say, "This is good and this is bad," or "I live better here than there," because they can't reason. They know nothing. The Campa is like a child, and I think that the Constitution declares him to be a child. He has an infantile mind.[38]

The idea that Indians are childlike, in both good ways and bad, has a long history in the New World. In the sixteenth century, the Franciscan friar Gerónimo de Mendieta described mission Indians as children, "soft wax" to be molded through paternalistic education by monks.[39] Four centuries later, the Lima daily *La Prensa* used similar language to portray what it saw as the Asháninkas' childlike susceptibility to the enticements of left-wing agitators:

> The offers that they [the communists] make to the Campas are almost infantile. Joined with promises to give them land and treat them better, they tell them that when the revolution triumphs, they will all be able to own cars, pickups, and heavy trucks. And that their children will be able to become engineers and doctors. . . . Their children are going to study together with whites and have the same education as whites.[40]

An account that dismisses the promise of Indian education and admittance to the professions as "infantile," as the article in *La Prensa* does, reveals the deep currents of racism that shaped relations between Indians and whites in Peru. What the article's author has missed entirely, however, is the symbolic significance that property, especially trade goods, held for Asháninkas.

Many Peruvians believed that Asháninka support for the MIR guerrillas was based on the guerrillas' "trickery" and "deception," which took the form of unrealistic promises of material goods. General Armando Artola repeats this claim in his book ¡Subversión!, in which he states that the Indians joined the Túpac Amaru after being paid with rifles and trifles. "In fact," he continues, "with the exception of the headmen, [the Indians] didn't understand what the campaign was about until very late." Since an ingenuous materialism was at the root of their allegiance, Artola argues, Asháninkas proved willing to desert the revolutionaries when the army offered them "radios, machetes, carbines, flashlights, etc."[41]

For whites, the transfer of machetes and other machine-made goods lay at the heart of the economic arrangements that would bring "progress" to the Amazon. The guerrillas offered the Indians the same goods to join them in a struggle of national liberation. For the Indians to be seduced by this ploy was, from the white perspective, prima facie evidence of their childlike nature, their lack of a "sense of value" and the ability to discriminate between one sophisticated ideology and another.

Asháninkas saw the exchange—and the meaning of trade goods themselves—in an altogether different light. Goods stand in a metonymic relationship to the European world and its power over native peoples. Asháninka mythology establishes that machetes, cloth, and other trade goods were once controlled by Inca, who was captured by sinister whites after they emerged from the underworld. When the oppressive system that currently exists is overturned by a spirit-hero, Indians will again govern the production of goods and whites will be reduced to the poverty they deserve. So from the Asháninka point of view, promises of material goods were entirely appropriate to a vision of apocalyptic transformation and the launching of a new era of social justice. This is not to deny that Indians wanted the goods *as goods*. But the goods defined a semiotic field much larger than immediate material needs.

In puzzling out the jumbled intertextuality of the MIR-Asháninka alliance, it is difficult to determine who was more responsible for the apparent overemphasis on the immediate material rewards of rebellion. To some extent, Asháninkas must have distilled the MIR's abstract revolutionary slogans to something more meaningful in native terms. At the same time, the MIR was not above engaging in its own forms of strategic oversimplification.

In his small office in an Andean town, the former MIR guerrilla Elías Murillo explains that the Marxist must reconcile his sophisticated creed with the atavistic beliefs of the peasantry:

> So this belief in the Inkarrí, the Inca King, has always existed, no? This will never be erased from the minds of the people. . . . But from time to time come personages who seek the well-being of the people. They go from town to town saying, "Now the revolution is coming, now we'll make our own government, now no one will be exploited." So the people form their own concept, their own idea. Do you believe that the Shining Path teaches Marxist-Leninist thought? No. They simply speak of the old order and "that we must change this, that we'll govern ourselves." So the people say, "Ah, this is a good man, he's the son of the mountain gods," or something. They say, "We've got to protect him, to give him what little food we have."

Even before its contact with Asháninkas, the MIR had developed a brand of Marxism that was stripped down and, in its own way, millenarian. Ricardo Letts and other orthodox Peruvian Marxists accuse Lobatón and the MIR of a "simplistic" view of revolution.[42] The party's members believed that guerrilla war could shortcut the long-term process of class struggle and arrive at an immediate redress of grievances. When confronted with potential allies about whose culture they knew little, the guerrillas doubtless made their already simple message even simpler.

After token resistance by elements of the Túpac Amaru, the last highland "security zone," Intihallamuy, fell to the army on August 11. A few days later, the military's campaign against the MIR's central front shifted its focus almost entirely to the jungle. With considerable publicity, the army moved a special unit of U.S.-trained Rangers from Huancayo to Satipo. Nine detachments—including Rangers, regular army units, Civil Guards, and Republican Guards—encircled the basin surrounding the Pangoa and Sonomoro rivers, cutting off guerrilla communication with MIR forces in the Department of Cuzco.[43]

As soon as its forces were deployed, the army attempted to distance Asháninkas and peasants from the MIR. The methods used to open this breach ran the gamut from blandishments to terror. In Mazamari, the Special Police Emergency Unit of the Civil Guard used U.S. funds to provide free medical care to Asháninkas and peasant farmers. The army began an intensive propaganda campaign in the rural communities of the province. Elías Murillo remembers how this worked:

Now they knew we were in the Campa settlements, and they threw out leaflets from helicopters offering thirty thousand soles [then worth more than $1,100] for each guerrilla. Today that amount would be equal to 30 million, even 50 million. A lot of money, tempting people to turn us in to the authorities.

Presumably judging that leaflets might have a negligible impact on illiterate Indians, the air force used loudspeakers mounted on aircraft to warn people to stay away from strangers and to report suspicious persons to the authorities.[44]

But there was no reluctance to extract information by more direct means. Alfredo Atiri recalls one "intelligence gathering" mission to the community of Sonomoro:

Within a week the troop of Rangers arrived. They came quickly. They had uniforms. Well armed. They were frightening! They brought us all together and told us: "You received these people. We ought to kill you too. You're all subversives!" That was the first time I'd heard that word, subversives. "What does it mean?" I thought. Then I found out. "Criminals, subversives," said the Rangers. They shouted at us and kicked us. . . . It happened that the Rangers grabbed a boy, one of my people, no? They hung him by his balls. Yes! With a rope they tied his testicles and hung him from a tree branch. While he was hanging there they made a fire underneath and smoked him. . . . The poor boy began to give names. Since he was half dead, he talked. And one of the names that he gave was my father's.

Deploying paratroop units, helicopters, and foot patrols on forced marches, the army moved quickly from place to place, harassing Indians and searching for caches of weapons.

In response to the increasing pressure, Guillermo Lobatón decided to attempt an assault on the Túpac Amaru's former highland base, Pucutá, in the hope of humiliating the army by striking a position now within its sphere of control. Leading a group of guerrillas back into the mountains, Lobatón attacked Pucutá before dawn on September 23. The guerrillas killed two soldiers and an officer but sustained three casualties themselves. Lobatón pulled his men back to the jungle, and the various detachments of the Túpac Amaru met at Shuenti on the Río Anapati. Upon receiving news of the encounter, the MIR's Central Committee tried to represent the battle as a triumph which "proved that the people can defeat any repressive force . . . if only the revolutionary organization manages to lead the masses and put them on the right path of guerrilla warfare."[45]

Despite the optimism of the party's propaganda, the Túpac

Amaru was in a bad state. For all his brilliance, Lobatón had no gift for dealing with rural people or with the peasant members of his guerrilla unit.[46] Elías Murillo remembers that by early October, Lobatón was "bitter" and "distant." "There were," he adds, "problems with food, ammunition, everything—wounded comrades here, hungry peasants there." Some sources claim that Lobatón and Velando had a falling out at this time, but the main tension seems to have been between Lobatón and Froilán Herrera, who was more aggressive, more disposed toward violence than either Lobatón or Velando. The younger comrades regarded the group's leaders—especially Lobatón—with an awe that approached reverence. According to Elías Murillo, "One thought of them as having a mystique, like a god, like a leader so very far above; they spoke another language."

Manuel Ashivánti's oral testimony includes an account of the conflict between Lobatón and Herrera. Lobatón, he recalls, was angry because Herrera had attacked the hacienda at Cubantía without his permission:

> *"Damn [Lobatón said], why did you do this? I didn't give the order to do this. Now they're going to kill the poor Indians. The Indians need to be taught first. They need to learn first, then they can attack." He almost killed Jaime [Froilán Herrera]. Well, he was Jaime's boss! Because Jaime had led my people when they still didn't know much.*

The insurgents were tired, sick, and hungry. The army had cut them off from the other guerrilla fronts and from their supporters in the city. They found themselves hounded from village to village through some of the roughest terrain in the Amazon. They suffered the disheartening sight of their leaders quarreling among themselves. Most telling, under the pressure of army harassment and air assaults, Asháninka support for the war of Itomi Pavá was slipping away.

SEVEN

White Angel

As the Túpac Amaru dropped into the jungles of Satipo Province, spectral foreigners appeared on the Amazonian stage. The Huancayo newspaper *Correo* reported that Che Guevara was personally directing the guerrilla campaign of the Túpac Amaru.[1] Fears of Che's participation in the struggle multiplied in October, when Fidel Castro announced that Guevara had left Cuba and gone underground to foment revolution elsewhere.[2] The *New York Times* News Service and Reuters were both to carry unsubstantiated reports that Che led the MIR guerrillas and that he had been captured by the army near Mesa Pelada in the Department of Cuzco.[3]

Yet most press accounts and local hearsay about mysterious foreigners concentrated on the role that *gringos*, especially Americans, allegedly played in the conflict. *Correo* reported that the SOS radioed by the besieged Cubantía hacienda had been picked up by an American missionary pilot, who flew overhead to see if he could provide assistance.[4] Widely circulated rumors held that missionaries of various denominations—especially American evangelicals—were helping to put down the insurgency. In a history of the Summer Institute of Linguistics (SIL), the largest American evangelical group operating in the Peruvian jungle, David Stoll suggests that the SIL may have been involved in the army's aerial loudspeaker campaign directed to Asháninka villages.[5] The Peruvian left was quick to identify these outsiders as agents of the CIA, whose power to sow the seeds of disorder was held to be nothing short of miraculous. Although the American advisors sent to train counterinsurgency troops in Mazamari kept a low profile, photographs of them surfaced in the Lima papers. *La Crónica*, for example, described them as battle-hardened veterans of guerrilla warfare in Vietnam; they have "an amazing ability to handle firearms, they are knowledgeable in judo, and during a lethal leap they can successfully shoot at a target."[6]

Nowhere in Latin America is the symbolic resonance of the gringo deeper or more contradictory than in Peru. Long before Pizarro's scruffy expeditionary force appeared on the Peruvian coast, the Incas venerated the figure of Viracocha, a fair-haired wanderer who brought a luminous civilization to the Andes and then vanished in the Pacific Ocean with a promise of future return. It is difficult, of course, to reconstruct the subtleties of a religion whose most sacred objects were raffled off to Spanish officers within days of Pizarro's triumph. But some anthropologists identify Viracocha as the deity of the outer or unknown world. By extension, he ruled over the outer limits of time, that is, the Andean past and future. The fatal vacillation of the reigning emperor, Atahualpa, in the face of an invasion by foreigners from the West may have been nourished by the possibility that these pale outlanders represented the promised return of Viracocha.[7]

Spanish rule brought an end to the reign of the Sun, the major Inca deity, and began the epoch of the viracochas. To this day, people of the light-skinned landowning class are politely addressed as *wiracocha* by Quechua-speaking Indians. Yet beneath outward deference to the viracochas lies a dark well of dread. Andean peasants believe themselves stalked by golden-haired phantoms, called *pishtacos*, who hunt travelers on wind-ripped highland trails. Pishtacos plunder their victims' corpses for blood or fat, substances that for Andean Indians embody the life force. A Peruvian scholar has argued that the colonial Spanish practice of using human fat to treat wounds gave birth to fears of pishtacos.[8] Since then, the symbolic contours of the pishtaco myth have changed with shifts in technology: once used to make candles for the church, the stolen fat now lubricates the machinery of northern factories or carries American rockets to the moon. Pishtaco fear lives on today as a powerful metaphor for the experience of Andean people, whose lives have been twisted and foreshortened by what they see as the mysterious power emanating from the gringo world.[9]

The Indians of Peru's tropical forests see Europeans through the lens of their own cultural experience. The Aguaruna of northern Peru, for example, think of *wíakuch*, viracochas, as people of great wealth who move easily through the social chaos of the jungle's frontier towns. These beings are powerful sorcerers who bear lone travelers off to viracocha cities hidden in cliffs or trees.[10]

Asháninkas have perhaps the most elaborate ideas about gringos of any Amazonian tribe, undoubtedly because of their centuries of contact with Andean peasants, as well as with the non-Indians who fill the pishtaco role: rubber-tappers, slavers, plantation owners, and foreign engineers.[11] Asháninka elders say that the primordial whites were fished from a jungle lake by the disobedient son of Inca, a powerful shaman and the source of material wealth. "On the fishhook appeared a viracocha, who was thin and pale, with a very long beard," explains one version of the myth. "After all the viracochas had emerged, their fathers came, those who are now Franciscans." The viracochas dismembered the Inca and began to enslave Asháninkas. The story ends with the lament, "If it hadn't been for the disobedient son of Inca, we would now have axes, machetes, steel knives, firearms, and clothing." Asháninka shamans were finally able to contain the homicidal frenzy of the viracochas, but whites retain control over the production of the trade goods that make life in the jungle possible.[12]

The symbolic burden of the gringo is not all negative for Asháninkas, especially as the Indians have come to distinguish between different categories of viracochas. Missionaries from the United States and Europe have had more success in evangelizing Asháninka communities than their Roman Catholic counterparts, because the Indians identify the latter with the colonists and landowners who are the cause of their present poverty.[13] The Indians now distinguish Spanish viracochas—who emerged from the water, which has a negative connotation—from other whites, especially evangelicals, who come to the jungle from the air, in airplanes, which links them to spiritual benefactors such as the *tasórentsi*.

Despite broad differences in language, culture, and historical contact, the symbolic archetype of the gringo—with its alternating guises of viracocha and predatory pishtaco—has made a transect of western South America, from the Pacific desert to the Amazon. For the people who inhabit these places, the gringo stands for power, danger, and an insatiable, ruthless hunger for life. The gringo's symbolic potency makes its presence felt in Peruvian elite culture as well. One sees it in the recurrent search for European immigrants to colonize the jungle, spawned by a hope that these gringos can lead Peru from the cul-de-sac of underdevelopment. As recently as 1963 the Peruvian government explored the feasibility of bringing five thousand French refugees from Algeria to colonize the Amazon, even as Peruvian peasants fought for lands that the government had ceded to the Peruvian Corporation, a British firm, in the nineteenth century.[14]

The most persistent rumor of gringo involvement in the guerrilla struggle of 1965 centered on an American named David Livingstone Pent, variously misidentified in the press as David Penn, David Livingstone, or Miguel Pend. On July 8, 1965, soon after the Túpac Amaru insurgency was underway in the sierra, an article appeared in *La Prensa* under the headline "In Pucallpa They Denounce Foreign Communist":

The North American-Peruvian communist David Pent has again come to the area of the Urubamba River, where he is stirring things up, according to information provided by farmers of the locality where Pent has some property.

Police sources have no information that this communist has returned to the country, from which he was expelled some time ago after it was proven that he had links to members of the extreme left, with whom he stirred up the situation. Pent is of North American origin but a naturalized Peruvian. He is married to a young woman from Loreto.

The informants, who are all responsible people, give assurances that Pent has secretly returned to the country, his arrival coinciding with a series of criminal acts committed by communist guerrillas in the central region of the country.

"Since this gringo returned to the country, one can observe a certain agitation among the peasantry of the Urubamba and the Upper Ucayali," manifested the informants, who, however, did not specify the source of their information, though they provided assurances that the news is trustworthy.

The newspaper *Correo* developed this theme more fully on August 11 in an article with the headline "Miguel Pend is Leader of Rebel Campas":

The loggers of the region of Masea [presumably Masisea] and Sepahua have denounced the collaboration of several hundred Campas with the guerrilla fighters. To arm the Campas, cases of rifles and ammunition may have been sent from the area of Inuya.

*According to what is now known, the Campas are trained and
led by Miguel Pend, "The White Angel," a naturalized Peruvian
of North American descent, who was deported from Peru for his
extremist ideas.*

Both of these news reports drew on hearsay about the insurgency that circulated widely at the time. These same tales
led the American social scientist David Chaplin to state, in a
scholarly appraisal of the 1965 guerrilla conflict, that "the
original assistance of campas [sic] had been enlisted on behalf
of the guerrillas through the efforts of a 'renegade' U.S. Protestant missionary."[15] Pent is most durably embroidered into
the mythic tapestry of 1965 through his appearance in two
works of fiction: Róger Rumrrill's short story "El viborero,"
in which Pent is thinly disguised as the American "Penny
David," and, at much greater length, in Manuel Scorza's
novel *La danza inmóvil*, where Pent appears under his own
name as a guerrilla leader. Both writers portray Pent as a
charismatic figure, a messiah, who had tapped a deep current
of utopian thought. In these accounts, the gringo is seen
through what Michael Taussig has called the "epistemic
murk" of Amazonian violence.[16] Can we give the stories any
credence?

Though his current whereabouts are unknown, David Livingstone Pent is, or was, a real person. Born in 1931, Pent
was the third of six children raised by Phillip and Rosine
Pent, American evangelicals who settled in the Amazonian
town of Iquitos. David and his siblings grew up in an aus-
terely Christian household. They were educated at home and,
to the extent possible, insulated from the relaxed standards
of life in the tropics. Nevertheless, says David Pent's sister,
Deborah Hudson, their parents worried that David and his
brothers were "becoming too Peruvian, too influenced by
Peruvian morality." She remembers David as the sibling who
spoke Spanish the best and who was "the most Peruvian of
all of us."[17] Javier Dávila Durand, a boyhood friend of Pent's,
agrees. "He was the only one of them who denied his Amer-

ican birth. 'I'm not a North American,' he would say to me, 'I'm Amazonian.' "[18]

The Pent household was strict, and none of the children were spared corporal punishment. Deborah Hudson remembers:

> There were too many don'ts in our household, and Dave was often in conflict with my father. It was a Christian home but perhaps not an understanding home. My father saw the boys falling into the morality of the Peruvians. Peruvian morality is different, you know, and they were becoming like that—especially Dave.

In his teens, David Pent was sent to the United States to renew his identity as an American and to complete his Christian education. By all accounts, David felt out of place in the United States. He was unable to settle down to his studies at the Philadelphia College of Bible, which he attended for a semester in 1948. "He had zeal but not discipline," his sister recalls. Reflecting on their common experience as boarding students, Deborah Hudson says that it was hard to feel at home in America after an upbringing in the Amazon:

> We were Americans but not Americans. Now they'd call what we experienced "culture shock." My brothers went away to boarding school and hated it. The confusion of coming back to the United States tempted us to return to Peru as missionaries simply because there was nothing else we knew how to do.

Deborah Hudson did eventually return to Peru, where she has lived for many years with her husband at the Yarinacocha base camp of the Summer Institute of Linguistics, the overseas branch of the Wycliffe Bible Translators.[19] The Hudsons have dedicated their lives to the SIL's effort to translate Christian Scripture into all the languages of Peru's jungle tribes.

What were other distinguishing qualities of David Pent, this young man caught between cultures? Deborah Hudson remembers with fondness her brother's excellent memory.

"He would memorize scripture, then take me aside so that I could listen to him recite it—whole chapters by memory." After so many years, she has little recollection of what David did immediately after leaving his American Bible college. Eventually, though, he returned to Peru with the idea of taking up missionary work himself. David's brother Joseph, who now works for a Christian service agency in Costa Rica, recalls that David was a man without fear as he undertook his evangelical travels in the jungle: "Dave was zealous in his preaching. Nothing frightened him. The power of the Catholic Church was extreme then, but he didn't hesitate to debate with priests."[20]

Jeanne Grover served for many years as a missionary linguist with the SIL. She recalls meeting David Pent at Yarinacocha, the organization's base camp, in 1954:

I, along with a whole group of new missionaries, arrived in Yarinacocha and was attending a party for all of us. Dave was present, probably reluctantly. He was a tall handsome blond, quiet and very solemn, about twenty-one or twenty-two years old. We were all slightly older than he chronologically, but he was lots older than we in so many other ways. He always impressed me as being morose, very low key and certainly with an entirely different agenda than any of us.[21]

Kenneth Kensinger also served as an SIL linguist in the 1950s, though nearly a decade of living with the Cashinahua Indians later convinced him to give up evangelism for the more speculative doctrines of cultural anthropology. Kensinger cannot summon up an image of the morose Pent seen by Jeanne Grover. The David Pent of his memory is charming and intense, and evidently conscious of his physical appearance. He and Pent didn't discuss religion or politics, but Kensinger found no reason to think of Pent as a religious zealot or, for that matter, as someone who had a "different agenda" than other people working at Yarinacocha.[22] He does recall him as a person who might have been able to use his charm to manipulate people, a view that Deborah Hudson corroborates. "David," she says, "could get people to do things for him."

In the mid-1950s, Javier Dávila Durand had much more contact with Pent than did his family, from whom he was increasingly estranged. Although Dávila and Pent had known each other in Iquitos, their paths crossed again in Atalaya, on the Río Ucayali, in 1955. Pent worked a farm on the Río Ene and asked Dávila to help him manage it. Dávila remembers Pent as having turned his prodigious memory for Scripture to a voracious hunger for poetry: "His vocabulary had been enriched by poetry and his conversation always began with a phrase or a verse of poetry."

Pent and Dávila soon moved their base of operations to a place called Charahuaja on the Río Tambo. Róger Rumrrill's short story turns Charahuaja into a jungle Shangri-la:

He easily learned the Piro and Campa languages and, dressed in a cushma the color of red achiote and preceded by five native sorcerers, he went from village to village predicting the return of the millenarian gods who had left a world polluted by whites with their firearms, their syphilis, smallpox, and influenza, contaminated by the White Plague, to live in the pure kingdom of Axpikondia.

Transformed into a spokesman for the return of the gods, into a prophet and at times almost into a demigod himself, Penny David lived in a place that figured on no map, on no itinerary, in no guidebook, but which was on the lips and in the memory of everyone: Charahuaja.[23]

Pent's actual activities at the Charahuaja farm, which he named "Fronda Alegre," were more worldly than Rumrrill's whimsical story suggests. There he ripened a scheme to separate American investors from their money. Using bait-and-switch tactics, he persuaded a Texan named Davis to put up approximately $40,000 for the exploitation of tropical hardwoods. Both Javier Dávila and Joseph Pent agree that David's motive was that of a modern-day Robin Hood: he used the

Texan's money to buy hundreds of yards of cotton cloth, crates of shotguns, and innumerable household goods to distribute among the Asháninkas who worked his land. And he built a house of such stupendous proportions that it is still legendary in the Upper Ucayali.

Like the other hacienda owners of the region, Pent secured Asháninka workers in two ways. Some came voluntarily, attracted by the manufactured goods he offered in exchange for labor. The rest were children purchased from Asháninka slave-raiders or from their parents, who sold them into servitude rather than see them killed as sorcerers. Pent's main Asháninka intermediary in these transactions was a headman named Inganiteri, whom Javier Dávila describes as "a leader of leaders, an infamous criminal, a man with only one eye, but dominated by David's personality." Inganiteri boasted a group of three hundred followers at the height of Fronda Alegre's prosperity.

Of the Asháninkas purchased by Pent, most seem to have been young girls, who formed what Javier Dávila describes as a harem. Dávila retains a vivid image of Pent's romantic life at Charahuaja:

David had patiently built up his harem of more or less twenty-eight Indian girls between twelve and fourteen years old; by fifteen they were too old. Among his favorites was an attractive brat with green eyes—an Asháninka with green eyes! David would take them all out in the afternoon to bathe in the creek, in Charahuaja Creek, which has crystalline waters. Right there he lathered them with soap. Then he took them to his room, where he rubbed them with talcum powder and delivered himself to his pleasures, as did all the hacienda lords on the Río Tambo.

But unlike these other landlords, claims Dávila, Pent genuinely loved his Indian mistresses: "He surrounded them with affection, with devotion, and he brought them ten thousand gifts."

In his novel *La danza inmóvil*, Manuel Scorza describes Pent's life in terms as extravagant as Dávila's:

Pent accepts no gifts. He buys the little Indian girls to save them. They fall irredeemably in love with him. The slaves are not slaves: they are wives. . . . And the splendor of the feasts returns, the true life of David Pent; the life of pleasure, by pleasure, for pleasure. Each night he sleeps with different wives. The great celebration that was always his life, interrupted only by sudden and brief trips to the United States. Each return implies more money: capital from new investors in Boston, Chicago, in Cleveland, convinced by him of the fabulous possibilities of Amazonian wood.[24]

It would be easy to dismiss these descriptions as male fantasies peopled by exotic and nubile adolescents. There is no shortage of hyperbole here, yet stories of sexual excess among local landlords are too sturdy to dismiss out of hand. The Tambo and Upper Ucayali had scarcely changed since 1900, when Pedro Portillo observed that "there are no laws, there are no authorities. . . . He who is strongest, who has the most rifles, is master of justice."[25] So Pent may well have been able to establish, at least for a time, his own amorous utopia at Charahuaja.

His utopian dream transcended the merely erotic. Like the Franciscans who preceded him on the Tambo, Pent's frequently stated goal was to deliver Asháninkas from poverty and ignorance, which were perpetuated by the draconian rule of mestizo landlords.[26] Using the hard currency provided by his American backers, he lavished trade goods on his Asháninka followers to such an extent that Indians began to migrate to Fronda Alegre from the farms of more miserly landowners. Javier Dávila remembers the trouble this caused:

The headmen fled from other haciendas and came in search of this patrón who was so generous with payment. David Pent broke with the traditional system of wages, which was traumatic for the

other landlords of that time. The Campa villages escaped in search
of Pent. Some landowners used force to prevent this flight, while
sentencing to death David Pent and those who worked for him. So
during this period we always went heavily armed. . . . It was
like the Far West.

After nearly three decades, Asháninka memories of Pent
and his utopia have been reshaped by the discourse of
ethnic assertion. Miguel Saviri, a native leader of the Río
Tambo area, remembers Fronda Alegre as a nightmare of
exploitation:

Well, I know something of the history of David Pent. He made
the natives work. He bought my people, natives, and made them
work for him. Men, women—he bought them and made them
work in his fields, building his house, fixing things. He paid them
with little things—clothing, little houses. It was terrible
exploitation.
You know how our grandparents were, no? When someone
died, they looked for the sorcerer who'd done the killing, until they
found the little boy or girl responsible. More often than not it was
a little girl. Then they grabbed them and took them to trade for
something. Long ago they killed them, but later they traded them
for cloth, pots, machetes, shotguns. Well, Pent bought boys and
girls, mostly girls. When they got older he made them his wives.
He had a lot of them![27]

Miguel and his brother were sold to Pent by a headman
named Severo Quinchoquer:

I and others tried to escape, but Severo's people pursued us and
grabbed us. They beat us pretty good. One of my brothers died
from the beating. It was slavery! They beat you if you tried
to leave.[28]

Despite Miguel Saviri's dyspeptic vision of Pent—which is,
after all, the memory of someone bought and sold as a

child—it seems likely that at least some Asháninkas saw in the charismatic gringo qualities of the amachénga or tasótentsi, benevolent spirits associated with prosperity. Anyone who visited Fronda Alegre, Indian or mestizo, was awed by the quantity of goods kept in its storehouses. At the same time, the local headman, Inganiteri, used Pent's wealth and quasi-mythical status to increase his own influence in the region.

By 1960, chilling rumors about David Pent began to circulate in Pucallpa, especially among the American missionaries at the SIL base in Yarinacocha. He was said to be a slave trader; he had set himself up as the "owner" of the Río Tambo, controlling all the river traffic that passed his house; he had begun to import carbines and automatic weapons with which to arm the Asháninkas; he was providing Asháninkas with military uniforms. These stories edged him into the space of Amazonian legend.

The sinister tales did nothing to improve Pent's relations with other *hacendados* along the Tambo. He also had to weather legal action brought by his American investors. The Pent family recalls that David's father bailed him out by paying off one angry victim. David also cultivated the friendship of politicians in Pucallpa and Iquitos, who apparently helped him dodge prosecution. Among his contacts, according to Javier Dávila, was Fernando Belaúnde Terry, soon to be elected president. This involvement in Peruvian politics was to prove his undoing.

In 1962 David met and married a young Iquitos woman, Nélida Rojas, who was known among David's friends as "Sophia Loren" for her striking beauty. Like many women, she was captivated by his charm and good looks. "Pent was outgoing," says Javier Dávila, "and when he met a girl he surrounded her with poetry. She was soon stuck on him."

Seated in a sparely furnished room in 1989, Nélida Rojas de Pent seems bewildered by her marriage to the romantic American twenty-seven years before. It is hard to see Sophia Loren in her ample figure and awkward attempts to find the right words to describe what happened so long ago. "We were married one Saturday, the fifth of May. I was nineteen years old. We woke up the next day, a Sunday, and they grabbed him. The police grabbed him. They accused him of being a communist."[29] After a marriage that lasted less than twenty-four hours, Nélida Rojas never saw David Pent again.

Scorza's novel and the oral accounts of family and friends hold that Nélida was the fiancée of a police officer when she met David. Nélida Rojas denies that a rejected suitor was involved in Pent's persecution, but the folklore of the region has elevated the conflict between the handsome gringo and the enraged policeman to an affair of honor in the Latin style. David had put up money so that his business partner, Mario Godeau Muñóz, could run for congress as a candidate for the leftist National Liberation Front (FLN). As a foreigner, Pent was barred from involvement in politics, and the discovery that he had paid for Godeau's legal registration as a candidate provided the pretext for his arrest. Deborah Hudson heard that the policeman and his friends savagely assaulted Pent as he and Nélida left the town hall after their civil wedding; Scorza's novel turns the contest into a fight to the death.

Even if the police had not intervened, Pent's strange empire at Charahuaja was foundering. "The situation on the Tambo was creating a climate of adversity," says Javier Dávila.

The people in the town of Atalaya began to ostracize Pent, to be hostile toward him. It was a town made up of families involved one way or another with the hacienda owners—even the Catholic Church was involved with them. They rejected Pent for being a Protestant. There was a climate of violence.

After his arrest, Pent was held incommunicado for several days and then unceremoniously deported to the United States. His wife, his considerable property, the utopian space of Fronda Alegre—all remained behind.

Pent's whereabouts immediately after deportation remain a mystery. He seems to have formulated a plan—one that eventually became an obsession—to return to Charahuaja and mete out vengeance to the enemies who had destroyed him. In 1963, Pent surfaced in Los Angeles, where a report about him appeared in the September 30 issue of *The Militant*, a Socialist Workers Party newspaper. The article describes the revolutionary activities of a "graceful young American" traveling under the alias McDonald:

> *McDonald worked with and speaks the dialect of the Campa Indians and fought on their side in a revolt against the landlords. The area McDonald comes from is just the other side of the mountains from the Concepción Valley where Hugo Blanco organized unions of peasants—for which he is now held in jail, facing death.*

It is not clear whether the implied link between Pent and Hugo Blanco, the Trotskyite peasant organizer, was made by Pent or his interviewer, though as an experienced seeker of the main chance, Pent was good at telling people what they wanted to hear. In the interview, Pent pledged to return to Peru to join the struggle to end the exploitation of Peru's urban and rural poor: " 'When I get back,' he said, 'the first thing I will do is get my ranch back from the army and distribute it among the peasants.' "[30]

Although twenty-five years have passed since the interview appeared in *The Militant*, the article's author, Della

Rossa, carries with her vivid memories of this romantic revolutionary and his lonely struggle against the Peruvian ruling class. "Pent first introduced himself to Oscar Coover in the Los Angeles office of the Socialist Workers Party," she recalls. "He wanted assistance in publicizing his cause, the struggle for land reform in Peru. He seemed sincere, so I decided to interview him."[31]

Rossa's conversation with Pent took place in his apartment in Hollywood, which she recalls as unpretentious. She remembers him as "vibrant," not so much good-looking in a classical sense as "charming and lively, someone who needed to gather people around him." Her suspicion that he might be a Lothario was provoked by the feminine undergarments scattered about the apartment, which Pent identified as belonging to his companion, "someone who helped him with his work." Yet he also described himself as married to a Peruvian, about whom he spoke with some affection.

Pent used a *nom de guerre* in the published interview, but Rossa does not recall him as being noticeably concerned about police surveillance or harassment. His knowledge of Marxism struck her as limited. He presented himself as sincerely committed to armed struggle but a trifle romantic in his notions of how it should be undertaken. Pent mentioned that he planned to have his Asháninka followers use poisoned arrows against the Peruvian army. Rossa later deleted this from the article "because it would have sounded too far out" for *The Militant*'s Trotskyite readership. After this single encounter, Pent apparently dropped from sight of party members—though not from the surveillance of the Federal Bureau of Investigation, which tracked Pent's movements on the grounds that he might be contemplating violations of the Neutrality Act.[32]

Pent's brother Joseph believes that David worked in Hollywood as a chauffeur for a movie actor. The Pent family also heard that David married a wealthy widow in New Orleans to extract from her the money he needed to return to Peru. During this period he had no direct contact with his family—

"David never kept in touch with us," Joseph Pent says—but he did correspond with Javier Dávila:

I was arrested in Lima after being compromised by a letter that Pent mailed to me, in which he talked of directing the guerrilla movements in Latin America from a base in Shumahuani, where there were enough cattle to feed the guerrillas who would move into the region. David indicated that he would take vengeance on those who'd betrayed him and who'd made false accusations to get him out of the country, generally the hacienda owners on the Ucayali. . . . I understood the psychological crisis he was going through, the process of hallucinations.

In 1963 and 1964, Pent made at least two attempts to return to Peru. Nélida, his wife of one day, recalls being notified at work that David had been detained at Jorge Chávez Airport in Lima while trying to enter the country. She held a secretarial position with the Investigative Police (PIP) at the time, and a high-ranking officer warned her to keep clear of her husband, who was promptly deported. Joseph Pent learned that David was jailed in Ecuador for several months, apparently after attempting a clandestine border crossing into Peru. In June 1964, Peruvian authorities notified the U.S. consulate of its intention to deport Pent yet again. Curiously, the Peruvians stated that Pent was definitely not involved in subversive activity.[33] James Haahr, who was the embassy's political officer at the time of the deportation, cannot recall being briefed on the Pent case, suggesting that it was treated as a purely consular matter of no political significance.[34] One might have expected the case to be more memorable, since the initial press accounts of Pent's arrest identified him as Dr. Josef Mengele, the Nazi war criminal. These erroneous reports were followed by hasty denials from the Minister of the Interior.[35]

Despite these setbacks, by late 1964 or early 1965 Pent had accomplished a clandestine entry and made his way back to the Río Tambo. But the world he returned to was not the lost utopia of 1962. Former employees had sacked his house for raw materials, which were sold off to settlers in Atalaya and nearby villages. His Asháninka women were gone. After the 1963 guerrilla incident in Puerto Maldonado, rumors of subversion were widespread in the Department of Junín. Nowhere had the situation changed more than in the local Civil Guard, which was on full alert for signs of subversion from abroad.

Pent walked into this transfigured world making no secret of his desire for vengeance and his romantic plan to liberate the Asháninkas from their oppressors. And he had antecedents—political connections to the left, a record of deportations. He was known to have stockpiled weapons for distribution to the Indians. Javier Dávila contends that these consisted of perhaps a hundred primitive front-loading shotguns and a handful of breechloaders and pistols. The alchemy of hearsay quickly transformed them into automatic weapons.

Once Asháninkas joined the MIR guerrillas at Cubantía, Pent became a threat of the first order. He was a gringo, imbued in the popular imagination with a natural ascendancy over the Indians. With this he could engineer a massive revolt of savages—for, in the words Manuel Scorza attributes to a fictional Pent, "ten thousand bowmen would have risen with us!"[36]

Hence the news reports, appearing in July and August of 1965, that tied David Pent to a Marxist insurgency about which he probably knew little. After an initial flurry of newspaper stories, Pent disappeared from press accounts until early December, when a series of contradictory articles materialized in the Lima and Huancayo dailies. On December 1, *La Crónica* alleged that "Livingstone," who directed guerrilla activities throughout Peru, was being sought by the FBI and Peruvian authorities:

> *Livingstone, who knows the southeastern Andean region well, has returned to Peru in a clandestine fashion. . . . He was*

*previously linked to an extensive contraband operation in arms
that entered the country from Desaguadero, coming from Bolivia.
He was also linked to the illegal importation of arms across the
Brazilian frontier, though this has not been clearly established.
Livingstone has been identified as the extremist responsible for
bringing into Peru most of the arms of Czech manufacture.*

Only two days later, the same daily implicated Pent in gun-
running on the Pacific coast, with the help of foreign sub-
marines of unknown origin:

*In this game, various hacienda owners are said to be involved,
among them the North American Livigstone [sic], who is said
to have encouraged the guerrilla fighters in the jungle.*

After placing Pent on the Peruvian coast for his rendezvous
with foreign agents, the December 4 issue of *La Prensa* returned him to the jungle, where Ranger units "pursue fugi-
tive guerrillas, among whom will be Lobatón Miller [sic] and
the North American communist David Livingstone Penn
[sic]." A December 3 article in the *Correo* of Huancayo mentioned that among the surviving Túpac Amaru guerrillas is
"an unidentified North American." The most bewildering
contradiction appeared a day later in *El Comercio*:

*Police of the Division of State Security and Foreign Affairs
informed journalists last night that the Communist David Livingstone Pen [sic] is not being sought in the country for the simple
reason that he is currently to be found working as a waiter in New
York City.*

By January 5, 1966, Pent had evidently forsaken Manhattan
for Satipo: *La Prensa* claimed that "Livingstone" had been
captured with Lobatón by the Forty-Third Infantry Brigade,
but provided no further details. The *New York Times* published the same story under the headline "American Called
Peru Bandit":

> *David Penn Livingstone [sic], the son of an American Protestant*
> *missionary and identified as a guerrilla leader in Central Peru,*
> *has been captured. . . . Livingstone, known to Indian tribesmen*
> *in the area, was deported from Peru in 1962 but had returned*
> *clandestinely.*[37]

La Tribuna of January 7 noted that "with respect to the capture of the North American David Livingstone, who has
been identified for some time as a dangerous agitator in the
service of communism, there is no official information." The
same news item elevated Pent to the status of an "American
industrialist" who was expelled from the country several
times.

Here Pent's trail vanishes, both in the Peruvian media and
for members of his family. His name appears in none of the
official army communiqués during the counterinsurgency,
yet rumors circulated that he was killed by Rangers. The David Pent of Scorza's novel dies a victim of love and jealousy—
the love of the Iquitos woman who runs off with him, the
jealousy of the police officer cuckolded by the handsome
gringo. "The worst thing that I did in my thirty years of
service," confesses one of the policemen who kills Pent in
Scorza's work, "was to pulverize the face, pulverize the body,
convert into a sorry sight this gringo, who was, I swear . . .
made of God's own porcelain."[38]

Javier Dávila was probably the last of Pent's friends to see
him alive:

> *So the police sent a unit and captured Pent. They took him to*
> *Pucallpa, and I went to visit him. At that moment he was shaving,*
> *and he'd had them bring him a barber, so there he was with that*
> *face he had, pink and handsome. We hugged each other as we'd*
> *always done, and he asked me to tell Mario Godeau to sell his*
> *motorboat because he needed the money to buy his air ticket when*
> *they expelled him. . . . But he was never deported, because*
> *four or five months later, when there were guerrillas in Chaupi-*

Asháninka family. Taken in early twentieth century by the German photographers Krohle and Hübner. Location unknown. (Courtesy Gastón Garreaud)

Asháninkas on Sunday outing at headquarters of Perené Colony. Photograph taken in 1910 by C. L. Chester. (National Anthropological Archives, Smithsonian Institution, Photo No. 89–22036)

Portrait of Carlos Fermín Fitzcarrald, rubber baron of the Upper Ucayali River. (From Ernesto Reyna, *Fitzcarrald, el rey de caucho,* 1942)

Portrait of the *cacique* Venancio with his wives and children. Venancio was Carlos Fitzcarrald's principal Asháninka employee. Taken circa 1900 on Río Tambo. (From Pedro Portillo, *Las montañas de Ayacucho y los ríos Apurímac, Mantaro, Ene, Perené, Tambo y Alto Ucuyali*, 1901)

Mestizo colonists, Río Apurímac, ca. 1900. (From Pedro Portillo, *Las montañas de Ayacucho y los ríos Apurímac, Mantaro, Ene, Perené, Tambo y Alto Ucuyali,* 1901)

Asháninkas at a Perené Colony coffee camp, 1910. (National Anthropological Archives, Smithsonian Institution, Photo No. 89–22035)

Mestizo women on a festive excursion hold Asháninka artifacts. Photograph entitled "Picnic on the Paucartambo," taken by Fernando Garreaud, ca. 1905. (Courtesy Gastón Garreaud)

Portrait of Asháninkas published in F. A. Stahl's *In the Amazon Jungles,* 1932. Stahl's original caption identifies subjects as "a band of murderers organized . . . for the purpose of stealing children, after killing the parents." Río Perené, ca. 1928. (Courtesy Orlando and Grace Robins)

F. A. Stahl baptizes Asháninka convert near Río Perené, ca. 1928.
(Courtesy Orlando and Grace Robins)

Guillermo Lobatón in Europe, ca. 1959. (Courtesy *Caretas*)

Guillermo Lobatón (center) with other members of Túpac
Amaru guerrilla column, 1965. To Lobatón's left is Máximo
Velando; to his right is Máximo Félix Lazo Orrego. (From
Peruvian Ministry of War, *Las guerrillas en el Perú y su represión,*
1966)

Civil guards board transport plane in Satipo during counterinsurgency campaign against Túpac Amaru column of MIR, 1965. (Courtesy *Caretas*)

Luis de la Puente, commander-in-chief of the MIR, at the headquarters of his guerrilla column at Mesa Pelada, Department of Cuzco, 1965. (Courtesy *Caretas*)

Press photograph of bridge partially destroyed by MIR's Túpac
Amaru column, June 1965. (Courtesy *Caretas*)

Asháninkas watch parachute training at base camp of the Special Police Emergency Unit, a branch of the Peruvian Civil Guard trained in antiguerrilla tactics by the U.S. Agency for International Development. Mazamari, Satipo Province. Peru, late 1965-early 1966. (Courtesy U.S. Department of State)

U.S. military advisor with members of Civil Guard counterinsurgency force during parachute training. Mazamari, Satipo
Province. Peru, late 1965–early 1966. (Courtesy U.S. Department of State)

Portrait of David Pent in the Peruvian jungle, ca. 1960, exact location unknown. (Courtesy Joseph B. Pent)

David Pent (in khakis, far left) with unidentified colonists and
Asháninkas, ca. 1960, location unknown. (Courtesy Joseph B.
Pent)

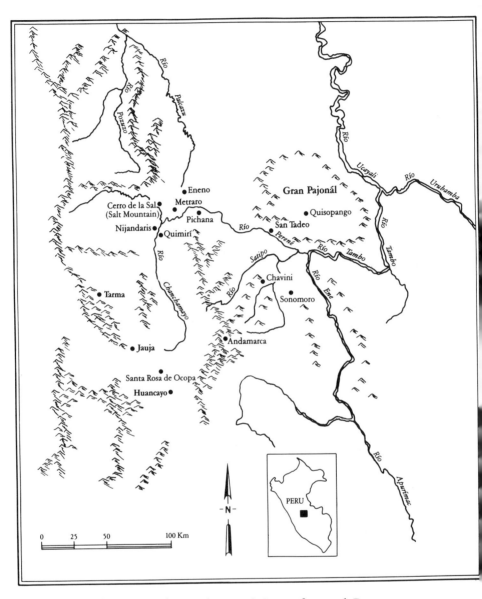

Principal towns and Franciscan missions of central Peru, seventeenth and eighteenth centuries.

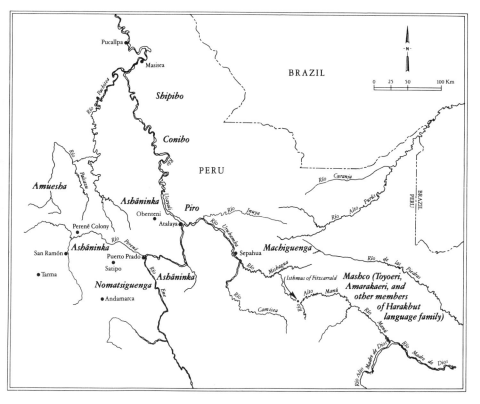

Approximate location of the major tribal groups of the central Peruvian Amazon, late nineteeth-early twentieth centuries.

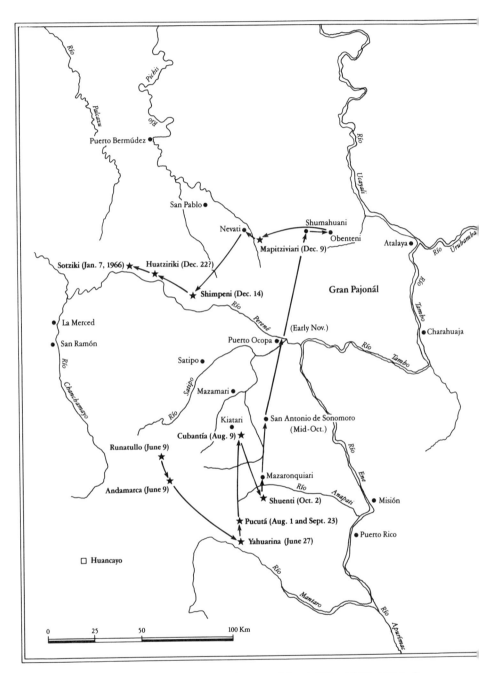

Movements of Túpac Amaru column of the MIR, 1965–1966. Stars
mark sites of MIR raids or combat with counterinsurgency forces.

*mayo [Department of Cuzco], I read a newspaper report that the
American guerrilla David Pent was among the dead. Years later
I discovered that this hadn't happened. They simply threw him
out of an airplane because they considered him a threat to the
Peruvian state.*

Joseph Pent also heard tales of a violent end. The brother of
a family friend claimed to have seen secret military records
proving that David was thrown from a helicopter somewhere
over the jungle. As he was hurled from the aircraft, the soldiers shouted to him: "If you love the Campas so much, you
can have them." Yet family members also dimly recall receiving phone messages from David months after the antiguerrilla campaign. Pent's sister Deborah believes that David
may have turned his hand to diamond hunting or gold mining elsewhere in South America. An uncle said that he had
seen an interview with David on NBC News sometime in
the late 1960s.[39]

In the family's recollection of these scattered contacts there
is an unsettling vagueness that one hardly expects of people
determined to probe the disappearance of a missing brother.
The years, of course, have dulled the memory of specific
details and blunted the impact of the family's loss. But with
David Pent's choice of a life so at odds with that of his siblings, the conclusion is inescapable that for them he was, in
a profound sense, dead long before he vanished from the Río
Tambo. Deborah Hudson, a devout and reflective woman,
sees the violence surrounding his life and disappearance as the
result of his failure to come to terms with God:

*A person can have knowledge about God but not know him
personally. If you don't know our Lord and Saviour Jesus Christ
personally, it is easy for Satan to take control. You either belong
to Christ or to Satan, one or the other. Dave had bitterness in his
heart about our family, and this bitterness gave Satan a foothold.
A person who has known God, who has been brought up in a*

Christian household, can fall deeper into sin than one who hasn't. My brother should have let himself be healed by scripture.

There is another view. One of the characters in Scorza's novel insists that Pent's actions be seen as heroic rather than as self-indulgent or sinful. Instead of an evil gringo, "exploitative and abusive to the point of caricature," Pent "appeared as the North American who instead of exploitation brought civilization to the jungle."[40] He was, in other words, an amachénga—a helpful spirit—rather than a sinister pishtaco.

Without David Pent's own voice to guide us, we can only guess at his motives. One divines in Pent's story the contradictions of his upbringing. He rejected the strict fundamentalism of his parents' home for a life without boundaries—that of a white man uncoupled from white society, a Christian hidden from the sight of God. Even as Pent contributed to the enslavement of Asháninkas, he seems to have been angered by the abuses heaped on them by the hacienda lords of the Río Tambo.[41] Hence his attraction to the idea of redirecting American venture capital—the purest expression of the forces that would strip the land and the people of their resources—to the enrichment of the Indians and the defeat of the landlords. But at some point, Pent lost himself in the thicket of his own delusions, for arrows and poisoned darts cannot defeat carbines and napalm. His obsession with returning to what was for him the utopian space of Fronda Alegre blinded him to the intensifying struggle of other myths—the messianic dream of communism and the counterdiscourse of anticommunism—that loomed on the horizon.

If Pent himself remains silent, the conflicting stories about him speak eloquently of the collective representations of his time. Peruvian reporters and novelists assumed that Pent possessed a natural ascendancy over the Indian and mestizo peoples of the Tambo. This ascendancy was alternately political, economic, intellectual, or sexual; it was the destiny of the gringo, these narratives imply, to dominate the darker masses through the strength of intellect or passion. This domination took forms that were either sinister or heroic— more properly, an oscillation between the two in an orrery of Amazonian conquest—but they were always larger than life, just as the amachénga and the pishtaco are larger than life. Hence the persistence of discordant stories of Pent's end: dying for his Marxist creed at the hands of the counterinsurgency forces or finished off, with equal brutality, in a crime of passion. What we will never know is the extent to which David Pent himself shared in, and was a victim of, these fantasies of domination.

EIGHT

Death of a Chronicle Foretold

In 1984, Eduardo Fernández interviewed Luis Shintori far into the night. A reserved man, slight of build, Shintori is one of the most forceful Asháninka leaders living near Cubantía. His reputation as a leader comes in part from experience in the world outside of Asháninka communities, in part because of his demonstrated willingness to kill.

Eduardo, Shintori, and a party of Shintori's relatives and friends had been drinking manioc beer for hours as Shintori recorded the story of his life. The atmosphere of the gathering was jovial until Eduardo asked Shintori about the events of 1965. All talk suddenly ceased, until Shintori's wife cried out, "Now tell him about how the guerrillas fooled you!" An unmistakable edginess set in. The others present, who numbered nearly thirty, began to shout at each other in anger. Men picked up their bows and arrows. The Asháninka man who had accompanied Eduardo to Shintori's house blanched, then quietly suggested that it was time to leave. To return to the place where they would sleep, both men had to cross a river by balancing on a rain-slick log in absolute darkness. Safely across, Eduardo's guide reminded him that Shintori was an *ovayeri*, a killer. They were lucky to have gotten away before violence detonated in the group. Twenty-five years after the guerrilla struggle, feelings still run high between Asháninkas who stayed with the Túpac Amaru and those who cooperated with the government's counterinsurgency campaign.

As units of the Peruvian army ringed and then penetrated the valleys of the Ene and Pangoa rivers in late August of 1965, the military tried to incorporate Asháninka guides—experts in the region's challenging jungle terrain—into the campaign against the Túpac Amaru. In his description of the counterinsurgency effort, General Artola claims that army intelligence officers called a meeting of Asháninka headmen, during which the Indians promised to collaborate with the armed forces.[1] We have not been able to verify this assertion. There is no question, however, that when help was not volunteered, the army tried to extract it through threats. Shortly after the militarization of the region, some Asháninkas began to assist the army by identifying communities where the guerrillas had taken refuge and by furnishing the names of those who assisted the Túpac Amaru. This fragmentation of support was caused in part by contradictory Asháninka responses to shamanic revelation.

In the developed world, popular interest in shamanism has grown enormously in the past decade. With it has come a sentimentalization of the shaman's place in the life of native peoples.[2] Although it is true that shamans are often respected elders who use a traditional idiom to give meaning to current events, they are also political beings. Their vocation forces them to tangle with explosive issues—life and death, public loyalty and secret betrayal—that project them into the arena of power.

Among Asháninkas, as among many other Amazonian peoples, shamans do not live in the society as a whole but among a particular segment of it. Their authority is spiritual, but it is given shape by a network of kinsmen, friends, followers, patients, and—at its outer boundaries—by enemies and detractors.[3] So there are limits to the receptiveness of people to the pronouncements of any shaman, no matter how much events initially tend to bear out his revelations. Shamans always have enemies, either because of their own actions or those of their close kin. Shamans are empowered by politics but also constrained by it.

The shaman Ernesto Andrés had followed a centuries-old pattern of using revelation to give a culturally appropriate meaning to an unusual event, in this case the sudden appearance of Guillermo Lobatón and his promise to end the abuses Asháninkas had endured for so long. Ernesto had, in a sense, appropriated the guerrillas rather than the other way around. He acknowledged their power, welcomed it, and turned it to the service of issues meaningful to his people. His specific vision was shaped by the latent pattern of Asháninka millennialism that manifested itself as early as the 1740s, from the support for Juan Santos Atahualpa to the movements engendered by Carlos Fitzcarrald and Ferdinand Stahl: an outsider speaking the language of dramatic social change is identified by Asháninkas with the Son of the Sun, who has the power to reverse the injustice that the Indians face each day of their lives.

Asháninka narratives about messianic figures note that someone always doubts the savior. Edilberto Shirinti recalls that a shaman named Pichari, whom some people regarded as a powerful spirit, claimed to be able to bring down the dead from a special tower in his house. But a man named Augustín had his doubts:

One night Pichari said that a dead woman would come. He climbed the ladder to the top floor, and right away the house began to shake. A woman came down. She was beautifully dressed, with feathers on her chest. The woman came down and spoke!

"Damn," Augustín thought, "how could this be? Let's see if it's true." They grabbed her like this. "Boom," two men threw

her to the ground and took off her clothes. And it was Pichari himself![4]

Similar skepticism arose in the 1950s during the movement associated with the foreign missionary whom the Indians remember as "Werner Bulner." Marta, a Nomatsiguenga woman, recalls that her relatives joined Bulner at his mission on the Río Ene because they thought he was Itomi Pavá. She now believes that he was a false prophet:

Lies, lies. He wasn't the Son of the Sun. All those who come here just try to trick us. They lie to us, saying they come to help. But they won't help, they're just here to abuse us![5]

Luis Shintori was one of those who followed Bulner to the new mission. He recalls that people began to doubt Bulner when he chided them for drinking manioc beer. "My people like their customs," says Shintori. "Why should they leave their customs? That's why people no longer wanted him to stay."[6]

Thinking about this and other cases of false shamans and messiahs, Edilberto Shirinti concludes: "There are always some who don't believe."

Manuel Ashivánti was one who doubted the vision of Ernesto Andrés in 1965, but he had decided to bide his time and see whether events would bear out the shaman's claim. When the guerrillas failed to defend Asháninka villages from army repression, his doubts grew—not doubts in the reality of Itomi Pavá but in the veracity of Ernesto and his prophecy.

In part, Ernesto was a victim of the lore that gave meaning to his revelation. Those who believed in Itomi Pavá expected the helpful spirit to transform their world in one rapid crusade. As the struggle dragged on, their faith wavered.

By the end of September, the patrols of Rangers and other counterinsurgency forces had intensified to the point that the villages of Boca Kiatari, Cubantía, Anapati, and other settlements in the Sonomoro valley were at least sporadically abandoned by their inhabitants to avoid persecution. People hid in the forest, making do as best they could. Pedro Kintaro watched from a hiding place as Rangers burned his village and made off with all the livestock they could grab. Indians were detained, some never to be seen again by their relatives. Kintaro remembers:

Look, we were alone, our village burned, the fields abandoned, nothing to eat. Our children began to get sick from walking in wet clothes in the forest. Our wives began to complain, "Why have you let them fool you? How are we going to live now?" Everything that the shaman had said, that the guerrillas were going to defend us, that they were going to finish off the exploiters—nothing! We were worse off than before. Not even anything to eat. And police everywhere. Where were we going to go?

There were also personal reasons for ambivalence about members of the Túpac Amaru. Some people allege that Froilán Herrera was making amorous advances to a daughter of the headman Alberto Yorini, an impropriety that could not have come at a more sensitive time in relations between the Indians and the MIR. Yorini began to distance himself from the guerrilla cause and ultimately came to serve as an important intermediary between the army and pro-MIR Asháninkas.

The guerrillas suspected that the prompt arrival of Ranger patrols at some of their camps could only mean that they had been betrayed by an Indian. Elías Murillo remembers that one Asháninka asked to be allowed to go to Salt Mountain to collect salt, which the guerrillas needed badly. He thinks that this trip was a pretext for the Indian to inform the authorities of the Túpac Amaru's location: "He's the one who brought the army to our camp. But the comrades executed him, in 1968 or 1969, when we were in jail after the guerrilla war."

Perhaps drawing on rumored fissures in Asháninka support for the guerrillas, Huancayo's *Correo* reported in late September that Indians and revolutionaries were squaring off for a fight. "Two hundred Indians led by the cacique José Alberto Pirichico declare their own war. . . . From Gran Pajonál, with poisoned darts, machetes, and old carbines, the Campas advance on the guerrillas," the headlines claimed. The article alleged that the guerrillas executed four Indians for betraying the Túpac Amaru, which then triggered reprisals from two hundred "fierce Choviaros" from the Gran Pajonál. The article's unidentified author then let his flair for the dramatic wrestle free of even modest constraints:

> *The guerrillas, emaciated, with torn clothing, hungry, are falling back with machine guns at their sides. New encounters are foreseen, and it is feared that the struggle will be fierce and unequal. The primitive but well-aimed arrows will whistle in the tangled jungle. And with a symphony of death, machine guns will return the crossfire, reverberating in the stillness of the Green Hell.*[7]

When queried about these events by journalists, Hércules Marthans, Inspector General of the Investigative Police, would say only, "I know nothing about it."

By August the Peruvian congress was taking the insurgency seriously enough to pass legislation making it a capital offense to "betray the Fatherland and take up arms on behalf of foreign powers." At the same time, the government issued special war bonds to support counterinsurgency efforts "in defense of national sovereignty." Among the first to make a patriotic contribution to the war effort was Pedro Beltrán, director of the Lima daily *La Prensa*, who bought bonds worth a million *soles*.[8] The Belaúnde administration was by this time struggling against fierce conservative criticism within the congress. The president's Popular Action Party was accused of harboring communists and of failing to act decisively against the guerrillas.

The public profile of the MIR, meanwhile, had never been higher. In a shrewd analysis of the guerrilla struggle written in 1966, the deputy chief of mission of the American Embassy, Ernest Siracusa, observed that by mid-September of 1965, the MIR had "harvested considerable publicity and resultant prestige both in Peru and abroad; had succeeded initially in creating an atmosphere of uncertainty and concern throughout the country; and . . . allow[ed] the left in Peru to gain the sympathy of a few intellectuals by claiming repression on the part of the Government."[9] Among those intellectuals was the so-called "Paris Group," a circle of Peruvian expatriates who voiced their approval of the MIR's insurgency in a letter published in the magazine *Caretas*. Their communiqué closed with an offer of "moral support to the men who now deliver their lives so that all Peruvians can live a better life."[10] A prominent member of the Paris Group, the writer Mario Vargas Llosa, confessed in a letter to his friend Francisco Moncloa that he "has a bad conscience to be living outside of Peru now. I wish I were there to help in some way."[11]

Once the government recognized that it was dealing with a real guerrilla threat, it laid plans for strikes against the other fronts that the MIR claimed to be organizing. The most important was in the Department of Cuzco, where Luis de la Puente and a force of perhaps forty guerrillas hoped to direct an uprising in the Convención Valley from the MIR's "security zone" at Mesa Pelada, a remote mountaintop east of the town of Quillabamba. The names used by the guerrillas of the southern front suggest the millennial currents within MIR ideology. The Mesa Pelada camp was called *Illarec ch'aska*, a Quechua term meaning "morning star," to symbolize the dawning of a new day. De la Puente's column took the name Pachacutec after the Inca ruler who consolidated the Inca state into an empire. Pachacutec itself comes from the Quechua word *pachacuti*, an apocalyptic rupture of time leading to a new era.

Although de la Puente's unit had not yet undertaken military action, the government feared that a guerrilla front in La Convención could prove to be a serious threat because of the valley's history of peasant unrest. An assault on the southern MIR front might also net de la Puente himself, severing the party from its highest-ranking leader.

The Mesa Pelada command post proved to be the MIR's Achilles heel. The guerrillas hoped that the site's natural defenses, as well as the minefields they had laid around their camps, would make Mesa Pelada impregnable to government attack. In late August the army quickly surrounded the escarpment, cutting off supplies and isolating de la Puente from his peasant supporters. The notoriously unpredictable Cuzco weather permitting, jets could bomb and strafe guerrilla positions with impunity because the area was only sparsely inhabited by civilians. The army also used 120mm mortars to harass guerrilla encampments as its forces enveloped Mesa Pelada. There are allegations, never answered by the armed forces, that peasant suspects captured by the army were used as human minesweepers—that is, forced to walk over the MIR minefields until something exploded.[12]

The biggest blow to the guerrillas was the defection of one of their comrades, Albino Guzmán, who revealed the location of weapons caches and other sites important to the guerrillas' survival. In press accounts, Guzmán and two other presumed guerrillas renounced "the extremist tendency that agitators have begun to propagate internally with the aid of red countries." Even the American ambassador allowed, in a telegram to Washington, that the tone of the statement suggested the confessions had been composed by army propagandists.[13]

If Lobatón and the other members of the Túpac Amaru were able to receive news about the fate of their comrades in other MIR fronts, it couldn't have encouraged them. Official army sources announced that Luis de la Puente died on or about October 23 as he and his men tried to break out of the blockade around Mesa Pelada. The American journalist Norman Gall, who interviewed peasants near Mesa Pelada a few

days after de la Puente's death, reported that soldiers captured
the MIR leader while he drank condensed milk in a tent. Before being taken into custody, Gall wrote, de la Puente "only
asked to be allowed to finish his milk." The next day, the
government reported de la Puente dead in battle.[14] Documents released by the State Department suggest that de la
Puente perished under circumstances different from those reported by Norman Gall or by the army. On October 30, an
unidentified informant interviewed by V. P. Randolph III,
the U.S. Embassy's second secretary, spoke in considerable
detail about de la Puente's death:

*[Name excised] said that de la Puente and Ruben Tupayachi
(well-known Quechua Indian communist and son of a communist)
had actually been captured by the Army and brought into Quillabamba about October 8, heavily guarded and with bags over
their heads to prevent their identities from becoming known. Shortly
afterwards, Minister of Government Alva Orlandini, War Minister Arbulú and Army Commanding General Doig all travelled
to Quillabamba to interrogate de la Puente. After extracting what
they could, de la Puente, Tupayachi, and two other captured
guerrillas . . . were taken out into the backcountry and suitably
dispatched.[15]*

The MIR's northern front, under the command of Gonzalo
Fernández Gasco, never saw action at all. The army combed
the backlands of the Department of Piura for weeks, beginning in October, and although patrols managed to capture a
few guerrillas, Fernández Gasco and most of his men assid-
uously avoided contact until they could cross the border into
the safety of Ecuador.

An unexpected development was the opening of a fourth
front in the Department of Ayacucho, led by Héctor Béjar
and members of the Army of National Liberation (*Ejército de
Liberación Nacional*, or ELN). After protracted negotiations,
the ELN and MIR agreed in early September to join forces
in the guerrilla struggle. Although Béjar and the ELN "lib-

erated" a hacienda in La Mar Province by killing its owners, the ELN never posed a serious military threat to the government. The army concluded that cleanup operations in Ayacucho could wait until it had dealt with the more formidable guerrilla threat posed by the Túpac Amaru.

On the first of October, Lobatón and most of the guerrillas of the Túpac Amaru were in the community of Shuenti, on the Río Anapati. A few days earlier, two army detachments, Loma and León, had begun a sweep down the Río Anapati from Puerto Rico, in the course of which they killed Asháninka sentries manning observation posts at Alto Sumabeni, Alto Tinkabeni, and Shenquiari. Learning of their approach, Lobatón, Velando, Herrera, and a mixed force of guerrillas and Asháninkas attempted without success to outflank the approaching troops. On October 2, commandos of the León detachment assaulted Shuenti. The encounter was a disaster for the insurgents. Casualty figures vary, but officially the army killed eleven guerrillas and captured seventeen. The commandos suffered three casualties.[16] Since the available documents name only two of the fallen guerrillas, Máximo Lazo Orrego and "the fierce Campa Priori," it is likely that many of the other dead and wounded were Asháninkas. (Indian dead were rarely considered worth identifying in official communiqués.) The magazine *Caretas* claimed that the only food the army found in the guerrilla camp was lima beans and some boxes of gelatin.[17]

For the rest of October the Túpac Amaru managed to avoid head-on encounters with the army. The guerrillas slowly retreated northward from Shuenti toward the Río Perené. Alfredo Atiri, then a young man in a mission school who happened to be visiting his family, witnessed the arrival of the guerrillas in his village:

They came on the trail from Anapati and Cachingarani. One day they came. There I met Froilán Herrera. He was a young man then. . . . "Brothers," I said to them, "what's your purpose in coming here?" We were drinking manioc beer. Since it was the full moon, we were having a drinking party. That's our custom, no? Well, they greeted me politely and we received them.

Later I asked them, "Why have you come here? What's your purpose? Are you civil guards?" "No, we aren't civil guards," they answered. "We're here to protect you from those who abuse you—the ones who deal in coffee and the merchants who trick you. From those who exploit you and your people . . ."

In truth, I didn't understand much of what they said. Neither did my father. They used words we'd never heard before.

The next day they left. They stayed with us just a day and a night. They were very suspicious.[18]

They had reason to be uneasy, for the army was close behind. Several days after the guerrillas' departure, a Ranger unit stormed into Atiri's village and tortured a young man until he divulged the names of people with whom the guerrillas had spoken during their visit. Alfredo and his father Antonio were among about a half-dozen men arrested for collaborating with the subversives:

We didn't know why they had captured us. We didn't understand. Everything was shouts and threats. They pointed rifles at our heads and then laughed. Our custom is that when people come to our villages we offer them food and beer. If there's meat or fish, you share that too. You offer whatever there is in the house. If the visitor is polite, if he greets you properly, you treat him well. He'll do the same for you some other time. That's our custom. That's why we treated the guerrillas well. And for this they took us prisoner—for our hospitality!

Yet Alfredo also remembers that his father believed in Ernesto's vision of the guerrillas as helpful spirits. Antonio Atiri's involvement with the Túpac Amaru went beyond simple hospitality, though it isn't clear whether he actually took up arms with the rebels.

The guerrillas made their way down the Río Sonomoro to settlements near the Río Perené. Again they were assisted by a local headman, this time the elderly Choviante, who in his day was a feared warrior. On November 2, Choviante helped the guerrillas cross the treacherous Perené, apparently east of the Franciscan mission at Puerto Ocopa.[19] They began the arduous ascent into the Gran Pajonál, a region that had given Juan Santos Atahualpa shelter in the eighteenth century.

Choviante's connection with the guerrillas cost him his life. He died in an application of the "Law of Flight" (*ley de fuga*), the rule allowing the authorities to shoot fleeing prisoners. The army began to cite the Law of Flight with numbing regularity to account for the deaths of captive suspects. Eugenio Sarove, a Spanish hacienda owner who before his death owned land in Kiatari, recalled with admiration the application of this policy:

> *Well, nothing was known about prisoners. There were rumors about the Law of Flight . . . But the only thing is, ¡macho! they didn't let even one live! They finished the guerrilla war here in the jungle.*[20]

Edilberto Shirinti remembers:

> *Choviante was also in the guerrilla war. He was the guide who led the guerrillas, because they couldn't walk by themselves. The soldiers asked him: "Do you know Lobatón Milla?" "Yes," he said. "Are you his buddy?" Choviante denied it. "No," he said. They grabbed him, they handcuffed him with another Asháninka, and they took them away. They beat them. There's an Asháninka who says they beat him every night with their rifle butts. They made him cry out, they did everything to him. They took him to Puerto Ocopa, where there was a camp of soldiers.*
> *The priest at Puerto Ocopa didn't want to see so many dead there. He asked the soldiers to free the Asháninkas. He said that*

they shouldn't kill the Indians because "they are ignorant and don't know what they're doing."

"Alright, we'll release them," said the army captain. That night they took Choviante and his companion to the banks of the Río Tambo. They sat them there, while the soldiers pretended to ignore them. . . . Everything was quiet there in the dark, and Choviante was handcuffed to his companion. Seeing that no one was watching them, they ran toward the water. Just when they started to run, the guards fired bursts with their machine guns and killed Choviante's companion. Choviante made it to the water, still tied to the dead man. He swam as long as he could, then got out. The soldiers chased him along the riverbank, and there they shot him. They threw his body into the river and told the priest, "We let him go, and he left by the river." But there downriver, near a place called Coriteni, the bodies fetched up on a tree trunk. That's where my countrymen found Choviante and his companion. The two were murdered by the soldiers.[21]

Padre Donato Lecuona, who came face to face with the Túpac Amaru in mid-November of 1965, now lives in retirement in the northern Spanish town of Vitoria. Perhaps because of his experiences in Peru and, more recently, his life amid the struggle of Basque separatists, Lecuona wasn't eager to talk about soldiers or guerrillas when Eduardo Fernández called him from Madrid in July 1988 to request an interview. Eduardo took the night train to Vitoria and met the priest at the Franciscan residence. Lecuona, an angular, balding man, relaxed visibly when Eduardo mentioned that he was an Argentine descended from *gallegos*, immigrants from Galicia in northern Spain. They began a walking tour of Vitoria, alternating quick visits to the city's churches with stops at wine bars. As they rambled, Lecuona told the story of his life as a missionary in Peru's Gran Pajonál.

Padre Lecuona was only seventeen when he came to Peru

as a Franciscan novice. He freely admits that despite two decades of life with Asháninkas he scarcely knows anything
about them. Yet twenty-five years later, he remembers viv-
idly the arrival of the Túpac Amaru at his mission station:

> In 1965, we knew that there were guerrillas. People were
> uneasy, and the Indians talked all about it. One day a native came
> running and shouted, "A white man has fallen." We thought that
> a plane had crashed. They're always crashing, aren't they? We
> grabbed our rifles and went into the jungle where the Indian had
> directed us. We hadn't gone far when we met a stranger, a high-
> lander. Castro, who administered the farm at Shumahuani, asked
> him, "Aren't you a guerrilla? You'd better come with us to Oben-
> teni." But the highlander answered him, "Be careful with me. I'm
> just a messenger, and back there at the camp there are many more
> people."
> So we let him go and returned to Obenteni. . . . We had
> some arms at the mission, just Mausers from Argentina. They
> were ancient but still formidable. They'd given us the arms to
> defend ourselves from the savages. That's the way we thought
> about things then. Well, I took a Mauser and put it in my bedroom.
> Before dawn the next day, they called from outside my house:
> "Padre, come out! We're the guerrillas."[22]

Among the revolutionaries was an articulate black man who
seemed to be the group's leader:

> There was a zambo, a black man, who pointed a machine gun at
> me. I wanted to say "Jesus have mercy on me" because I thought
> they were going to kill me, to riddle me with bullets. Then the
> black man said, "Well, Padre, we won't hurt you if you don't try
> anything. All right?"

The commander, who identified himself as Guillermo Lobatón, silenced the mission's shortwave radio by removing
some tubes, then marched Lecuona into the village. Lecuona
asked the Mother Superior, Sister Ricarda Fernández, to pre-

pare food for the rebels. Froilán Herrera·arrived and threatened the priest, saying that he "wanted to wear the Franciscan's cassock"—in other words, to kill him. Lobatón warned
Herrera to leave the priest alone.

The meal went well, though at one point Lecuona had to
advise the loquacious Mother Superior that this was not a
good time to express her admiration for General Franco or to
criticize the behavior of communists during the Spanish Civil
War. The guerrillas rested after breakfast, leaving Lecuona
alone in his house.

There was a tense moment several hours later when Lobatón found Lecuona with a letter the priest intended to send,
via Ashániyka courier, to the missionaries at Puerto Ocopa,
apprising them of the situation. Without losing his composure, Lobatón made himself comfortable in the priest's quar-
ters. They fell into a friendly debate about the role of Pope
Pius XII in the persecution of the Jews during World War II.
Lecuona offered Lobatón a book on the subject and, to the
priest's surprise, Lobatón accepted it. They talked of Lobatón's studies at San Marcos University, the dreadful years of
work in the used newspaper trade in Paris, his visits to East
Germany and Cuba. "He told me," remembers Lecuona,
"that they were going to close the circle, to change the structure of Peru. He spoke of things like that, of justice and of
exploitation, but with great simplicity."

The rest of the "occupation" of the mission by the Túpac
Amaru, which according to Lecuona lasted three days, was
marked by the same relaxed cordiality of the priest's first encounters with Lobatón.[23] On Saturday the guerrillas and local
residents faced off for a game of soccer, during which Lecuona and Lobatón sat by the playing field and talked. "I can't
remember who won the match," says Lecuona. The next day,
the priest asked permission to say Mass. He invited the guerrillas to attend, reminding them that they were in considerable danger:

"May we enter with our weapons?" one of them asked me.
"Of course," I said, "that way Our Lord will be better protected."

*And most of the guerrillas came into the church to hear Mass.
Lobatón didn't come in. He listened from outside. Then I began
my sermon. I read from the Book of Amos, which provides a
justification for young people to take up arms against injustice. I
spoke of inequality and poverty—the Christian message. Lobatón
came into the church and knelt. To end the service I said a prayer
for the guerrillas who had died in defense of a noble cause. Everyone
prayed. When I finished the Mass, the guerrillas got into line
outside and shouted, "¡Viva la guerrilla!" They congratulated
and thanked me for the sermon, raising their weapons in the air.*

The guerrillas departed Obenteni the next morning, moving in the direction of Shumahuani. "I'm going in this direction," Lobatón told the priest. "If they ask you where I went,
tell them I went the other way." "Priests don't lie," answered
Lecuona. Lobatón said nothing, recalls Padre Lecuona: "He
understood and left." Lecuona later heard that the guerrillas
killed a steer at Shumahuani and spitted it there so everyone
could eat. They also took some horses for the trip to Puerto
Bermúdez.

After Lobatón and his men left the mission, Padre Lecuona
waited for a time, then dispatched a written message to the
Franciscans at Puerto Ocopa, notifying them of the guerrilla
occupation. The priest at Puerto Ocopa radioed the message—in Latin, so that it wouldn't be overheard by the military—to his counterpart in San Ramón. From there it was
relayed to Lima in the Basque language, again to avoid
interception.

Padre Lecuona's most vivid memories are of Lobatón
himself:

*When I spoke to him he struck me as a sincere man, and one
who'd suffered. When they arrived over the mountains, on trails
that only the natives use—living on manioc "thanks to his Campa
brothers," as Lobatón put it—I realized that they simply wanted
to escape. They were exhausted, disillusioned. Lobatón was
very sick. One noticed that he was suffering. Once he told me that
his sisters were religious. We spoke about religion, about God,*

*but also about injustice and socialism. I interrupted him and said,
"You are a good Christian." He was very moved. I could almost
see the tears. He was suffering.*

The Peruvian armed forces had cut a swath through the
peasantry with napalm and aerial bombardment. They were
now closing in on the guerrillas. The military's honor was at
stake, for a few poorly armed insurgents had tied up the
armed services for many weeks and taken a heavy toll in lives.
There would be few survivors among the guerrillas. Whether
this was the result of an explicit policy of liquidation is
known only to the officers in charge, though in a recent interview an officer who fought the Túpac Amaru stated his
conviction that "the best subversive is a dead subversive."[24]
What the army released to the public was a series of increasingly unbelievable stories to account for the deaths of all the
key members of the Túpac Amaru.

The first to fall were Máximo Velando and Juan Paucarcaja.
They had separated from the column led by Lobatón in the
first week of November and marched in the direction of
Puerto Bermúdez, apparently with the idea of laying the
groundwork for an escape. Some sources suggest that Lobatón planned to take the town and then use the private planes
that were based there to fly the surviving guerrillas to safety.
The more imaginative press accounts identified their ultimate
destination as Cuba, but it is more likely that they sought to
cross the frontier into Brazil or Ecuador or, alternatively, fly
to the Peruvian coast, where they could lose themselves in
one of the country's larger cities.

Velando and Paucarcaja came to the settlement of San Pablo, a short distance south of Puerto Bermúdez. Official military sources state that they were betrayed by an Ashaninka,
taken into custody December 2 or 3 by the police, and transferred by airplane to Satipo. A source sympathetic to the MIR

makes the plausible claim that the pair was captured around November 24 and held prisoner—presumably for interrogation—for over two weeks.[25] Peruvian officials eventually announced that Paucarcaja was shot while trying to escape. General Artola's account follows the official version of events:

> *At four in the morning on December 6 . . . Paucarcaja attempted to flee, pursued by the rest of the guards roused by the shouts of the sentry, and since he didn't obey the order to halt and he was near the thick vegetation into which he could disappear, he was killed by the guards.*
>
> *Meanwhile, in his cell Velando lost all hope and attempted to kill himself by striking his head against the wall, which produced grave fractures of the cranium, resulting in his death while he was being transferred to Huancayo.[26]*

During his 1969 trial for participation in the guerrilla struggle, the peasant José Miranda Balbin told a different story of Velando's death:

> *We arrived at the base and they blindfolded me. They'd taken us from the Satipo jail [bound for Huancayo], but I don't remember whether it was the third or fourth of December. When I arrived at the airplane, they took off my blindfold and threw me inside; I heard a burst of machine-gun fire and then they threw in the bloody body of Velando . . . Velando's head was destroyed and he had five bullet holes. They uncovered his head so I could see it. It was destroyed, and blood oozed out.[27]*

When Velando's body was released to his wife Carmen, she also received his wristwatch and wallet, which contained 170 *soles*, "as proof of the honesty of the armed forces."[28]

As the army began to harvest guerrilla captives, people in Satipo heard that the suspects were thrown from helicopters over the jungle, in some cases while still alive. The farmer

Juan Saavedra remembers having a few drinks with a lieutenant involved in the counterinsurgency operation:

> He said to me, "I've captured three guerrillas." There were two men and a woman. He had them there [in San Ramón de Pangoa]. They interrogated them. The guerrillas said nothing. The woman was nice looking but tough. Very committed. "They'll kill me, but I won't talk," she said.
> Committed. She didn't talk. What happened is that they put her into a helicopter, flew away, and came back empty a half hour later. That's why I think that they took them up in the helicopters to make them talk. And if they didn't, they were pushed out.

Alfredo Atiri believes that this is what happened to his father, Antonio. Both were in police custody when a colonist identified Antonio Atiri as a guerrilla. The police released Alfredo and promised to liberate his father within two months.

> The colonel told me, "We're taking him to Lima to process him for the trial." I waited two months and then came to look for him. I looked everywhere, but nobody would tell me anything. When I complained too much they threatened to kill me . . . I learned later that they took my father up in an airplane and threw him alive into the jungle. They killed a lot of people like that, throwing them alive from airplanes.

Lobatón and those who remained with him traveled slowly from Shumahuani in the general direction of Puerto Bermúdez. The army, however, was now aware of their presence in the Gran Pajonál and implemented a new strategy of small-unit mobility. Seven commando units—presumably elements of the Second Light Division—were deployed on the Pajonál and moved quickly from place to place in helicopters.[29] The unit called Relámpago approached Nevati on December 9 and caught up with the guerrillas in the nearby community of Mapitziviari. The commandos killed two Indian sentries, named Camaytiri and Gerónimo, before they could sound the alarm.[30] The government claims that in the ensuing fire-fight, eight guerrillas died, with only one army casualty.

Lobatón and about fourteen others continued their retreat to Nevati, where they must have heard about the fate of Velando and Paucarcaja and of the danger that awaited them in Puerto Bermúdez. They turned south toward the Perené, presumably with the hope of recrossing the Perené and es-caping to Satipo. The army tracked them to the communities of Miritiari and Piñango. The guerrillas' retreat was hindered by the rainy season, which began in earnest in November. Larger rivers had become impassable without special equip-ment or a high-powered boat.

Blocked by the violent waters of the Perené at Miritiari and La Cascada, Lobatón and his men doubled back to Shim-peni, deeper in the forest. There they were surprised by the commando unit Flecha on the fourteenth, but the encounter produced no recorded casualties on either side.

Any semblance of consistency in the few published sources about the insurgency vanishes at this point. Some versions have the Túpac Amaru splitting up, presumably on the as-sumption that the rebels would be more likely to survive if each set his own course.[31] Other accounts keep the dimin-ished and battered column—reduced to fewer than a dozen men—together until the end. Whatever the guerrillas' strat-egy for survival, they must have known that their prospects were bleak. Isolated on the fringes of the Gran Pajonál, their only choices were to follow the Perené downriver toward the Tambo or upriver to more populated areas in Oxapampa Province. They opted for the latter. Without their Ashaninka supporters, who had all deserted or been killed by comman-dos, the members of the Túpac Amaru depended on Froilán Herrera's familiarity with the region.

After a week of evasive movement through the jungle on

a course roughly parallel with the Perené, Herrera and several other guerrillas fell into the army's hands at Huatziriqui. The government claimed that Herrera died in combat on December 22, but a U.S. Embassy cable sent to Washington on December 28 states that he was captured on December 21 and executed shortly thereafter.[32] General Artola claims that one of the guerrillas with Herrera, César Toro, "met a horrible end at the hands of the Campas." Toro, Artola adds, "had thirty-eight arrows in his body."[33] It is hard to see this claim, for which there is no supporting evidence, as anything other than an attempt to contrast the "surgical" quality of the army's extermination methods with the atavistic killing technology of the Indians.

Lobatón dodged the commandos for another two weeks. The War Ministry's report states that on January 7, 1966, "Lobatón and the few who accompanied him fell after confronting one of the combat teams near the Río Sotziqui."[34]

The day after Padre Lecuona's message about the occupation of the mission reached Lima, the army sent a helicopter to Obenteni. The officer in charge was a colonel known as "Silver Fox." He ordered his men to confiscate the mission's rifles, accusing Lecuona of cowardice because he had failed to use his Mauser against the rebel column. Then the soldiers began a campaign of "intelligence gathering":

They began to mistreat people in Obenteni. They tortured Campa children who had been guides for the guerrillas. They hung them upside down from trees. For days on end they hit and insulted them. The soldiers threatened to take me up in the helicopter. This colonel, the Silver Fox, specialized in applying the Law of Flight. He said, "And what will we do with this one?" Since the pilot knew me, he interceded on my behalf, so they didn't throw me out. Without him, they would have done it!

They took me to Satipo and turned me over to the priest in charge
there. The colonel told him, "I bring you a black sheep."

No doubt Lecuona was protected by his status as a priest.
Eventually the Church sent him back to Spain. Before leaving, he paid a visit to Lobatón's wife, Jacqueline, who had
been imprisoned after the outbreak of the guerrilla war:

I told her everything I knew. By then the news had come out
that Lobatón was dead. She told me, "My husband can't have
died." She sat silently for a while, then looked toward the vase in
which she kept a rose bud. The flower was withered and sad-
looking. Then she said, "My husband is dead."

A curious feature of the army's communiqués and official
reports is that they fail to stitch Lobatón's death into their
narrative of communist subversion and revolutionary cowardice. Lobatón simply disappeared at the end of the campaign. The government never produced his body, nor did it
make any effort to reconcile the different stories—official and
otherwise—of his end. It is as if there was a conscious attempt to avoid closure of any sort, thereby denying others,
especially the Peruvian left, the opportunity to appropriate
the story for their own purposes. In this sense, the Peruvian
counterinsurgency presaged the strategy of making people
vanish—turning "disappear" into a transitive verb—that was
applied so ferociously in Argentina in the 1970s.

The army's attempt to deny narrative closure to Lobatón's
life was countered by stories of what really happened to the
guerrillas, especially the Túpac Amaru's leader, that still circulate among Asháninkas and other residents of Satipo Province. People with whom we spoke agree that an Asháninka
man informed on the guerrillas, resulting in their capture and
execution. One widely circulated variation on this theme

holds that the informer was paid with thirty *calaminas*, pieces of metal roofing material. The parallel to New Testament messianism and the treachery of Judas Iscariot is obvious. Versions collected by the Danish anthropologist Søren Hvalkof describe a death of mindless brutality and degradation: "The Rangers tortured some of the *guerrilleros*, castrated them, and forced them to swallow their own testicles, which caused some laughter among the Asháninka men who told me the story."[35]

Non-Indians, even those unsympathetic to the Túpac Amaru, tended to see Lobatón's death in a more heroic light. *La Prensa* of January 19, 1966, stated that Lobatón suffered a bullet wound in the hip during an earlier shootout with the army. Rapidly losing strength, he ordered his men to make their escape. "However, all refused to abandon him, and the Campas were kept under close surveillance by the guerrillas to make sure they didn't denounce his presence to the authorities." Three days later, the article contended, the remaining nine guerrillas were killed in a clash with the army. Huancayo's *Correo* embellished this final encounter with a show of revolutionary defiance:

> *Lobatón, the man who spoke seven languages and traveled through many countries in Europe and Asia, defended himself until the end. He emptied his gun, even though he was mortally wounded. Close-quarters machine-gun fire ended his life when he shouted at the top of his voice, "Long live the Revolution! Long live the Revolution!"*[36]

A soldier claiming to be an eyewitness to Lobatón's capture told a journalist in 1990 that "Lobatón acted like an academic, with the style of an educated person, despite the circumstances." He was, the man remembered, "quite tranquil."[37] A more sardonic version of this story, told by a Spaniard close to military sources during the insurgency, has the wounded Lobatón captured by the commandos. A high-ranking officer arrives by helicopter to interrogate him. Lobatón answers all questions with a self-assurance that enrages the officer, who tells Lobatón that he is "a filthy communist and a traitor to his country." Maintaining his composure, Lobatón replies that "now they'll stop talking about Ingrid"—referring to the spectacular Ingrid Schwend murder trial in Lima—"and start talking about socialism." In the face of this defiance, the officer orders Lobatón taken up in a helicopter and thrown out over the jungle.

Another narrative left unfinished in January of 1966 was that of David Pent. Newspaper articles placed him with Lobatón and Velando in December. The *New York Times* reported him captured on January 6. The armed forces neither confirmed nor denied his participation in the last days of the Túpac Amaru. The MIR and other leftist parties kept silent about Pent. He was, after all, a North American in a period when anti-*yanqui* rhetoric had reached its apogee.

"Of the Asháninkas who died," says Pedro Kintaro, "I don't remember all their names." A few stay with him:

> *The first was Piori Changueti. He died at Alto Anapati. They captured and killed him when the helicopters landed. Another who died was Guillermo Chimanga, who was thrown from an airplane. Then Romulo Pachacama, part Asháninka and part highlander, who died in Chiriari. Another was Rosaria, a woman from here. Then the mother of José Quintimari. They shot her and said that the Rangers had taken her to Lima to be cured, but she never came back. At Puerto Ocopa they killed Nicolás and Choviante. Then Fernando Chanqueti and Mapasi, killed near Puerto Bermúdez.*

The fate of Ernesto Andrés, the shaman who had identified Lobatón as a helpful spirit, was much like that of Lobatón himself. The police arrested Ernesto along with four other men, including Pedro Kintaro, as the insurgency drew to a close. Manuel Ashivánti describes their interrogation by the police:

[The policeman demanded:] "Who spoke to God?" "Him!"
[one of the Asháninkas] said, pointing at the shaman. . . .
Ernesto, the sheripiari, *never came back. They say that he was*
killed, but it's not known. Did they really kill him or not? They
killed him in jail, that's what people say . . . All the people
blamed him for being the leader, the one who tricked us, the one
who said that Itomi Pavá had arrived, the guerrillas. No one
knows where Ernesto went. Could he still be alive, or is he dead?

NINE

Beyond 1965

With the death of Guillermo Lobatón, the Peruvian government declared the MIR's act of revolutionary boldness a failure. Héctor Béjar's ELN column in Ayacucho, which had shrunk to thirteen guerrillas, scattered after an encounter with the army on December 17, 1965.[1] Three of Béjar's comrades escaped to Bolivia, where they later died with Che Guevara. Béjar himself eluded capture for several months, enough time for intellectuals abroad to stir up considerable support on his behalf. Fearing bad publicity, the army refrained from meting out the same punishment to Béjar and the surviving leaders of the MIR that it had dispensed to Guillermo Lobatón and Luis de la Puente.

The armed forces lost no time in boasting about their achievement:

"Mission accomplished," we say to the Government and to the Peruvian people at the conclusion of the anti-guerrilla campaign. . . . It has been proven that the Peruvian people re-

ject communism and will not assist its ominous designs to deliver the country to foreign powers.[2]

The staff of the U.S. Embassy in Lima was equally pleased that Peru had succeeded in neutralizing the guerrilla threat. In a report prepared for the State Department, the embassy's deputy chief of mission, Ernest V. Siracusa, called the conflict "a blessing in disguise," first because Peru's most militant group of leftists had been destroyed, second because it made the "Peruvian Government and people conscious of the nature of the communist threat to their country." Siracusa asserted that Peru was the only country in the world that had defeated a communist guerrilla movement without foreign support, a point that must have reassured State Department officials worried about the spread of communist movements elsewhere. Even Siracusa voiced a word of caution, however, by noting that the failure of Peru to address long-term social grievances helped to "provide the breeding ground for discontent and promote the opportunity for continuous exploitation by communism."[3]

Despite the general elation within the Peruvian armed forces, some senior officers took a more sober view when tallying the results of the conflict. The government had spent over $10 million to subdue scarcely a hundred poorly armed revolutionaries. At least three thousand soldiers and policemen were deployed in the departments of Junín and Cuzco, and estimates of the total force strength directed to the counterinsurgency campaign range as high as five thousand. Air force planes logged thousands of hours of flight time. The government admitted that security forces suffered thirty-eight dead; it has never released definitive information on other casualties. Had the guerrillas been able to attract strong support from peasants in their areas of operation, the cost in lives and scarce economic resources would have been far higher.[4]

In his concluding remarks on the campaign against the Túpac Amaru, General Artola claims that the army treated
Asháninka communities "with special care" and that the Indians were paid compensation "for those who lost their lives,
regardless of which side they belonged to."[5] In fact, the hunt
for Asháninkas believed to have aided the guerrillas continued on even after the death of the Túpac Amaru's leaders.
Antonio Atiri and Ernesto Andrés were held for an unknown
length of time before their execution. And although Pedro
Kintaro had been briefly captured and released by Rangers
while the fighting was still underway, he found himself in
custody again in March 1966, accused of killing Ismael Castillo during the ambush at Cubantía:

> *I was in my field with my wife, the one who's now dead. I*
> *awoke early to go cut* ungurave *palm, but I'd dreamed that*
> *a* sabayunga *worm had stung me. I thought, "Why did the*
> sabayunga *sting me in my dream? Something's going to happen."*

Later that day, two policemen came to his house, explaining that they had orders to take him to Satipo:

> *I took off my clothes and put on my cushma. Then I grabbed*
> *my daughter and said, "Daughter, you stay here. I'm going, and I*
> *don't know whether I'll come back. I think I'm going to die."*
> *My little daughter began to cry, then my sister, my brother-in-law,*
> *my wife. Everyone wept. They took me to Satipo with my hands*
> *tied behind my back, pushing me. "Now, make your declaration!"*
> *they shouted. They hit me—kicks, knees to the groin, everything.*
> *The commander shouted at me and put his revolver here, at my*
> *head. They made me stand up and another policeman kneed*
> *me like this. Uhh! Blood, vomit, I threw it all up. The commander*
> *threatened me with his revolver again. "Pum!" The revolver*
> *went off. But there was no bullet, it just made a sound! I thought,*
> *"Now I've had it."*

Kintaro's interrogation continued for two weeks. He
learned that another Asháninka and three colonists from the

highlands had accused him of Castillo's murder. Eventually the death threats stopped, and he was taken to jail in Huancayo, then to several prisons in Lima. Kintaro's imprisonment lasted eight months. Upon his release, he had to be hospitalized for treatment of injuries suffered during interrogation.

Why weren't more Asháninkas arrested and jailed with Kintaro? The answer, like many aspects of this history, is not clear. The authorities seem to have been genuinely confused about the role of the Indians in the conflict. The convoluted plot of millennial prophecy and its betrayal outstripped the limited interpretive ability of the police and army. Influenced by the prevailing view that Indians were social children, they assumed that few, if any, of the Asháninkas fully understood what had happened. Asháninka headmen wise in the ways of whites were quick to exploit this belief. In his efforts to mediate between the army and his people, Alberto Yorini stressed the ignorance of those who sided with the Túpac Amaru. Pedro Kintaro reconstructs Yorini's plea to the local army commander:

The guerrillas have fooled my people. They tricked them. My people are innocent, they are illiterate. They don't know how things are. They don't know civilization.

The statements Kintaro imputes to Yorini, and which other witnesses have corroborated, mimed the convictions of local landowners and dampened the government's interest in finding more Indian scapegoats. And in a sense, Asháninkas did *not* understand the MIR, nor had they fully imagined the forms of destruction that the struggle would bring down upon their heads.

The chief irony of the 1965 insurgency was that its long-term impact on the Peruvian armed forces was the exact opposite of what the U.S. Embassy had anticipated.

Some of the officers of the Peruvian general staff saw the success of the counterinsurgency as proof that repression was the way to silence the voices of communism. Ambassador Frank Ortiz, who served in the U.S. Embassy in Lima during the 1970s, recalls an encounter with a general in the Peruvian army during a party in honor of Ortiz's appointment as ambassador to Uruguay. The general offered Ortiz advice on how to handle the growing urban guerrilla problem in Montevideo. "During the guerrilla war in Peru," he said, "when a guerrilla killed a soldier, especially an officer, the army found a member of the guerrilla's family and killed him in reprisal." "I tell you this," the officer concluded, "so the U.S. will know the right way to handle the situation in Uruguay. That's how we handled it in Peru."[6]

The view that insurgencies should be managed through draconian internal measures was articulated most eloquently by General Carlos Giral Morzán, director of Peru's influential Center of Advanced Military Studies (CAEM). Giral Morzán saw guerrilla struggles in Latin America as an extension of the international conflict between communism and democracy, a Cold War analysis encouraged by the United States and adopted by military governments in Brazil and Argentina. This position found growing favor in the Belaúnde government, which after 1965 was pushed steadily to the right by the conservative opposition in the Peruvian congress, an unstable coalition of the formerly revolutionary APRA party and the Odriist National Union.[7]

A different vision of the causes of communist subversion was developing among younger officers. To counter the *guerra de guerrillas*, the army had organized a sophisticated system of internal intelligence operations, the Army Intelligence Service (SIE). Previously, army intelligence had directed its attention to external threats, especially the armies of Chile and Ecuador, rather than to the destabilizing social

forces within Peru itself. The SIE used its considerable mus-
cle to squeeze information out of leftists and peasants during
the counterinsurgency, information that was turned against
the guerrillas of the MIR. But even as the officers of the SIE
applied ruthless repression to the people of Cuzco and Junín,
they were being educated in the grim realities of rural life in
their own country. General José Graham was later to remark
that "the guerrillas were the bell that awakened the military
to the reality of the nation."[8]

The senior officer who was most influential in shaping the
analysis of the increasingly radicalized junior officers was
General Edgardo Mercado Jarrín, later to serve as Minister
of External Relations, head of the military's Joint Command,
and prime minister. Although recognizing that communists
were actively projecting their ideology in the international
arena, Mercado Jarrín saw that injustice and social inequality
provided the medium in which revolutionary movements
could thrive. In his view, the promises of communism could
be preempted by reforms that reduced class conflict and encouraged national unity. Mercado Jarrín's position was progressive and profoundly nationalistic, and he stood opposed
to the "internationalization of repression" advocated by the
United States and implemented in the use of the Interamerican Peace Force during the 1965 crisis in the Dominican
Republic.[9]

Although the counterinsurgency campaign of 1965 convinced elements of the army of the pressing need to address
the internal causes of subversion through broad social reforms, the post-1965 Belaúnde government lost the political
leverage it needed to achieve them. Belaúnde's Popular Action party split into conservative and progressive factions as
the country's economic situation deteriorated. Corruption
and inefficiency within the civilian government—symbolized
by a 1968 contraband scandal that implicated high-level officials of Popular Action—appalled military officers committed to social discipline. And it was discipline that had better come quickly, for as the years slipped by without reform,

the possibility of another, far bloodier, guerrilla uprising loomed ever larger.[10]

The event providing the symbolic spark for military intervention was the ratification of a new agreement between the government of Peru and the International Petroleum Company. Under pressure to settle the IPC dispute quickly so that foreign capital could flow more freely into Peru, the Belaúnde government agreed to terms that commentators from both ends of the political spectrum described as "humiliating." Among other concessions, the government waived IPC payment of $144 million in back taxes previously assessed by a Peruvian court. It also made a "moral commitment" to cede the company exploration rights to a million hectares of Peruvian jungle known to contain petroleum deposits.

The strangest moment in the IPC controversy was the so-called "page eleven scandal." Carlos Loret de Mola, who represented Peru during the final stage of the negotiations with the IPC, claimed to have signed an eleventh page in the agreement that stipulated the price at which the Peruvian government would sell its crude oil to the IPC for refining. The IPC insisted that this page was a figment of Loret de Mola's imagination, an assertion that the Belaúnde government declined to contradict. Loret de Mola resigned his position as president of the national petroleum company, and a few days later he went public with his claim that an important page of the treaty had been removed, to the advantage of the IPC. Though the existence of the disputed page was never definitively established, the scandal contributed to a public perception that the Belaúnde government had sold out Peru in its negotiations with the American oil concern.[11]

The public revelation about "page eleven" occurred on September 10, 1968. In the early morning hours of October 3, army tanks surrounded the presidential palace. Officers escorted President Belaúnde to a plane bound for Buenos Aires. Six days later, troops occupied the IPC plant on Peru's north coast. The newly formed Revolutionary Government of the Armed Forces confiscated all IPC assets as security against repayment of the $690 million the government now claimed it was owed by the company.[12]

The head of the new military government was General Juan Velasco Alvarado. At his side during the coup was a group of colonels who had held important positions in the Army Intelligence Service during the counterinsurgency of 1965. Their goal, according to the military historian Victor Villanueva, was to "overcome the oligarchy, eliminate it as a power group . . . [and] to organize, discipline, moralize civilians." In short, the military wanted to create "a new society in the image of, and similar to, the armed forces, neither communist nor capitalist."[13]

The coup was a blow to United States foreign policy. The embassy's pleasure over the defeat of the MIR turned to grim disappointment as a democratically elected government fell before a military junta with a strong left-wing orientation. The nationalization of the IPC forced the invocation of the Hickenlooper Amendment, which halted U.S. aid to governments seizing the property of American citizens or corporations. Ambassador J. Wesley Jones recalls ruefully: "If I'd only left Peru a year earlier, before the coup, I'd have gone out in a blaze of glory." As it was, Jones spent his last year in Lima dispatching curt notes of protest to the Peruvian government.[14] Relations deteriorated further in 1969, when the so-called "Tuna War"—a dispute over Peru's assertion of a 200-mile fishing-rights zone off its coastline—heated to the boiling point. In May of that year, the United States halted military sales to Peru. Peru retaliated by ordering the withdrawal of the American military mission. Cordial relations between the two countries were not restored until well into the 1970s.

Even before Guillermo Lobatón and his comrades in the Túpac Amaru gave up their lives, other leftist parties in Peru had begun to mount critiques of the MIR's "hegemonist" and "vanguardist" uprising. Few would openly condemn such a splendid example of revolutionary courage, for to do so would be to collaborate with the oligarchy and the military. Instead, the largest Marxist parties issued communiqués that, under the pretense of lending moral support, conveyed petulant disapproval.

The pro-Soviet Communist Party of Peru (PCP), for instance, opened its declaration of July 2, 1965, by stating that the guerrilla movement of Andamarca could not be classified as "communist," as the government alleged, because the PCP had not organized it. The PCP's Maoist splinter faction was even more sanctimonious, calling attention to the "mostly petit bourgeois extraction of the Movement of the Revolutionary Left" and, even worse, "the APRA origins of most of its members," which prevented the MIR leadership from recognizing the pro-China faction of the PCP as the only party espousing true Marxist-Leninist thought. The support of both blocs of the Communist party was limited to condemnation of repressive measures the government had taken against peasants and MIR sympathizers. Some of the Trotskyite parties were more sympathetic to the MIR's position, though their membership was too small for them to become major players in the ensuing conflict.[15]

As the insurgency passed into history, more thoughtful reflections on the failure of the MIR appeared in print. There was general agreement that the MIR had failed to forge strong links to the rural masses and that it had ignored radicalized populations in factories, slums, and universities. From the tactical point of view, the MIR placed too much faith in fixed guerrilla bases; the party's "security zones" in Pucutá and Mesa Pelada proved to be easy targets for air force jets. Junín and Cuzco were not the Sierra Maestra of Cuba, safe refuges from which guerrillas could hit strategic military targets. It would take more than three small guerrilla fronts to overburden an army as large and well-equipped as Peru's.[16]

Recently published interviews with MIR insiders—all of

whom survived 1965 because they had been assigned to supporting roles in urban areas—raise the possibility that Guillermo Lobatón took the Túpac Amaru into action without the prior authorization of Luis de la Puente. Héctor Cordero, a highly placed member of the MIR, met with de la Puente at Mesa Pelada in May of 1965, at which time it was decided to "slow slightly the process of armed struggle in order to find a more propitious moment." This decision couldn't be communicated to Lobatón in time to prevent the Túpac Amaru from raiding the Santa Rosa mine in June. Once the guerrillas took to the field in Junín, the other MIR columns had to support their comrades.[17]

The 1968 coup d'etât of the armed forces threw the Peruvian left into even greater disarray than usual. The very institution that Marxists had for decades condemned as retrograde was implementing many of the social changes espoused by the left: nationalization of the IPC, land reform, a dramatic break with the United States, and a crusade to erase the political power of the aristocratic families that had ruled Peru for more than a century. The revolutionary government provided employment for many of the country's college-educated leftists in an organization called SINAMOS (National System of Social Mobilization), founded in 1971, which sent its personnel to rural villages to foster community development. In the long run, SINAMOS proved as paternalistic as other government agencies committed to a top-down model of development. Whatever its failings, however, the creation of SINAMOS marked the first attempt by a central government to link the country's remote communities to decisions in Lima.

The events of 1965 came to the public eye one last time in February 1969, when the police brought fifty-odd "guerrillas"—mostly peasant farmers—to trial on diverse charges stemming from the insurgency. The dazed peasants, in some cases wasted by chronic diseases acquired during their years of detention, scarcely looked the part of ruthless insurgents. When they could be made to talk at all, they haltingly spoke of their own torture, the rape of their wives and daughters by civil guards, and summary executions of other suspects. It was a public relations disaster for the government, which after the 1968 coup had little stomach for punishing either rustics or the middle-class guerrilla leaders—Héctor Béjar and Hugo Blanco among them—whose imprisonment had become a cause célèbre among North American and European intellectuals. The Civil Guard tribunal declared some of the defendants innocent; others were handed prison sentences as long as fifteen years. On December 22, 1970, President Juan Velasco attempted to close this chapter of Peruvian history by declaring a general amnesty for all those implicated in the guerrilla war of 1965.[18]

Jacqueline Eluau, Guillermo Lobatón's widow, was not about to end her involvement with Peru until she knew how and where her husband died. In 1967, a Chilean journal, *Punto Final*, speculated that Lobatón might still be alive, held prisoner by the Peruvian government.[19] In the next issue of the same publication, Jacqueline described her return to Junín in search of answers to the many questions about Lobatón's fate. Her essay is revolutionary rhetoric at its most floridly romantic:

> *Endless paths have carried the exploits of the rebels, lovers of justice and defenders of the happiness of children's hearts. . . . A name vibrates on lips made nearly immobile by chewing coca leaves: LOBATON, Guillermo Lobatón, indelible shadow and, at the same time, hope of the peasant.*[20]

Prevented by the authorities from pursuing Lobatón's shadow further than Andamarca in 1967, Jacqueline took up the search for his trail again in 1970. This time she was guided by members of the MIR freed by the general amnesty, as well as by others new to the movement. According to Elías Murillo, who accompanied Jacqueline on this pilgrimage, they armed themselves with weapons cached in the mountains in 1965. But Jacqueline proved to be a burden, conspicuous to potential informers and unable to match the pace of her comrades on the difficult trails. She insisted that they follow the exact route of the Túpac Amaru whenever possible, no small feat in view of the continuing military presence in the area. Growing tensions within the column—related in part to Jacqueline's strong will, uncongenial to men accustomed to more complacent women—might have led to mutiny had not Jacqueline fallen into the hands of the police at the Alegría Hacienda. She was taken to Lima and promptly deported.[21] We are left only with the defiant questions she penned in 1967:

What truth is there in the different versions spread in pamphlets and communiqués about the death of Guillermo Lobatón? What is the meaning of the shameful contradictions of the military, of the government in general, when they claim that the warrior has died? . . . Without a doubt, a deception of the people. A deception of History.

The disputes within the Peruvian left sparked by the guerrilla war of 1965 were nowhere more intense than among the provincial party organizations that found themselves pushed aside from high-level debate in Lima. One of the provincial activists who played a prominent role in the debate was a young philosophy professor named Abimael Guzmán. Guzmán taught at the National University of San Cristobal de Huamanga, located in the city of Ayacucho, capital of a highland department that was, and is still, among Peru's most destitute.[22]

The venomous feud between pro- and antiguerrilla factions, and the final failure of the Túpac Amaru and other insurgent columns, doubtless had a major impact on Abimael Guzmán. After 1965, he moved ever closer to the Maoist view that revolution must begin as a popular war in the countryside that will eventually sweep the cities, the chief repositories of decadent bourgeois thought. By 1969, Guzmán had burned his bridges to orthodox communism and formed his own sect, called the "Communist Party of Peru for the Shining Path of Mariátegui" in homage to the founder of Peruvian socialism. This small splinter party has come to be known simply as the Shining Path (*Sendero Luminoso*).

Although the revolutionary government hoped to raise living standards in poor regions such as Ayacucho, its efforts were sluggish and ineffective. The traditional landlords, meanwhile, had gone into decline, leaving a power vacuum into which the Shining Path stepped during the 1970s. Guzmán drew students of peasant extraction into the party, trained them in Maoist political thought, and sent them back to their communities to spread a vision of revolutionary change. Unlike the MIR guerrillas of 1965, the Shining Path put down deep roots in the countryside. Party members could speak Quechua. They dressed as peasants—in many cases *were* peasants. And they were under no illusion that the revolution would happen in a month or even a decade. Central to the Shining Path's organizational tactics was absolute secrecy, which according to one observer was a direct reaction to the MIR's lax internal security in 1965, "when everybody seemed to know everything."[23]

The Shining Path first elbowed its way into the popular imagination in 1980, when activists hung dead dogs from street lamps on one of Lima's principal avenues. The dogs carried placards denouncing Deng Xiaoping's betrayal of Maoism. This macabre propaganda statement was followed by straightforward acts of revolutionary violence, first in Ayacucho and then in other highland departments, with steadily increasing pressure on Peru's cities—most notably, attacks on power lines that regularly plunged Lima into darkness. By the mid-1980s, deaths linked to Shining Path violence and the government's equally brutal efforts to put down the insurgency numbered more than five thousand, dwarfing the casualty figures from 1965. In the first two months of 1990, political violence claimed more than five hundred lives.[24]

The Shining Path may be the first revolutionary movement in the modern world to shun public statements. The total mass of its communiqués and official texts would scarcely outweigh the small bag of coca leaves carried by most Ayacucho peasants. Children living in the zones controlled by the Shining Path are taught to revere "*Presidente* Gonzalo"—as Abimael Guzmán has come to be known—even though the specific content of his message is still a mystery. Perhaps, as one Peruvian anthropologist has said, the Shining Path is silent because it "considers itself the representative of a world that has been stripped of speech."[25] Presidente Gonzalo's text is violence itself. With the fervor of medieval cabalists, Peruvian and foreign intellectuals struggle to interpret cryptic messages in the party's savagery, as well as in the reciprocal cruelty of the government's response.

Persistent speculation focuses on the millenarian message that the Shining Path may, or may not, be spreading to the peasantry. The notion that revolutionary violence in the Andes has a ritualistic or mythical undercurrent was advanced in an influential essay published in 1983 by Mario Vargas Llosa.[26] Subsequent research has linked the Shining Path to Andean myths of millennial renewal, as well as to the darker mythic tradition of the homicidal pishtaco.[27] As in 1965, it is unclear whether the millenarian message comes from the guerrillas themselves or from the peasants' interpretations of the events taking place around them.

The emergence of Shining Path violence contrasted with the behavior of the mainstream left, which threw itself into electoral politics after Peru returned to democratic rule in 1980. Not all Marxist parties, however, were content with the democratic process. A new militant group called the Túpac Amaru Revolutionary Movement (MRTA) took up arms in 1982, initially operating in Peru's largest cities. In 1987, the MRTA established a revolutionary front in the Department of San Martín. News photos of the guerrillas are eerily similar to images of the Túpac Amaru column of 1965, though the MRTA is equipped with arms far superior to the museum pieces carried by Lobatón and his men.[28] The similarity is more than accidental, for late in 1986 the remaining members of the MIR announced that they were merging with the MRTA. Their unity was to be based on "the goal of socialism and the inevitability of armed struggle."[29] One of the few survivors of the Túpac Amaru, Antonio Meza, died with his MRTA comrades in May 1989 when a truckload of guerrillas was ambushed by the army.

The MRTA and the Shining Path owe their growth to the precipitous decline of Peru's debt-ridden economy. They also feed on the expansion of illicit coca farming and cocaine refining in Peru's central jungle region. The cocaine trade creates a climate of lawlessness in which insurgents thrive; the guerrillas become protectors of peasant coca farmers, whose livelihood is threatened by Peruvian police at the behest of the United States. Coca production also yields a flood of hard currency that guerrillas siphon off for their own purposes.[30] Parts of Amazonian Peru are now effectively severed from civil control, save whatever form of "people's government" the MRTA and Shining Path have been able to impose on the areas under their authority. Meanwhile, the government of the United States seems determined to play into the hands of the guerrillas by encouraging a "Vietnamization" of key coca-producing areas: building new military bases in the jungle, sending in Special Forces units to train their Peruvian counterparts, and refurbishing attack jets and patrol boats that can intercept shipments of cocaine.[31] Guillermo Lobatón could hardly have imagined the improbable conjunction of forces and events that would produce today's Peru: the leftist military coup of 1968, the emergence of a rural insurgency led by backwoods militants, and the spectacular growth of the cocaine trade. One suspects that the courtly Lobatón, a man who could put aside the cares of a guerrilla war to debate church history with a Franciscan at a remote mission outpost, would find the ruthlessness of his contemporary counterparts troubling. In the persistence of the struggle, however, Loba-tón might see a vindication of the MIR. The former guerrilla Elías Murillo speaks for his fallen leader when he insists that "the important thing is that we sought the experience, for better or for worse. . . . We acted on what we believed." "The truth of the matter," he emphasizes, "is that time will tell. If we were right, if we took a correct and just path, then time will tell."

Of the key players of 1965, the United States may have been the one to learn least from the experience. There was, as embassy documents reveal, awareness of the need to combat guerrillas with social reforms and economic development as well as with military readiness. An employee of the AID public safety program who traveled through Cuzco during the insurgency, for instance, reported to his chief that the peasants around Mesa Pelada failed to rally around the MIR because they "have never had it so good in terms of government programs"—referring, among other things, to agrarian reform measures implemented by the Belaúnde government.[32] Yet in practice those who saw subversion in strictly military terms had the upper hand.

Research on effective ways to counter leftist insurgencies was conducted under the aegis of a special initiative of the Advanced Research Projects Agency (ARPA), part of the Department of Defense. The program was called Project Agile.

Speaking to the Armed Services Committee of the House of Representatives in 1967, a spokesperson for the Department of Defense portrayed Project Agile as a research effort that included "quick fix hardware engineering and testing" as well as assessment of "the longer range problems of actual or potential subversive wars."[33] Agile's purview also encompassed "applied behavioral science." The spokesperson noted that ARPA was receiving much useful information on Thai village life from social scientists affiliated with the Stanford Research Institute—data that would supposedly help in U.S. efforts to prevent communist infiltration there.

Project Agile reports that have made it into the public domain range from the prosaic ("The Utility of Horse Cavalry and Pack Animals in Counterinsurgency Operations in the Latin American Environment") to the nearly hallucinatory. In the latter category falls a research paper on the smell receptors of *Lucilia sericata*, a species of blowfly, and their ability to detect human beings, part of American efforts to develop remote sensing systems that would alert security forces to guerrilla infiltration.[34] Other reports assess problems of radio communication in tropical forests and the use of defoliants—specifically the highly toxic compound known as Agent Orange—in denying cover to insurgents.

This passionate involvement with technical solutions to insurgencies led the United States to defeat in the Vietnam War. The most perceptive American soldiers came to see that materiel alone could not win the struggle, but their views went unheeded by senior officers and civilian policymakers.[35] Identifying infiltrators, for instance, was only half the problem. The real challenge was to create a system in which infiltrators would be unwelcome in peasant communities; the peasants had to be backed by honest and efficient security forces. People needed more attractive options than the violent overthrow of the state.

In the immediate aftermath of 1965, Asháninkas of the Río Perené saw modest improvement in their lives. The landowners who returned to their farms after the death of Guillermo Lobatón were understandably reluctant to antagonize

Indian workers. Pistol-waving bravado was replaced by a more conciliatory attitude. The realities of land ownership remained unchanged, however, and underneath the genial manner of mestizo settlers persisted the same paternalism and prejudice.

This situation was changed by sweeping reforms imposed by the revolutionary government, the most important of which was the Law of Native Communities (Legal Decree 20653). The statute recognized "native communities" (*comunidades nativas*) as social units with a high degree of autonomy, including a legal right to maintain local custom. More important, native communities could seek land titles, which were to be inalienable and held collectively by community members. As soon as the law went into effect, employees of the government's social mobilization agency, SINAMOS, traveled to Asháninka villages to explain how Indians could begin the complex process of laying claim to their lands and shepherding the documents through the Peruvian bureaucracy.

In the first years after the law was in effect, the government titled Asháninka communities at a brisk pace. As of 1976, thirty-four communities had received titles to territories varying in size from 188 hectares to more than 10,000.[36] The measure brought little satisfaction to Asháninkas in heavily colonized areas, whose land grants were pathetically small. But it held out the prospect of a better future for more remote communities in possession of enough land to meet the foreseeable needs of their members. The government also took steps to increase the number of schools and health posts in Asháninka communities.

Yet even as Asháninkas received the legal protection they had sought for so long, other government policies created new threats. Highway construction accelerated the movement of colonists to Satipo Province. An extensive agrarian reform redistributed land but also promoted the idea that land should be owned by those who use it—"use" being defined as deforestation and conversion of jungle to agricultural fields or pasture. This vision could not easily accommodate the Asháninkas' system of shifting agriculture, with its dependence on long periods of fallow.

As the revolutionary government moved to the right in the late 1970s, the land titling process slowed, then virtually halted. Asháninka communities submitted all the necessary documents to the Ministry of Agriculture but were then told that the titles could not be issued "because of problems in Lima."[37]

In response, Asháninkas threw themselves into the political arena by grouping their villages into local federations—numbering at least eight by the end of the 1980s—that affiliated themselves with pan-Indian organizations at the national and continental levels. Although most of these federations are precariously financed and subject to abrupt leadership changes, they provide an effective forum for presenting Indian grievances to the government. They have also become a training ground for young leaders, who quickly learn the subtleties of lobbying and manipulation of the media. These native politicians, nearly always literate and bilingual, have increasingly challenged the authority of traditional headmen.

Peru's return to democratic rule in 1980 brought with it a further retreat from the progressive Indian policies of the early 1970s. As recently as 1984, a young Asháninka man was sentenced to two years in prison for the local equivalent of statutory rape, because he had sexual relations with a fourteen-year-old girl, hardly a deviant practice in communities where girls are often married after their first menstruation.[38] In 1982, the president of the National Institute of Flora and Fauna (INFOR) visited an Asháninka community on the Río Ene to study land conflicts between Indians and colonists. His report on the situation there alleged that some Asháninkas "are found in a completely savage state, in extreme cases living totally naked"—an assertion as improbable among Asháninkas as it would be, say, among members of a fundamentalist congregation in Lynchburg, Virginia.[39] In 1985, the Danish anthropologist Søren Hvalkof reported that Asháninkas denouncing land invasions by colonists or abuses of labor contracts by non-Indian landowners were harassed by local authorities in the Gran Pajonál. During such harassment, Indians were occasionally "whipped with a dried bull penis." One can hardly imagine a more crudely expressive symbol of political domination.[40]

By the late 1970s, the Perené Valley's economic boom, largely the result of government attempts to improve conditions in the region after the 1965 insurgency, had begun to falter. Competition for scarce farmland pushed farmers onto the steepest hillsides, where gravity and tropical rains carried away the thin topsoil. Agricultural production declined sharply through most of the region. In 1980, the government integrated the Perené Valley and neighboring regions into a unified development effort, the Pichis-Palcazu Special Project, funded by foreign governments and multilateral lending organizations such as the World Bank.[41] In the Perené Valley, the project's principal aim has been to squeeze higher levels of production from disappearing soils. The construction of new roads has boosted migration to frontier areas occupied by Asháninkas and neighboring Indian peoples. These new pressures on the land have been only partially offset by renewed titling efforts for native communities, initially promoted by the World Bank and later carried out with the support of several foreign aid organizations.[42] Despite the massive infusion of capital, a visitor to the Perené Valley today sees hillsides stripped of forest, the sharp red of the lateritic soil clearly visible in land slips and deep erosion cuts. With the loss of watersheds that once braked runoff to the regional river system, the Perené runs with unprecedented ferocity, now posing an even greater danger than it did in earlier centuries.

The only growth industry in the Peruvian jungle is cocaine. Cocaine producers are not noted for their scrupulous recordkeeping, so no one knows how much raw coca leaf and processed cocaine paste come from the valley of the Perené and its tributaries. Anecdotal evidence, however, indicates that coca cultivation has expanded significantly from the modest levels of the 1970s, especially along the Pichis, Ene, and Tambo rivers. The economic opportunity presented by coca brings more outsiders to the surviving pockets of untilled land, most of which are occupied by Asháninkas.[43]

The spreading insurgencies of the Shining Path and the MRTA have added another destabilizing force to the Asháninkas' current situation. Beginning with widely spaced and selective assassinations of Asháninka leaders, the Shining Path has intensified its attacks against Asháninka communities that refuse to obey the guerrillas' directives. In April of 1990, as many as forty Indians were killed when a Shining Path column assaulted the Asháninka village of Naylamp in Satipo Province. In other parts of Asháninka country, guerrillas of the MRTA have begun the forced recruitment of Asháninka youths.

Late in 1989, the Asháninka encounter with the MRTA took a sharp turn—which, it turned out, was defined by the insurgency of 1965. MRTA guerrillas kidnapped an Asháninka leader named Alejandro Calderón Espinoza near the town of Puerto Bermúdez. The MRTA, a group whose political genealogy links it directly to the MIR, questioned Calderón about his alleged involvement in the capture of Máximo Velando and Juan Paucarcaja in 1965, then condemned him to summary execution. In a communiqué explaining the killing, the MRTA noted that "Calderón was subjected to the verdict after evaluating his behavior during the events of 1965." "He was," the communiqué says, "found guilty."[44]

Asháninka reaction to the killing was explosive. In the words of the popular press, the Indians "declared war on the MRTA." On or about December 26, 1989, hundreds of Asháninka men stormed the town of Puerto Bermúdez, detained the town officials (who were then accused of supporting the guerrillas), and rounded up dozens of MRTA suspects. Press reports coming from Puerto Bermúdez alleged that a score of guerrillas were subjected to "popular justice," including execution. As of mid-January 1990, Asháninka militias were still in control of the town and the surrounding area. The Peruvian government was slow to send army units to restore civil control or to take custody of the alleged MRTA suspects in Asháninka hands.[45]

Press coverage of these events scarcely differed from that of a quarter-century earlier. Reporters stressed the prevalence of bows and arrows—especially poisoned arrows—among Asháninka fighters. Members of the Asháninka militia from the Gran Pajonál were still portrayed as the "fiercest," "most primitive," and "most uncontrollable." Although emphasizing the supposedly atavistic quality of Asháninka dress and weaponry, however, the journalists of 1990 were amazed at every turn by the sophisticated organization imposed by Indian leaders, who appointed a "General Staff" and issued safe-conduct passes to accredited members of the press.[46] It is still too early to say where this violence will lead or whether it is driven by the millennial impulses that figured in the uprising of 1965.

The hardships faced by Asháninkas invite gloomy predictions that their society is headed for extinction. Ecological catastrophe, political violence, poverty—all are threats with which Asháninkas contend today. Yet Asháninka culture is not an unyielding object but a flexible set of dispositions, ideas, and social arrangements. By responding creatively to new circumstances, Asháninkas have sustained a distinctive way of life despite four centuries of contact with the West. Above all, their history has endowed them with a diamond-hard will to survive and with the patience to wait for a final settling of accounts.

TEN

Coda: Amazonian Indians and the Millennial Dream

The Asháninka of eastern Peru are by no means the first Amazonian people to await a tumultuous reversal of their fortunes. In 1549, Spanish settlers encountered a group of Tupinamba Indians near Chachapoyas in the Peruvian Andes. The Tupinambas had trekked there from Brazil, crossing the continent in search of the Land Without Evil, an earthly paradise described in their mythology.[1] More than three centuries later, a Baniwa Indian prophet named Venancio Kamiko (later known as Venancio Christo) began to preach among the Indians of Venezuela's Upper Río Negro region. Venancio had been told in a dream to inform his people that they must deny their labor to whites. Later he took on a priestly role, organizing feasts and wedding ceremonies while predicting the destruction of those who refused to heed his message.[2] In 1912, the anthropologist Curt Nimuendajú observed a group of Guaraní Indian pilgrims who had migrated to the Brazilian coast. They sang and danced for days, expecting at any moment to fly away to the Land Without Evil. When hope exhausted itself, they blamed their failure on contamination by European clothing and food, which made them too heavy to take wing.[3] In 1946, scores of Tukunas from western Brazil participated in a mass migration toward a place where they believed spirits would shower them with trade goods.[4]

In these displays of unwarranted hope some anthropologists see the abandonment of indigenous religions in favor of Judeo-Christian notions of salvation.[5] Others perceive elements of social disorganization, resistance, or the enactment of unconscious patterns codified in mythology. Most interpretations start from the assumption that millennial movements are freakish intervals in which stable societies somehow come unglued.[6] The foundations of indigenous life crumble when the natives observe sharp differences in wealth between conqueror and conquered or experience the traumatic effects of a radical change of values, as when, for example, Christian missionaries oppose the keeping of more than one wife by native headmen.[7]

As we learn more about Amazonian prehistory, it becomes increasingly doubtful that millennial dreams are solely a product of the Conquest. Amazonian societies have not existed in a state of untrammeled sameness. Recent archaeological research shows that many parts of the region experienced social changes that would have confronted egalitarian tribal peoples with highly stratified chiefdoms, perhaps precipitating cultural crises long before the arrival of Europeans.[8]

Nevertheless, the crisis cults about which we know the most have occurred in response to European contact. Indians identify the arrival of Europeans, who bear terrifying epidemics and act as agents of sweeping social change, with the instantaneous transformations already well established in Amazonian myth and legend. Amid such chaos, native peoples find it necessary to rethink their own institutions and beliefs.[9]

When Indians tear their traditions apart, they may turn to the symbols and paraphernalia of Christianity, the conqueror's religion, in search of raw materials with which to build a new order. The incorporation of Christian symbolism into a millennial vision is, according to some scholars, a form of "acculturation" that launches native peoples on the path to cultural impoverishment.[10] More compelling is the contrary view—that these movements attempt to wrestle Christianity away from whites, reshaping it to meet the Indians' own spiritual needs. Theological purity is a Western obsession. Most New World peoples are comfortable with the exchange of religious knowledge between societies. The seizure of elements of the conqueror's religion is only the first step in a process of adapting native culture to new realities. The leaders in this venture are often shamans, the members of the society most thoroughly versed in traditional religious practice. The Indians' "Christianity" may emerge in an indigenized form, with a meaning all its own.

Wealth is another preoccupation of millennial movements. Although few fully developed cargo cults have unfolded in Amazonia, the Indians' millennial reflections often fix on the power that gives outsiders control of trade goods in such abundance. Native peoples must also ponder the future place of whites in the Amazonian social order. Some groups, such as the Asháninkas under Juan Santos Atahualpa, hope to expel whites forever. In other parts of Amazonia, believers expect to *become* whites. Still others, such as the Guaraní Indians whom Curt Nimuendajú observed on the Brazilian coast, hope to escape the ordinary world altogether. In every case, participants in crisis cults express their view that the status quo is intolerable.

In sum, Amazonian millennial movements represent experiments in social change undertaken by peoples who believe that history is made in explosive bursts rather than in slow waves. Some movements have been dismal failures, even to their adherents. Yet in all cases the affected tribes seem to gain something from the experience. They learn that whites are vulnerable when native peoples stand united, or that the forced imposition of alien ideas can, in some circumstances, best be opposed by maintaining traditional religious practices in ways that elude detection by outsiders. They come to realize that wholesale rejection of traditional social arrangements does not lead instantly to increased wealth. The bitter experience of state repression may teach them the value of what James Scott calls "everyday forms of resistance," tactics that frustrate control without provoking the use of force.[11] The price paid for these lessons—in lives, in social disorder, in acutely demoralizing experience—has sometimes been high. It is not ours to say whether it has been worth it.

Asháninkas have been more likely than other Amazonian peoples to turn their dream of millennial change into violent action. It is well to keep in mind, though, that some Asháninka crisis cults—notably the movement inspired by the missionary F. A. Stahl in the 1920s—were peaceful affairs. Whatever violence marked them was initiated by worried settlers, not by Indians.

Whether violent or peaceful, all Asháninka millennial episodes involved the appropriation of foreign ideas and their reconfiguration within a native idiom. We will probably never untangle the strands of Franciscan, Andean, and Amazonian thought that came together in the eighteenth-century rebellion of Juan Santos Atahualpa, nor will we ever fully understand how the Asháninka rebels of 1965 interwove shamanic prophecy with the MIR's brand of utopian Marxism.

Similar riddles confront us in the Asháninkas' equivocal alliances with charismatic outsiders—Juan Santos, Fitzcarrald, Stahl, Pent, and Lobatón. We doubt that any of these men fully understood the uses to which their leadership was put by native shamans, who were under pressure to validate their own spiritual insight by providing solutions to the urgent problems of the moment. The charismatic outsider offered leadership that could, for a time, transcend long-standing feuds and grievances, bringing people together into powerful alliances. Like other Amazonian peoples, though, Asháninkas value above all else their freedom—the "ancient liberty" about which Spanish chroniclers speak with such scorn. "There are always those who doubt," Asháninkas say, expressing their recognition that the seeds of an alliance's dissolution are ready to germinate at a moment's notice.[12]

The corrosive influence of doubt may have passed unnoticed by outsiders who saw the motives of their Indian followers through the lens of a very different cultural experience. Could Guillermo Lobatón, for instance, have fully grasped the reasons for the Asháninkas' move away from the Túpac Amaru at the end of the 1965 insurgency? It seems unlikely. Juan Santos, David Pent, Guillermo Lobatón—all experienced a period in which they approached the status of gods for the Indians. Asháninka enthusiasm then exhausted itself, leaving the leaders alone and used up, endowed only with utopian dreams, victims of an indigenous political process they were ultimately unable to fathom.

Pichári is a shaman from the Río Berta. His isolated homestead commands a view of the valley below. The visions granted to him during tobacco-induced trances nourish the tradition of prophecy that led his people into the struggle of 1965. Thinking of the upheavals he has witnessed during his long life, Pichári tries to understand the demolition of his ancestors' world:

My grandfather told me that one day the white people would come here, where we live. Then we would cease to see forests, he said. They would cut down the trees to plant their crops. They would capture us to work as their slaves. We would work for nothing. We would have to clear their fields. They would take our land.

That's the way it will be, he said. And that's how it was. That's how it is. I've seen it.

For Pichári, part of the blame for this misfortune rests with the Asháninka people themselves, for they have failed to obey the command of Tasórentsi, God, to live in peace among themselves. "If we had obeyed," he muses, "we would live happily, singing our songs. Those who live in the sky would come to visit us." Yet the whites, despite claims of moral superiority, suffer from the same inability to obey their religious principles. Pichári notes with bitterness that "they say we have to live according to the 'sacred scriptures,' but they kill among themselves. They fight, they steal. We're going to end up just like them."

This disorder began with the arrival of the Spanish:

If the Spanish hadn't come, we would now have our own factories and the whites would be our peons. They would work to give us money. But no, they took away our knowledge. Otherwise we would know how to do all that they do.

Pichári's cheerless prophecy reflects the death of the tropical forest that has been the Asháninkas' source of life. Every year he sees the soils grow poorer and game animals more scarce. Yet Pichári doubts that this turmoil and unhappiness will last forever:

I know that the world will end someday, just as my grandfather told me. All the injustice will end. First our manioc crops will fail. The time is coming when we'll die of hunger. Once we had much game here: monkey, tapir, deer, bear, many birds and fish. But long ago someone predicted we would die of hunger. I heard my grandfather say the same thing. "The animals are going to disappear," he said. "You'll suffer from hunger!"
And all this is coming to pass. Now I see it happening. But if we follow the path of Tasórentsi, he will take us away.

Despite the failure of the prophecies of 1965, despite the death that rained down on Asháninkas moved by a belief in millennial change, Pichári continues to await an apocalyptic transformation that will move his people from chaos to order, from privation to plenty. He reads local events for signs that this difficult chapter of Asháninka history approaches its end:

Just the other day, a dead man came back to life in Cubantía. That's when I began to understand that the time is near. As my grandfather told me, there will come a day of darkness, without daylight, without sun. When you see these strange things, it's because the end approaches. We'll be changed into something else.

These things haven't yet happened, these things that are just the warnings. Perhaps I won't see those yet to happen. They'll be seen by my children or by you. But I tell you that it will be this way. Because that's the way my grandfather told it. Meanwhile, I wait. I live here far from everything, where the whites don't bother me.

Notes

INTRODUCTION

1. Interview, 18 December 1986.

2. *Area Handbook for Peru* 1972: 337.

3. Asháninka often appears as "Asháninca" in Spanish. Here we follow the more common English usage. Occasionally ethnographic sources use other spellings, including "Ashéninka" and "Ashaninga."

4. Influential works on revitalization movements and crisis cults include La Barre 1971, Wallace 1956, Wilson 1973, and Worsley 1968. Space considerations prevent us from mentioning the many other important works on this subject.

5. See, for example, Wilson 1973: 502.

6. Quoted in Lan 1985: xvi. Lan's study of the links between spirit mediums and ZANLA guerrillas in Zimbabwe is arguably the best study available of the connections between a traditional religious system and a "rational" movement of national liberation.

7. Marzorati 1989: 102.

8. See Taussig 1987: 74–83.

9. For an extended discussion of this issue, see Hill 1988.

10. Sahlins 1985: 54–55.

11. In particular, we would like to note that our account focuses on the history of these events as related by male participants. Women's views of the insurgency are almost impossible to find in official documents, canonical histories, and the accounts of the Peruvian left. With few exceptions, Asháninkas described the events as being

essentially a male affair. No doubt Asháninka women might see things in a different light.

12. For the low figure, see Uriarte 1976; Hvalkof (1989: 145) argues that 45,000 is a "very conservative estimate" of the contemporary Asháninka population and that, in fact, the population is much higher. Note that both of these figures include estimates of the Nomatsiguenga population as well as that of the Asháninka.

13. In this book, we do not analyze cultural differences within the Asháninka population as a whole. Weiss 1975, for instance, makes a distinction between the River Campa—the population along the Apurímac, Ene, Perené, and Tambo rivers—and the Pajonál Campa, who live in the area known as Gran Pajonál. He and other authorities believe the Nomatsiguengas, who live along the Anapati, Mazamari, Alto Pangoa, and Sonomoro rivers, to be a Machiguenga population, though they are culturally almost indistinguishable from their Asháninka neighbors and are identified as "Campa-Nomatsiguengas" by other anthropologists familiar with the region. Because of uncertainty about the ethnic status of Nomatsiguengas and, more important, because documents and oral histories relating to the guerrilla war of 1965 rarely distinguish Nomatsiguengas from Asháninkas, we use "Asháninka" as a cover term that includes the Nomatsiguenga people.

14. Basic monographic sources on the Asháninka include Bodley 1971, Chevalier 1982, Elick 1969, Varese 1973, and Weiss 1975.

15. Elick 1969: 165; Weiss 1975: 270.

16. Quoted in Weiss 1975: 493.

17. Ibid., 225.

18. *Ayahuasca*, which comes from a vine of the genus *Banisteriopsis*, is called *kamárampi* in Asháninka. Leaves of the species *Psychotria viridis* may be added to the beverage to increase its potency. For details see Weiss 1975: 245.

19. Weiss 1975: 407.

20. Elick 1969: 236.

CHAPTER 1: TO FILL THE GRANARIES OF HEAVEN

1. Jiménez de la Espada 1965, Tomo II: 102–103.

2. Ibid., 104.

3. Varese 1973: 115–126; Fernández 1986c.

4. Quoted in Varese 1973: 120. Based on this passage, Varese

suggests that the language is indeed Campa rather than Amuesha, because Campa phonology is more similar to that of Spanish than is Amuesha.

5. Font in Varese 1973: 125.

6. See Fernández 1987b: 337.

7. See Varese 1973: 139–144.

8. Quoted in Loayza 1942: 146–147.

9. Izaguirre 1922, bk. 2: 163; see also Amich 1975 [1771]: 45.

10. Ibid., bk. 2: 173.

11. Wolf 1982: 112–114.

12. Details of the life of Bohórquez and his assumption of the title of Inca in the Calchaquí Valley come from Miller 1975.

13. Santos (1986: 124) argues that the "Francisco Bohórquez" mentioned by Franciscan observers is really Pedro Bohórquez. The latter may, in fact, have changed his first name to hide his true identity during the scandal over the failure of the first Paitití expedition.

14. Wolf 1959: 160, 164.

15. Amich 1975 [1771]: 52.

16. Izaguirre 1922, bk. 2: 227.

17. Amich 1975 [1771]: 73.

18. Ibid., 74.

19. Ibid., 118.

20. Ibid., 41–42.

21. Ordinaire 1988 [1892]: 128.

22. For details of the Franciscan administrative apparatus and the growth of the Ocopa mission center, see Lehnertz 1974.

23. Tibesar 1952: 30–31.

24. For an inventory of religious objects at one eighteenth-century mission see Lehnertz 1974: 298; inventories of trade goods for distribution to Indians can be found in Lehnertz 1974: 309–310.

25. Amich 1975 [1771]: 155.

26. For details of the satellite villages of San Antonio de Eneno, see Tibesar 1952: 27–28.

27. Jay Lehnertz (1974: 95–96) provides documentary evidence that the first Franciscan entry into the Pajonál occurred in 1723, not in the 1730s as is usually stated.

28. Loayza 1942: 51.

29. Lehnertz 1974: 104.

30. Izaguirre 1922, bk. 2: 84–85.

31. Ibid., 87.
32. Lehnertz 1974: 113.
33. Amich 1975 [1771]: 149.
34. Lehnertz 1974: 63.
35. Ibid., 390. Zarzar (1989: 26) and Tibesar (1952: 37) provide much higher population totals for the Franciscan missions, but we judge Lehnertz's figures more reliable.
36. Tibesar 1952: 36, n. 55; 37.
37. Izaguirre 1922, bk. 2: 210.
38. Amich 1975 [1771]: 541. The editors of this edition do not make it clear whether this particular scheme applied in the early eighteenth century or whether it postdates Amich's contribution. Lehnertz 1974: 67-68 includes the text of an equally rigorous schedule that was definitely employed in the Franciscan missions of the 1740s.
39. Quoted in Lehnertz 1974: 84.
40. Lehnertz 1972: 117. See also Tibesar 1952 and López 1922.
41. Varese 1973: 146, 149.
42. Amich 1975 [1771]: 46.
43. Lehnertz 1974: 45-48, 115.
44. There is a discrepancy in the name of the community where Fray Santiago Vázquez encountered Juan Santos. Most sources refer to the place as Quisopango, yet the friar's own report, as rendered in a letter by Padre Joseph Gil Muñoz (Castro Arenas 1973: Documento No. 1, I-IV), identifies it as Siniaquí, possibly a corruption of Simaqui or Shimaqui, the name of a nearby river.
45. Quoted in Castro Arenas 1973: Documento No. 1, II.
46. Amich 1975 [1771]: 156-157.
47. Loayza 1942: 6.

CHAPTER 2: RETURN OF LORD INCA

1. Fray Santiago Vázques de Caicedo, quoted in Castro Arenas 1973: 84-85, translation by the authors.
2. Marqués de Villa García in Loayza 1942: 12-13.
3. Ibid., 10.
4. Amich 1975 [1771]: 161.
5. Loayza 1942: 24.
6. Ibid., 34.
7. There are significant discrepancies in descriptions of the size

of Bartoli's (or Bártuli's) contingent. Amich 1975 [1771]: 164 states that Bartoli and his forces numbered seventy-one; Varese 1973: 192 says eighty-one; the account of Troncoso's secretary states that the number is ninety-six, thirty-two of whom were "distributed in various occupations of the company, and others sick" (Loayza 1942: 45).

8. Loayza 1942: 48.

9. Cited in ibid., 65–67.

10. Vallejo Fonseca 1957: 243.

11. Varese 1973: 177.

12. Details of Anson's attack on Paita can be found in Laughton 1899.

13. Cited in Castro Arenas 1973: 15.

14. Varese 1973: 179.

15. Cited in Castro Arenas 1973: 11.

16. Loayza 1942.

17. Castro Arenas 1973: 132.

18. This theme is discussed in Varese 1973: 299–308 and Castro Arenas 1973: 27–28.

19. Phelan 1970.

20. Alvarez 1989: 5; see also Zarzar 1989.

21. For a brief summary of the saint's life, see Thurston and Attwater 1956: vol. 3, pp. 93–95.

22. Silverblatt 1988.

23. Izaguirre 1922, bk. 3: 117.

24. Amich 1975 [1771]: 140, 149.

25. Lehnertz 1974: 72.

26. Tibesar 1952: 35–36.

27. Cited in Izaguirre 1922, bk. 3: 116–117.

28. Varese 1973: 202.

29. Loayza 1942: 204.

30. Ibid., 208.

31. Castro Arenas 1973: 132.

32. Loayza 1942: 233.

33. Varese 1973: 203.

34. Castro Arenas 1973: 148.

35. Izaguirre 1922, bk. 3: 182–183.

36. Wertheman 1905: 202.

37. Castro Arenas 1973: 148.

38. Varese 1973: 205.

39. Ortiz 1961: 63.

40. Cited in Fernández 1987*b*: 338.

41. The complete text of this version of the Inca myth is presented in Fernández 1987*b*.

42. Sources on the myth of Inca among the Asháninka and neighboring groups include Weiss 1975 and 1986, Fernández 1984*b* and 1987*b*, and Varese 1973.

43. Important sources on the Inkarrí myth and its implications include Fernández 1987*b*, Flores Galindo 1988, Gow 1982, Ossio 1973, and Stern 1987.

CHAPTER 3: AMACHÉNGA

1. Herndon and Gibbon 1854: 85.

2. Ibid., 85.

3. Wertheman 1905: 191–193.

4. Quoted in Manuel Manrique 1982: 21. Although the Perené tract amounted to half a million hectares, the total concession made to the Peruvian Corporation was 2 million hectares. For details see Barclay 1989.

5. Bodley 1971: 10; Manuel Manrique 1982: 39.

6. This and all subsequent uses of the term "white" in this work should be understood to refer to the social category *blanco* or *civilizado* ("civilized person") as defined by Spanish-speaking Peruvians. In the Amazon, the term *blanco* is contrasted with *indio* ("Indian"), *chuncho* ("jungle Indian"), *salvaje* ("savage"), or *nativo* ("native").

7. Manuel Manrique 1982: 45.

8. Bodley 1971: 10–15; Shoemaker 1981; Elick 1969.

9. See Taussig (1987: 70–71) for information on the fluctuating rates of payment to rubber workers. Because payment was usually made in the form of goods (whose prices were wildly inflated by traders) rather than in cash, it is nearly impossible to arrive at an accurate figure for actual production costs. Guillaume (1888: 65) provides information on the rates paid by a German rubber merchant on the "Río Palcaza" [sic] that would suggest that his Asháninka tappers made much less than 10 percent of the market price for latex.

10. Guillaume 1888: 65.

11. Quoted in Taussig 1987: 20. Taussig's book is an unmatched source for a comprehensive analysis of Rubber Boom violence.

12. Sala 1897: 66.

13. Ibid., 67.

14. Quoted in Bodley 1971: 104.

15. Fuentes 1908, quoted in Fernández 1986b: 57.

16. Varese 1973: 246.

17. See Bodley 1971: 102–106 for details of intratribal slave raids.

18. Sala 1897: 96, 104, 115, 99.

19. Ibid., 127. See also Mendoza 1966.

20. Weiss 1975: 258.

21. Ibid., 263.

22. Sala 1897: 140–141.

23. Reyna 1942: 21.

24. Ibid., 43. Other sources on Fitzcarrald include Valdez Lozano 1944 and Junta de Vías Fluviales 1904. The screenplay of Werner Herzog's film *Fitzcarraldo* (Herzog 1982) takes great liberties with geographical and ethnographic reality—if reality can be said to exist in the Amazon.

25. Reyna 1942: 86.

26. Valdez Lozano 1944: 23.

27. Ibid., 13–14.

28. Ibid., 53–54.

29. Ibid., 5–6.

30. Portillo 1901: 40.

31. Portillo 1905: 492.

32. Guillaume 1888: 59, 65.

33. Wertheman 1905: 203.

34. Sala 1897: 159.

35. Guillaume 1888: 266.

36. Ibid., 70.

37. Ortiz 1961: 95.

38. Bodley (1971: 110) cites higher casualty figures for this encounter: four settlers and thirteen Asháninkas killed. An attempt to reestablish the Pangoa colony in 1914 reportedly resulted in fourteen settlers killed.

39. Ibid., 109–110; see also Elick 1969: 14–15.

40. Ortiz 1961: 257.

41. Reynolds 1930: 13–22.

42. Shoemaker 1981: 83–92.

43. Figures for the colonist population are from Shoemaker 1981: 84; the Asháninka population figure comes from Bodley 1971:

21, which was based on his work in the 1960s. Both figures must be regarded as rough estimates.

44. Multiple interviews, 1984.

45. Ibid., 1982–1984.

46. Quoted in Fernández 1988: 32.

47. Weiss 1975: 293. See also Pérez Marcio 1953 for a missionary's account of the fate of Asháninka children believed to be sorcerers.

48. Quoted in Shoemaker 1981: 190.

49. The principal sources on the history of the Peruvian Corporation are Manuel Manrique 1982 and Barclay 1989.

50. For details, see Barclay 1989: 213–233.

51. Bodley 1971: 147–188. This does not count two mission communities he lists as "abandoned" and one community identified as "independent."

52. Elick 1969: 16.

53. Sabaté 1925: 80–81.

54. Stahl 1932: 75.

55. Ibid., 86.

56. Bodley 1972: 224.

57. Ibid., 225–226. Maps of the region use the place names La Cascada and Las Cascadas with equal frequency.

58. There is a discrepancy in the available accounts of this missionary's name. The oral history of the mission included in Fernández 1986a states that the missionary's name was Werner Bulner. Ortiz 1976: 614, which presents the 1962 itinerary of Fray Pio Medina on the Río Ene, identifies the mission site as being under the direction of someone named Botne. Both accounts agree that the missionary brought together a large number of Asháninkas and that the mission was abandoned precipitously. In Fray Medina's words, the missionary "became disillusioned and abandoned everything, even the landing strip."

59. Multiple interviews, 1985.

CHAPTER 4: TOWARD ARMED STRUGGLE

1. Details of the Schwend-Sartorius case can be found, for example, in the article "¿Víctima o victimaria?" in *Caretas*, 26 May–7 June 1965, pp. 44–51, 56.

2. See Chaplin 1968 for a discussion of Peru's economy in the 1950s and early 1960s.

3. Campbell 1973: 45.

4. Huizer 1972: 121. Even *Time* magazine expressed dismay at the inequitable distribution of land in the early 1960s, noting that "1.4 percent of the Peruvian population owns 80 percent of the nation's arable land" (*Time*, June 22, 1964, p. 49).

5. See, for example, Lear 1962: 57; *Caretas*, 5 April 1965, pp. 7–9, "En pleno 1965: un hacendado es conducido en andas por sus indios."

6. Chaplin 1968: 395; Gall 1966: 145. In his study of the Peruvian left, Ricardo Letts (1981) is forced to divide the many factions into "galaxies." He lists thirty-four leftist parties, but there are undoubtedly more.

7. Gall 1966: 149.

8. Data on APRA influence in the Peruvian Workers Confederation are from an undated memorandum circulated to U.S. embassy staff, presumably in 1965, file number 71D203x14521.

9. Béjar 1969: 51. Sources on the genealogical relationship between APRA and leftist groups advocating armed struggle include Campbell 1973, Chaplin 1968, Gall 1966, and Gott 1973.

10. Galeano 1987: 10.

11. Quoted in Hodges 1974: 172.

12. For details of Che's vision of the revolutionary "New Man," see Hodges 1974: 165.

13. Agee 1975: 142.

14. See Brun 1987*c*.

15. Editorial Research Reports 1967: 532.

16. Quoted in Brun 1987*b*: 17.

17. Béjar 1984: 10.

18. Sources on Hugo Blanco and the Convención Valley include Béjar 1969, Campbell 1973, Chaplin 1968, Gall 1964, Gott 1973, Hodges 1974, Neira 1968, and Villanueva 1967.

19. Quoted in Gott 1973: 376.

20. In another of the organizational twists and turns characteristic of the Peruvian left, the POR created a revolutionary front called the Leftist Revolutionary Front (FIR) in 1961. In addition to elements of the POR, the FIR included a splinter faction from the Communist party (CP), members of CP Youth, and elements of Cuzco's Rebel APRA party (Hodges 1974: 113).

21. For details, see Hodges 1974: 113–116, Villanueva 1967: 97–101, and *La Prensa*, 6 May 1962. The SLATO holdup of the Banco de Crédito was subsequently fictionalized by Thorndike and Avendaño in *Abisa a los compañeros, pronto* (1976). Their novel forms the basis of a feature film of the same name released in 1980.

22. See, e.g., Hodges 1974: 116.

23. Ministerio de Guerra 1966: 23.

24. Gall 1964: 67. Condoruna (1966) alleges that 200 peasants died at Chaullay, but we have not been able to locate sources that corroborate this high estimate.

25. Béjar 1987: 14.

26. This position is taken by Ricardo Letts (Pumaruna 1967) but contradicted by an ELN document presented in Gott 1973: 393–394. For a detailed description of the ELN's plan of action, see Béjar 1969.

27. Sources on de la Puente's life and the formation of the MIR include Béjar 1987, Condoruna 1972, Eluau de Lobatón 1970, Gall 1967a, Gilly 1963, Gott 1973, Nelson Manrique 1984, Ministerio de Guerra 1966, and Pumaruna 1967.

28. De la Puente 1965: 23–24.

29. For details of the MIR's programs and publications, see Béjar 1969, Campbell 1973, Gott 1973, Lobatón 1970, Mercado 1967, and Pumaruna 1967.

30. This and all subsequent statements by Albert Brun are, unless otherwise indicated, taken from the transcript of an interview conducted on 22 July 1987.

31. Salazár Bondy 1965: 170.

32. Ricardo Gadea, in Cristóbal 1984: 19. This work is the major source of biographical information on Velando used here.

33. Morón Ramos 1975: 186–187.

34. Most of our information on the MIR-Barbie connection comes from the interview with Albert Brun mentioned above. See also Brun 1987a: 20.

35. Surprisingly little quantitative information on the strength of the guerrilla forces is available in published sources, even those of the military. Artola Azcarate 1976 is unusual in providing data on force strength that seems carefully calculated despite the author's view of the rebels as diabolical communists. In his description of the ELN forces preparing an independent guerrilla campaign in the

Department of Ayacucho, Héctor Béjar (1969: 132) admits that the organization's size was whittled down to thirteen by the time it came into direct confrontation with the armed forces.

State Department documents from 1965 and 1966 propose wildly varying estimates of MIR force strength. An AID document (NARA 286-75-074, Box 5-F4) dated January 1966 states that the MIR had "more than 600 members" who had "received guerrilla and terrorist training in Cuba, China, and North Korea since 1963." An embassy memorandum prepared by Ernest V. Siracusa, then Deputy Chief of Mission, puts national MIR membership at 1,200; Siracusa states that the central front of the MIR guerrilla force, called the Túpac Amaru, numbered between 25 and 30, "of whom 10–15 had been trained abroad" (U.S. Department of State, memorandum dated 23 June 1966). In the first days of the insurgency, a memo of the embassy's counterinsurgency group (20 July 1965) comes up with an estimate ten times higher than Siracusa's: 150 MIR members trained abroad. Later in the same year, the embassy plausibly estimated that the MIR had 125 activists in the field (Airgram A-308, 5 December 1965).

36. Quoted in Mercado 1967: 127.

37. Mariátegui 1971 [1928]: 29.

38. Quoted in Baines 1972: 56. See also Flores Galindo 1988 regarding links between Mariátegui and the emerging *indigenista* movement of the 1920s.

39. Billie Jean Isbell's ethnographic study of a highland community in Ayacucho (Isbell 1978) analyzes in some detail the Indians' suspicious attitude toward "progressive" reforms implemented by well-meaning outsiders in their community during the 1970s.

40. Quoted in Mercado 1967: 139. For discussion of the blindness of leftists to questions of Indian ethnicity in the 1960s, see Gros 1981.

41. See Béjar 1969: 105.

42. Ibid., 130–132.

43. The interviewee whom we call Elías Murillo was officially pardoned for his involvement in the guerrilla war, but he requested anonymity because, as an active participant in the current struggle, his Marxist ideology has undergone considerable change since 1965.

44. Interview, 14 July 1987.

CHAPTER 5: TÚPAC AMARU

1. For background on peasant unrest elsewhere in central Peru see Mallon 1985 and Smith 1989.

2. Artola Azcarate 1976: 51.

3. Guardia 1972: 48.

4. Interview, 14 July 1987.

5. Ibid.

6. Sources are inconsistent about Lobatón's matronym, citing it as Milla and Mille with equal frequency; occasionally it even appears as Miller. The most detailed published information on Lobatón's life can be found in Eluau de Lobatón 1970; other sources, which contain information of varying accuracy, include Gott 1973 and Ministerio de Guerra 1966 as well as newspaper accounts of the insurgency.

7. Eluau de Lobatón 1970: 38.

8. Interview with Jacqueline Eluau, 14 July 1988.

9. For information on Lobatón's time in East Germany, see Eluau de Lobatón 1970.

10. Interview with Ricardo Letts Colmenares, 25 July 1987.

11. *Correo*, Huancayo, 26 June 1965, p. 2.

12. Ministerio de Guerra 1966: 46.

13. Eluau de Lobatón 1970: 119.

14. Letter dated 20 August 1965, in possession of authors. Quoted with permission of Mario Vargas Llosa.

15. Lobatón in Gott 1973: 422.

16. Sources include Gott 1973, Guardia 1972, Ministerio de Guerra 1966, *Actualidad Militar* 1965a, and Artola Azcarate 1976.

17. *Presente* 1965: 20.

18. *La Prensa*, 15 June 1965 and 17 June 1965.

19. TOAID 828, 8 January 1965; TOAID 1583, 4 June 1965.

20. Beecher 1964. See also Shafer 1988 and Wolpin 1972.

21. Mercado Jarrín 1967: 27. See also Villanueva 1971: 147–150.

22. Villanueva 1971: 149.

23. From an OPS document cited in Shafer 1988: 86. For a general overview of the performance of Peruvian police and the creation of an antiguerrilla force in the Civil Guard, see Laughlin 1975, a personal memoir written by the director of the OPS program in Peru during the guerrilla struggle.

24. OPS file 527-062-1-50132, dated September 1965.

25. Agee 1975: 55.

26. AIDTO 1024, 16 June 1965.

27. TOAID-A 1711, 25 June 1965.

28. Letter written by David Laughlin for OPS files, 12 August 1965, and other documents.

29. Letter from ˝Ted Brown, AID-Washington, 9 December 1965.

30. Rodríguez Beruff (1983) argues that some sectors of the Peruvian military appropriated a counterinsurgency orientation with considerable enthusiasm, though his assessment is not necessarily incompatible with Villanueva's assertion that there were elements of the military high command that saw counterinsurgency warfare as a second-class form of military activity.

31. Rodríguez Beruff 1983: 181–182; Villanueva 1971: 151.

32. Quoted in Rodríguez Beruff 1983: 167.

33. Ministerio de Guerra 1966: 37.

34. Ibid., 37.

35. Artola Azcarate 1976: 49.

36. For details of Project Camelot and a sample of critical writing related to it, see Horowitz 1974.

37. See, for example, *La Prensa*, 28 August 1965, "EU Investiga en Perú Reacción del Pueblo a la Acción Cívica."

38. State Department cables dated 28 and 31 August 1965; 12, 18, 23, 25, and 26 February 1966; as well as a telephone interview of Milton Jacobs on 19 September 1988. Alexander Askenasy did not respond to our letter requesting information about Task Colony. The description of Task Simpático is from Blumstein and Orlansky 1965: D-4.

39. Rodríguez Beruff 1963: 175.

40. Barber and Ronning 1966, Waggener 1968. See also Shafer 1988 and Wolpin 1972.

41. State Department memorandum written by Ernest V. Siracusa, 23 June 1966.

42. Ministerio de Guerra 1966: 57. Other sources that provide data on the early stages of the counterinsurgency campaign are *Actualidad Militar* 1965, Añi Castillo 1967, Artola Azcarate 1976, and Gott 1973.

43. See, for example, State Department memorandum of the Special Group (Counterinsurgency) dated 22 July 1965 for discussion of the Peruvian request for napalm.

44. Villanueva 1971: 152, 156; interview, 25 July 1987.

45. Telegram, SECSTATE Washington 301, 25 August 1965, p. 4.

46. Interview, 14 July 1987.

CHAPTER 6: ITOMI PAVÁ

1. Interview, 18 December 1986.

2. Various interviews between 1982 and 1984.

3. See, for example, Eluau de Lobatón 1970: 61, 80. The author states that the MIR had made a "profound penetration" into local peasant communities, including Asháninka ones.

4. Interview, 14 July 1987.

5. Cristóbal 1989: 19.

6. Interviews with Juan Saavedra [pseudonym] and Eugenio Sarove, September 1987.

7. Interview, 16 August 1988.

8. Interview, 28 December 1984.

9. *La Prensa*, 15 and 17 June 1965.

10. Artola Azcarate 1976: 59, 67.

11. Ibid., 67–68.

12. Official documents and press reports are inconsistent about the exact date of the Cubantía raid. Some accounts state that the attack was on August 9, others on August 8.

13. *Correo*, Huancayo, 17 August 1965.

14. Artola Azcarate 1976: 69; *Actualidad Militar*, 31 August 1965: 3.

15. *El Comercio*, 14 August 1965.

16. *La Crónica*, 15 August 1965; *El Comercio*, 13 August 1965.

17. Interview, 1 May 1989.

18. This issue is outlined in a briefing paper for Sen. Robert Kennedy's visit to Peru dated 29 October 1965. In other documents, embassy staff members argue that Peru's anger over the grossly inadequate compensation paid by the IPC for its oil rights was unjustified because of the country's favorable balance of payments situation. The reason for the dispute, they contended, was strictly political: President Belaúnde was "trying to steal ammunition from the left to avert a Right wing-Communist alliance" (memo, Special Group [Counter-Insurgency], 22 July 1965, p. 3). What the embassy evidently failed to appreciate was that the pressure to expro-

priate the IPC was driven by nationalism rather than economic concerns: Standard Oil had provided Ecuador with Peruvian petroleum during the war between Ecuador and Peru in 1941 (see, for example, Moncloa 1977: 34).

19. Memo of the Special Group (Counter-Insurgency), 22 July 1965, p. 3.

20. Agee 1975: 271, 319.

21. Undated interview from *La Industria*, Trujillo, apparently published in 1982, found in archives of *El Comercio*, Lima.

22. Telegram, CINCSO FOR POLAD 116, 10 June 1965.

23. Telegram, CINCSO FOR POLAD 126, 19 June 1965.

24. Telegram to Secretary of State, 24 June 1965. The difficulty the United States had in convincing the Belaúnde government of the reality of a guerrilla threat calls into question Aranda and Escalante's assertion (1978: 92–93) that MIR camps had already been surveyed by government intelligence agents in late 1964 and early 1965.

25. Airgram A-308, 5 December 1965.

26. Ibid.

27. Memo, Special Group (Counter-Insurgency), 20 July 1965.

28. Memo by Ernest V. Siracusa, 23 June 1966.

29. We came across no information to support the assertion of Philip Agee (1975: 440) that the CIA "opened an outpost in the mountain village where the Peruvian military command had been set up," possibly Quillabamba in the Department of Cuzco. This outpost, he continues, "served for intelligence collection on successes and failures of the military campaign and for passing intelligence to the Peruvian military." In view of the number of excisions in the material released to us under the terms of the Freedom of Information Act, however, we cannot completely dismiss Agee's allegations.

The Reagan-era changes in the Freedom of Information Act have pulled many of the FOIA's teeth, and we have no doubt that the documents sent to us provide only a partial vision of U.S. activities in Peru in 1965–1966. Of the hundreds of pages of documents we received, large portions have been excised for reasons of "national security or foreign relations," "personal privacy," or simple "lack of relevance." The Department of Defense denied possession of any documents responsive to our research interests except a few unidentified records that it refused to release, citing national security concerns. As might be expected, the Central Intelligence

Agency proved the most impermeable of all, declining to "confirm or disconfirm the existence or non-existence" of any information relevant to the MIR struggle of 1965.

30. Memo, 3 September 1965.

31. Memo by Ernest V. Siracusa, 23 June 1966.

32. Telephone interview of James C. Haahr, 12 September 1989; memo dated 13 August 1965.

33. Airgram A-729, 9 June 1966; Airgram A-300, 27 August 1965; memo 26 October 1965.

34. Gall 1965 and 1967*b*: 39.

35. Interview with Carlos Borda, 11 July 1987. A telegram from the AID-OPS personnel in nearby Mazamari reported "widespread belief that there were many guerrillas in the Mazamari/Satipo area" after the "guerrilla/Campa ambush" at Cubantía (TOAID A-300, 27 August 1965).

36. Artola Azcarate 1976: 67-68.

37. *Correo*, Huancayo, 16 August 1965.

38. Interview, 9 June 1987.

39. Phelan 1970: 61.

40. *La Prensa*, 31 May 1962.

41. Artola Azcarate 1976: 49, 66.

42. Interview, 25 July 1987.

43. Artola Azcarate 1976: 70.

44. Añi Castillo 1967: 202.

45. Quoted in Gott 1973: 429.

46. Although most of our sources for this assertion are from Asháninkas or informed non-Indians sympathetic to the left, Páez 1990 corroborates the observation with oral accounts from former members of the army's "León" detachment.

1. *Correo*, Huancayo, 19 June 1965, 20 June 1965.

2. Agee (1975: 449) reports that Che had dropped from sight about six months earlier and that one of the "pet projects" of the CIA was to determine his whereabouts. He further alleges that the agency released false and unfavorable publicity about Guevara "in the hope that he [would] reappear to end it."

3. *New York Times* News Service, 9 October 1965, supplement, p. 3., col. 1; *New York Times*, 11 October 1965, p. 14, col. 3.

4. *Correo*, Huancayo, 11 August 1965.

5. Stoll 1982: 150. See also the assertion by Chaplin (1968: 398) that the Peruvian army was "assisted by US Protestant missionaries familiar with the area."

6. *La Crónica*, 17 August 1965.

7. Randall (1982: 72) analyzes the complex historical relationship between the dynastic struggle of Huascar and Atahualpa and the symbolic dualism of Inti (the Sun) and Viracocha (the Creator God). "The Spaniards," Randall writes, "stepped into the middle of this transitional chaos. They had the amazing fortune to arrive from the Ecuadorian sea . . . the spot from which Viracocha walked out into the ocean. . . ." This led Atahualpa to conclude that they were Viracocha's messengers. It should be noted that some anthropologists doubt the authenticity of the "white god" image of Viracocha and consider it an example of what Søren Hvalkov (personal communication) calls "eurocentric projection."

8. See Oliver-Smith 1969: 364. Oliver-Smith obtains his information on the Spanish use of body fat from Morote Best 1952. Morote is now a prominent figure in the radical left of Peru and has been, in at least one published article (Shakespeare 1988), linked to the Shining Path.

9. Shakespeare (1988) and Degregori (1987) say that fear of pishtacos and the murder of suspected pishtacos have reached a veritable frenzy in Ayacucho today, an effect of the Shining Path insurgency and the government's brutal counterinsurgency efforts. A Lima daily recently carried a story about the capture of a band of pishtacos that allegedly operated near Satipo, killing as many as thirty people and selling their fat to manufacturers of beauty products in the United States (*Diario La República*, 13 May 1990, p. 30). Although evoking skepticism, the report suggests how deeply the pishtaco myth has woven itself into the fabric of Peruvian popular culture.

10. Brown 1986: 61.

11. Weiss (1975: 292) discusses the increasing penetration of pishtaco fears into the belief system of the riverine Asháninka. Søren Hvalkof (personal communication), who has undertaken extensive fieldwork among the Asháninka of the Gran Pajonál, finds that

"everyone talks about the pishtacos in the entire Asháninka territory. There are some very well known pishtacos in the Satipo-Chanchamayo region . . . The pishtaco myth is now also an Amazonian fact."

12. The portions of the myth cited here are from Fernández 1984*b*: 207–208. For other versions of the myth see *Amazonía Peruana* 1976, Fernández 1987*b* and 1987*c*, Varese 1973: 285, Weiss 1975 and 1986.

13. Fernández 1986*b*: 56.

14. *El Expreso*, Lima, 26 March 1963.

15. Chaplin 1968: 398. In correspondence Chaplin was unable to elaborate on the information provided in his 1968 article.

16. Taussig 1987: 121.

17. Interview, 21 July 1987. Aside from the interviewees mentioned in the following pages, our research on David Pent benefited from correspondence with and telephone interviews of Willard Kindberg and Mack Robertson, both of whom conducted missionary work among Asháninkas in the 1960s.

18. Interview, 27 May 1989.

19. For details of the origin and sometimes controversial activities of the Summer Institute of Linguistics in Latin America, see Stoll 1982 and Hvalkof & Aaby 1981.

20. Interview, 17 July 1989.

21. Letter, 7 July 1987.

22. Interview, September 1987.

23. This passage is from a book of Rumrrill's short stories entitled *Vidas mágicas de tunchis y curanderos*, published in Lima by the author in 1972, pp. 19–20, translation ours.

24. Scorza 1983: 143–145, translation ours.

25. Portillo 1905: 506.

26. Letter from Willard Kindberg, 30 July 1986, and telephone interview, 12 August 1986. Kindberg's impressions were corroborated by Javier Dávila Durand, Joseph Pent, and Deborah Pent Hudson.

27. Interview, 4 November 1988.

28. This account is echoed in Thomas Büttner's (1989: 284) description of Charahuaja: "They said that it belonged to a foreigner, Lucas Paine [clearly a corruption of Pent], who had his farm and enslaved the Indians so that they would work his lands. Some of the old people still remember the despot."

29. Interview, 25 July 1989. Nélida Rojas recalls the year of her marriage to Pent as 1961, but a U.S. consular document states that the formal order for Pent's deportation was issued by the Peruvian police in 1962.

30. Rossa 1963.

31. Letter dated 5 January 1988; telephone interview, 23 January 1988. According to Macy and Kaplan (1980: 208), the Federal Bureau of Investigation "was regularly burglarizing the offices of the Socialist Workers Party" in 1960 and presumably thereafter.

32. Because conclusive proof of David Pent's death does not exist, Pent's confidential FBI files were denied to us under the terms of the Privacy Act. The FBI did provide us with what it classifies as "public source material," mostly newspaper clippings about Pent's activities in 1964–1965. Although these documents are not in themselves especially informative, the heavily excised memoranda that accompany them establish that the FBI maintained a file on Pent (#105-110977) and that it suspected him of radical activities.

33. In telegram 1475, 12 June 1964, the U.S. Embassy notified Washington that "David Livingstone Pent to be deported basis illegal entry only not political grounds." The telegram continues: "Peru police official informs subject not considered Communist though formerly involved general political activity. [Words excised] no concrete evidence available establish subject involved subversive political activities or that he communist . . . Lacking passport for entry Chile by June 25, subject will be deported U.S."

The telegram implies that the U.S. Embassy would have denied Pent a passport if the Peruvian police had wanted him deported directly to the United States.

34. Interview, 1 May 1989.

35. Information on the confusion of David Pent with Josef Mengele is contained in Pent's FBI file (#105-110977). The story was reported in the *New York Herald Tribune*, 7 June 1964, and in the 7 June 1964 edition of the *Register*, a newspaper published in Santa Ana, California.

36. Scorza 1983: 60.

37. *New York Times*, 6 January 1966, p. 11, col. 6. On 5 January, the U.S. Embassy cabled Washington the story of Pent's alleged capture. The cable concludes: "Embassy has no confirmation this report and inclined to doubt its accuracy," after which approxi-

mately one line is excised (telegram USCINCSO 170, 5 January 1966).

38. Scorza 1983: 154.

39. Letter, 10 October 1986. Our search of the episodes of NBC News that have been taped and indexed by Vanderbilt University turned up no segments that correspond to the Pent family recollection, though these records have only been kept since 1968.

40. Scorza 1983: 155.

41. For reflections on Western representations of the power and danger of Amazonian natives, see Taussig 1987: 100.

CHAPTER 8: DEATH OF A CHRONICLE FORETOLD

1. Artola Azcarate 1976: 70.

2. See Brown 1989.

3. Brown 1988.

4. Various interviews in 1984.

5. Interview, 1985.

6. Interview, June 1983.

7. *Correo*, Huancayo, 29 September 1965.

8. *La Crónica*, 21 August 1965; *La Prensa*, 21 August 1965.

9. Ernest V. Siracusa, memorandum, 23 June 1966, p. 9.

10. Reprinted in Mercado 1967: 171–172.

11. Letter dated 20 August 1965. Quoted with permission of Mario Vargas Llosa.

12. Añi Castillo 1967: 201.

13. Telegram, SECSTATE Washington 419, 13 September 1965. See also Gall 1967a: 38.

14. Ibid.

15. Memorandum of conversation, 30 October 1965.

16. Sources include Añi Castillo 1976, Artola Azcarate 1976, and Ministerio de Guerra 1966. Artola Azcarate (1976: 73–74) asserts that the departure of Lobatón from Shuenti prior to the attack was a cowardly "betrayal" but provides no evidence to support this claim.

17. Quoted in Guardia 1972: 21. For details of the movements of the León detachment, see also Páez 1990.

18. Interview, 16 August 1988.

19. Artola Azcarate 1976: 75.

20. Interview, 9 June 1987.

21. Interviews, 1984.

22. Interview, 20 July 1988.

23. *El Comercio*, 10 December 1965, reports that the occupation of the mission began on November 28 and lasted ten days. Artola Azcarate (1976: 77) cites the same arrival date but claims that Lobatón and his men spent only one day in Obenteni.

24. Quoted in Páez 1990: 23.

25. Guardia 1972: 21.

26. Artola Azcarate 1976: 76.

27. Guardia 1972: 66.

28. Cristóbal 1984: 8.

29. Ministerio de Guerra 1966: 64.

30. Artola Azcarate 1976: 78.

31. Military eyewitnesses interviewed by Páez 1990 assert that the Túpac Amaru had split into three groups as early as October 1965.

32. Telegram, SECSTATE Washington 929, 28 December 1965.

33. Artola Azcarate 1976: 78.

34. Ministerio de Guerra 1966: 64.

35. Hvalkof's Asháninka informants in the Gran Pajonál also provided him with an account of the execution of Guillermo Lobatón that is very different from that of official documents or our own sources. They told him, among other things, that Lobatón and Herrera were captured together in Mapitzcviari, where they were marched to an open area, executed, and buried (Søren Hvalkof, personal communications, 13 April 1988 and 10 May 1990).

36. *Correo*, Huancayo, 9 January 1966.

37. Quoted in Páez 1990: 23.

CHAPTER 9: BEYOND 1965

1. Béjar 1969.

2. Ministerio de Guerra 1966: 70.

3. Ernest V. Siracusa, State Department memorandum, 23 June 1966, pp. 1–2, 14.

4. Sources on the impact of the guerrilla war include Rodríguez Beruff 1983 and Ernest V. Siracusa, State Department memorandum, 23 June 1966.

5. Artola Azcarate 1976: 79.

6. Interview, 8 February 1989.

7. Sources include Einaudi 1970, Einaudi and Stepan 1971, Kuczynski 1977, Moncloa 1977, Rodríguez Beruff 1983, and Villanueva 1971.

8. Moncloa 1977: 35.

9. See Mercado Jarrín 1967 and Rodríguez Beruff 1983.

10. This analysis of the 1965–1968 period draws on Niedergang 1971, Rodríguez Beruff 1983, and Villanueva 1971.

11. For details of the scandal and other aspects of the Peru-IPC negotiations, see Goodwin 1969.

12. Goodwin 1969.

13. Villanueva 1971: 158–159. See also Rodríguez Beruff 1983: 159–235.

14. Interview, 1 May 1989. See also Einaudi 1970.

15. For texts of these documents, see Guardia 1972: 23–29. Levano 1966 includes a more detailed critique of the 1965 struggle from the perspective of the official Communist party.

16. See Añi Castillo 1967, Condoruna 1966, Gott 1973, and Pumaruna 1967.

17. García 1989: 30. The interview with Cordero places the meeting at Mesa Pelada in May 1964, but this is clearly a typographical error. Cordero's comments are confirmed by an interview with Carlos Flores Borja (Bermúdez 1985), another MIR survivor.

18. See Adolph 1969 and Guardia 1972 for coverage of 1969 trial and testimony of the accused.

19. *Punto Final* 1967. The same article has a curious reference to "an uprising of the Campa Indians," but provides no further details.

20. Eluau de Lobatón 1967: 15.

21. Interview with Elías Murillo, 14 July 1987.

22. Palmer (1986: 128) identifies Guzmán as the local commander of the ELN's Huamanga command and claims he broke with the party over the question of the guerrilla war and *foquista* strategies of revolution. To our knowledge, no other source links Guzmán with the ELN; most identify him as a member of the Maoist faction of the Communist party, called PCP–Bandera Roja (Red Flag). Other sources consulted for our discussion of the Shining Path are Berg 1986, Bonner 1988, Chang-Rodríguez 1987, Degregori 1985, 1986, and 1990, McClintock 1984, Seligmann 1985, Shakespeare 1988, and Tarazona-Sevillano 1990.

23. Shakespeare 1988: 189.

24. Bourque and Warren 1989: 15; National Human Rights Co-ordinating Committee 1990.

25. Juan Ansión, in Flores Galindo 1988: 379.

26. Vargas Llosa 1983.

27. See Chang-Rodríguez 1987, Flores Galindo 1988, and Vargas Llosa 1983. The identification of the Shining Path—as well as the Peruvian army—with pishtacos is made in Degregori 1987. In a more recent publication, Degregori (1990: 21–22) argues that the Shining Path's utopian currents come not from pre-Hispanic Andean roots but from an "excess of reason" that has "turned [Marxist] science into religion."

28. For brief background materials on the MRTA, see Bourque and Warren 1989. Sources on the MRTA *foco* in San Martín include *Diario La República* 1987 and *Caretas* 1987.

29. Joint declaration of the MIR and MRTA, Lima, 9 December 1986.

30. On this issue, we must differ sharply from the opinions expressed by Edmundo Morales (1989), who in his otherwise useful book on the cocaine trade in Peru dismisses the existence of clear links between guerrillas and coca lords. Events since his fieldwork now make it impossible to sustain a belief in the separation of the two phenomena. See also Tarazona-Sevillano 1990.

31. *New York Times*, 22 April 1990, p. 1.

32. Telegram to Department of State, 28 September 1965.

33. All information about Project Agile was obtained from *Hearings on Military Posture and A Bill (HR 9240)*, Committee on Armed Services, House of Representatives, 90th Congress, 1967, pp. 1524–1547, as well as from a bibliography of unclassified Project Agile reports provided by the Defense Technical Information Center, Arlington, Va.

34. The report, written by H. A. Ellis, is entitled "Applicability of Olfactory Transducers to the Detection of Human Beings" (Report AD-469-274, Semiannual Technical Report, July 1965).

35. For an extended analysis of this issue, see Sheehan 1988.

36. Chirif and Mora 1976: 83–101.

37. Problems related to land titling, colonization, and land-use policies among the Asháninka are described in Chirif 1982, Hvalkof 1985 and 1989, and Trapnell 1982, as well as in other short articles too numerous to cite here.

38. Fernández 1984c.

39. Chirif 1982: 4.

40. Hvalkof 1985: 23.

41. See, for example, Swenson and Narby 1986.

42. In fairness to the Pichis-Palcazu Special Project, we should mention that it has titled many Asháninka and Amuesha communities during a period when land-titling of native communities elsewhere in the country virtually ceased. In some parts of the project area, the Pichis-Palcazu Special Project has experimented with new strategies to integrate native peoples into programs of forest protection and technical assistance. Information on titling efforts since the late 1980s comes from Foster 1990 and Hvalkof 1989.

43. See Macdonald 1985.

44. Quoted in Benavides 1990: 13. For details about the links between the MIR and the MRTA, see Chávez 1990.

45. The struggle between the Asháninkas and the MRTA was front-page news during the first weeks of 1990, and the sources we have used to prepare this brief summary are too numerous to mention here. Benavides 1990 presents a review and analysis of the struggle through July 1990.

46. See, for example, the running coverage of these events in *Diario La República*, 13–19 January 1990 and *Sí*, 15 January 1990. Equally violent encounters between Asháninkas and the Shining Path are described in Gorriti 1990, which was published too late for us to integrate into this assessment of the Asháninkas' current situation.

CHAPTER 10: CODA: AMAZONIAN INDIANS AND THE MILLENNIAL DREAM

1. Métraux 1941.

2. Hemming 1987; Hill and Wright 1988; Hugh-Jones 1981; Wright and Hill 1986.

3. Métraux 1941: 54.

4. Vinhas de Queiróz 1963.

5. Burridge 1985: 226.

6. Although most social scientists continue to look at millenarian movements as "outbursts" indicative of social imbalance, Schwartz

1976 convincingly argues the merits of reconceptualizing crisis cults as a form of social process.

7. Worsley 1968: 248.

8. The work of Anna C. Roosevelt (e.g., Roosevelt 1987) has been especially influential in the reassessment of Amazonian prehistory.

9. In a provocative analysis of Melanesian cargo cults, Nancy McDowell (1988: 124) asserts that the rapid social transformations associated with such movements may derive from underlying native assumptions about change. For many Melanesian peoples, she says, "there is no gradual, cumulative, evolutionary change; change is always dramatic, total, and complete." Nancy Farriss's (1987) work on Maya concepts of time and history analyzes the complex links between Maya notions of rapid social transformation, as expressed through prophecy, and rebellions in colonial Yucatán. More germane to the Amazonian case, Jonathan Hill (1988: 7) observes in the indigenous South American traditions a pattern in which "history is understood in relation to a few 'peaks,' or critical periods of rapid change, rather than a smoothly flowing progression."

10. Pierre Clastres (1987: 160–161), for instance, laments the creation of an "impoverishing syncretism where, under the mask of an always superficial Christianity, indigenous thought seeks only to postpone its own demise."

11. Scott 1985.

12. For a discussion of this issue, see Clastres 1987.

Bibliography

Actualidad Militar
   1965 Acontecimientos en la Sierra Central. *Actualidad Militar*,
       31 August 1965: 2–4.
Adolph, José B.
   1969 Diario íntimo de la crueldad. *Caretas*, 17–27 February
       1969: 18–20.
Agee, Philip
   1975 *Inside the Company: CIA Diary*. New York: Bantam.
Alvarez Sáenz, Félix
   1989 El milenarismo franciscano: Una aproximación. Unpub-
       lished paper.
Amazonía Peruana
   1976 Testimonios: Todas las escopetas me van a mandar los
       Tasorentsi. *Amazonía Peruana* 1: 133–136. Lima.
Amich, José
   1975 [orig. 1771] *Historia de la misiones del Convento de Santa
       Rosa de Ocopa*. Lima: Editorial Milla Batres.
Añi Castillo, Gonzalo
   1967 *Historia secreta de las guerrillas*. Lima: Ediciones Mas Allá.
Aranda, Arturo, and Maria Escalante
   1978 *Lucha de clases en el movimiento sindical cusqueño, 1927–
       1965*. Lima: G. Herrera Editores.
Area Handbook for Peru
   1972 Washington, D.C.: American University, Foreign Area
       Studies Division.

Artola Azcarate, Gen. Armando
1976 *¡Subversión!* Lima: Editorial Juridica.
Baines, John M.
1972 *Revolution in Peru: Mariátegui and the Myth.* Tuscaloosa: University of Alabama Press.
Barber, William F., and C. Neale Ronning
1966 *Internal Security and Military Power: Counterinsurgency and Civic Action in Latin America.* Columbus: Ohio State University Press.
Barclay, Frederica
1989 *La Colonia del Perené: Capital inglés y economía cafetalera en la configuración de la región de Chanchamayo.* Iquitos, Peru: Centro de Estudios Teológicas de la Amazonía.
Beecher, William
1964 Special U.S. Forces Make Gains in Curbing Latin Guerrilla Bands. *Wall Street Journal,* 18 February: 1, col. 4.
Béjar, Héctor
1969 *Perú 1965: Apuntes sobre una experiencia guerrillera.* Havana: Casa de las Américas.
1984 Aquellos años sesenta. *30 Días* 1(8): 10. July 1984. Lima.
1987 Tierra y muerte: 1965. *Agro, Revista del Banco Agrario del Peru.* February 1987: 13–16.
Benavides, Margarita
1990 Levantamiento de los asháninka del río Pichis: ¿organización nativa contra guerrilla del MRTA? *Página Libre,* 11 July 1990: 11–33. Lima.
Berg, Ronald H.
1986 Sendero Luminoso and the Peasantry of Andahuaylas. *Journal of Interamerican Studies and World Affairs* 28(4): 165–196.
Bermúdez, Alfonso
1985 Testimonio: La guerrilla 20 años despues. *Gente,* 28 November 1985: 20–23. Lima.
Bierhorst, John
1988 *The Mythology of South America.* New York: William Morrow and Company.
Blumstein, Alfred, and Jesse Orlansky
1965 *Behavioral, Political, and Operational Research Programs on Counterinsurgency Supported by the Department of Defense.* Washington: Institute for Defense Analyses.

(Available as Department of Commerce Document No. AD 467-894.)

Bodley, John H.

1971 Campa Socio-Economic Adaptation. Ph.D. diss., University of Oregon. Ann Arbor: University Microfilms.

1972 A Transformative Movement Among the Campa of Eastern Peru. *Anthropos* 67: 220–228.

Bonner, Raymond

1988 A Reporter at Large: Peru's War. *The New Yorker*, 4 January 1988: 31–58.

Bourque, Susan C., and Kay B. Warren

1989 Democracy without Peace: The Cultural Politics of Terror in Peru. *Latin American Research Review* 24: 7–34.

Brown, Michael F.

1986 *Tsewa's Gift: Magic and Meaning in an Amazonian Society*. Washington, D.C.: Smithsonian Institution Press.

1988 Shamanism and its Discontents. *Medical Anthropology Quarterly* 2: 102–120.

1989 Dark Side of the Shaman. *Natural History*, November 1989: 8–10.

Brun, Albert

1987*a* Barbie roba colecta nacional en Bolivia. *Diario La República*, 15 May 1987: 20.

1987*b* América lo llama Che. *Diario La República*, 5 October 1987: 15–17.

1987*c* ¿Che intentó armar guerrilla en el Perú? *Diario La República*, 11 October 1967: 14–15.

Burridge, Kenelm

1985 Millennialism and the Recreation of History. In: *Religion, Rebellion, and Revolution*, ed. Bruce Lincoln. New York: St. Martin's Press. 219–235.

Büttner, Thomas

1989 *La rojez de anoche desde la cabaña*. Lima: Editorial Colmillo Blanco.

Campbell, Leon G.

1973 The Historiography of the Peruvian Guerrilla Movement, 1960–1965. *Latin American Research Review* 8(1): 45–70.

Caretas

1965 ¿Víctima o victimaria? *Caretas*, 26 May–7 June 1965: 44–51, 56. Lima.

1987 Juanjuí: guerrilleros. *Caretas*, 9 November 1987: 8–10.

Castro Arenas, Mario
1973 *La rebelión de Juan Santos*. Lima: Carlos Milla Batres.

Chang-Rodríguez, Eugenio
1987 Sendero Luminoso: Teoría y praxis. *Nueva Sociedad*, May–June 1987: 152–162. Caracas.

Chaplin, David
1968 Peru's Postponed Revolution. *World Politics* 20: 393–420.

Chávez, Luis Alberto
1990 Ideólogo subterráneo. *Diario La República*, 22 July 1990: 24–25.

Chevalier, Jacques M.
1982 *Civilization and the Stolen Gift: Capital, Kin, and Cult in Eastern Peru*. Toronto: University of Toronto Press.

Chirif, Alberto
1982 Crónica de un atropello mal programado. *Amazonía Indígena* 2(4): 3–11. Lima.

Chirif, Alberto, and Carlos Mora
1976 *Atlas de Comunidades Nativas*. Lima: Sistema Nacional de Apoyo a la Movilización Social.

Clastres, Pierre
1987 *Society Against the State: Essays in Political Anthropology*. New York: Zone Books.

Condoruna, S. [Aníbal Quijano]
1966 *Las experiencias de la última etapa de las luchas revolucionarias en el Perú*. Lima: Ediciones Vanguardia Revolucionaria.

Cristóbal, Juan
1984 *Máximo Velando: el optimismo frente a la vida*. Lima: Ediciones Debate Socialista.
1989 Antonio Meza Bravo: El combate por la vida. *Cambio*, 25 May 1989: 18–20. Lima.

Deal, Douglas
1975 Peasant Revolts and Resistance in the Modern World: A Comparative View. *Journal of Contemporary Asia* 5(4): 414–445.

Degregori, Carlos Iván
1985 *"Sendero Luminoso": los hondos y mortales desencuentros*. Instituto de Estudios Peruanos, Serie: Antropología No. 2. Lima.
1986 *"Sendero Luminoso": lucha armada y utopía autoritaria*.

Instituto de Estudios Peruanos, Serie: Antropología No. 3. Lima.

1987 El Regreso de los Pishtacos. *Diario La República*, 27 September 1987: 27–30.

1990 *Qué difícil es ser dios: ideología y violencia política en Sendero Luminoso.* 2d ed. Lima: Zorro de Abajo Ediciones.

de la Puente Uceda, Luis F.

1965 The Peruvian Revolution: Concepts and Perspectives. *Monthly Review* 17(6): 12–28. November.

de Lamberg, Vera B.

1971 La guerrilla castrista en América Latina: bibliografía selecta 1960–70. *Foro Internacional* 12(1): 95–111.

de Onis, Juan

1965 Peru's Chief Says Reds Stir Unrest. *New York Times*, 22 July, p. 10, col. 2.

1966 Latin Military Tactics Blunting Castro-Style Guerrilla Warfare. *New York Times*, 30 August, p. 1, col. 1; p. 10, col. 1.

Diario La República

1987 Terroristas toman San José de Sisa. 9 November 1987: 19–22.

Editorial Research Reports

1967 Guerrilla Movements in Latin America. *Editorial Research Reports* 2: 519–536.

Einaudi, Luigi R.

1970 *Peruvian Military Relations with the United States.* Santa Monica, Calif.: Rand Corporation.

Einaudi, Luigi R., and Alfred C. Stepan III

1971 *Latin American Institutional Development: Changing Military Responses in Peru and Brazil.* Santa Monica, Calif.: Rand Corporation.

Elick, John W.

1969 An Ethnography of the Pichis Valley Campa of Eastern Peru. Ph.D. dissertation. University of California, Los Angeles. Ann Arbor: University Microfilms.

Eluau de Lobatón, Jacqueline

1967 Tras las huellas de Lobatón. *Punto Final* 34: 15–16. August. Santiago de Chile.

1970 Il processo guerrigliero e lo sviluppo della situazione peruviana. In: Lobatón, Guillermo, *Secondo Fronte: Teoría della guerriglia e appella alla lotta armata negli scritti del capo del Túpac Amaru.* Milano: Feltrinelli. 5–120.

Farriss, Nancy M.

1987 Remembering the Future, Anticipating the Past: History, Time, and Cosmology among the Maya of Yucatan. *Comparative Studies in Society and History* 29: 566–593.

Fernández, Eduardo

1984*a* El águila que comía gente y el origen de los Piro. *Amazonía Peruana* 10: 129–142. Lima: Centro Amazónico de Antropología y Aplicación Práctica.

1984*b* La muerte del Inca. Mitología Asháninca. *Anthropologica* 2: 201–208. Lima: Pontificia Universidad Católica.

1984*c* Encarcelado por amor. *Diario La República*, 11 November 1984: 35–38.

1986*a* *Para que nuestra historia no se pierda: testimonios de los Asháninca y Nomatsiguenga sobre la colonización de la región Satipo-Pangoa.* Lima: Centro de Investigación y Promoción Amazónica.

1986*b* El científico ante los problemas de la Amazonía. *Culturas indígenas de la Amazonía.* Madrid: Comisión Nacional Quinto Centenario. 51–59.

1986*c* Juan Font, "El Perulero." *Pueblo Indio* 8: 52–54. Lima.

1987*a* El pensamiento Asháninca y los recursos naturales. *Anthropológica* 4: 71–89. Lima: Pontificia Universidad Católica.

1987*b* Los Asháninca y los Incas: historia y mitos. *Anthropologica* 5: 333–356. Lima: Pontificia Universidad Católica.

1987*c* Aguilas, jaguares, Incas y viracochas: toponimia del territorio ashaninca. *Extracta* 6: 16–21. Lima.

1988 El territorio ashaninca en su frontera sur: distribución y límites. *Extracta* 7: 23–33. Lima.

Flores Galindo, Alberto

1988 *Buscando un Inca*, 3d ed. Lima: Editorial Horizonte.

Foster, Douglas

1990 No Road to Tahuanti. *Mother Jones*, July/August, 1990: 36–45, 64.

Fuentes, H.

1908 *Loreto, Apuntes geográficos, históricos, estadísticos, políticos, y sociales.* Lima.

Galeano, Eduardo
1987 "Cuidado, Viene el Che." Diario *La República*, 10 October 1987: 9–11.
Gall, Norman
1964 Letter from Peru. *Commentary* 37(4): 64–69. June.
1965 A Red Insurgency Jolts Latin America. *Wall Street Journal*, 8 November 1965, p. 16, col. 3.
1966 Revolution Without Revolutionaries. *The Nation* 203(5): 145–149. 22 August 1966.
1967a Peru's Misfired Guerrilla Campaign. *The Reporter* 36(2): 36–38. 26 January 1967.
1967b The Legacy of Che Guevara. *Commentary* 44(6): 31–44. December 1967.
García, Ivan
1989 Conversación con Héctor Cordero: testimonio de una experiencia guerrillera. *Entrevista*, 1 October 1989: 27–30.
Gilly, Adolfo
1963 Los sindicatos guerrilleros del Perú. *Marcha*, 23 August 1963. Montevideo.
1965a The Real Battle. *Atlas* 10(3): 171. September 1965.
1965b Guerrillas en el Perú. *Arauco* 5: 4–8.
Goodwin, Richard N.
1969 Letter from Peru. *The New Yorker*, 17 May 1969.
Gorriti, Gustavo
1990 Terror in the Andes: The Flight of the Asháninkas. *New York Times Magazine*, 2 December: 40–48, 65–72.
Gott, Richard
1973 *Rural Guerrillas in Latin America*. Harmondsworth: Penguin.
Gow, Rosalind C.
1982 Inkarri and Revolutionary Leadership in the Southern Andes. *Journal of Latin American Lore* 8: 197–223.
Gros, Christian
1981 Guérillas et mouvements Indiens paysans dans les années 1960. *Cahiers des Amériques Latines* 23(1): 173–201.
Guardia, Sara Beatriz
1972 *Proceso a campesinos de la guerrilla "Túpac Amaru."* Lima: Compañia de Impresiones y Publicidad.

Guillaume, H. A.
    1888 *The Amazon Provinces of Peru as a Field for European Emigration*. London: Wyman & Sons.
Hemming, John
    1987 *Amazon Frontier*. London: Macmillan.
Herndon, William L., and Lardner Gibbon
    1854 *Exploration of the Valley of the Amazon, Made Under the Direction of the Navy Department*. Washington, D.C.: Robert Armstrong, Public Printer.
Herzog, Werner
    1982 *Fitzcarraldo: The Original Story*. San Francisco: Fjord Press.
Hill, Jonathan D.
    1988 Introduction: Myth and History. In: *Rethinking History and Myth: Indigenous South American Perspectives on the Past*, ed. Jonathan D. Hill. Urbana: University of Illinois Press. 1–17.
Hill, Jonathan D., and Robin M. Wright
    1988 Time, Narrative, and Ritual: Historical Interpretations from an Amazonian Society. In: *Rethinking History and Myth: Indigenous South American Perspectives on the Past*, ed. Jonathan D. Hill. Urbana: University of Illinois Press. 78–105.
Hodges, Donald C.
    1974 *The Latin American Revolution: Politics and Strategy from Apro-Marxism to Guevarism*. New York: William Morrow & Company.
Horowitz, Irving Louis, ed.
    1974 *The Rise and Fall of Project Camelot: Studies in the Relationship Between Social Science and Practical Politics*. Cambridge, Mass.: MIT Press.
Hugh-Jones, Stephen
    1981 Historia del Vaupés. *Maguaré* 1: 29–51. Bogotá.
Huizer, Gerrit
    1972 *The Revolutionary Potential of Peasants in Latin America*. Lexington, Mass.: Lexington Books.
Hvalkof, Søren
    1985 Urgent Report on the Situation of the Ashaninka (Campa) Population, Gran Pajonál, Central Peruvian Amazon.

Unpublished report, Council for Development Research, Danish International Development Agency. Lima.

1989 The Nature of Development: Native and Settler Views in Gran Pajonál, Peruvian Amazon. *Folk* 21: 125–150. Copenhagen.

Hvalkof, Søren, and Peter Aaby, eds.

1981 *Is God an American?: An Anthropological Perspective on the Missionary Work of the Summer Institute of Linguistics.* Copenhagen: IWGIA and Survival International.

Isbell, Billie Jean

1978 *To Defend Ourselves: Ecology and Ritual in an Andean Village.* Austin: University of Texas Press.

Izaguirre, Padre Fray Bernardino

1922 *Historia de las misiones franciscanas y narración de los progresos de la geografía en el oriente del Perú.* Lima: Talleres Tipográficos de la Penitenciaría.

Jiménez de la Espada, don Marcos, ed.

1965 Misión y entrada de los Andes de Xauxa. *Relaciones Geográficas de Indias—Peru.* II: 102–105. Madrid: Editorial Atlas.

Junta de Vías Fluviales

1904 *El Istmo de Fiscarrald.* Lima: Imprenta La Industria.

Kuczynski, Pedro-Pablo

1977 *Peruvian Democracy Under Economic Stress: An Account of the Belaunde Administration, 1963–1968.* Princeton: Princeton University Press.

La Barre, Weston

1971 Materials for a History of Studies of Crisis Cults: A Bibliographic Essay. *Current Anthropology* 12: 3–44.

Lan, David

1985 *Guns and Rain: Guerrillas and Spirit Mediums in Zimbabwe.* Berkeley, Los Angeles, London: University of California Press.

Laughlin, David L.

1975 *Gringo Cop.* New York: Carleton Press.

Laughton, John Knox

1899 *From Howard to Nelson: Twelve Sailors.* London: Lawrence and Bullen.

Lear, John
1962 Reaching the Heart of South America. *Saturday Review*, 3 November 1962: 55–58.

Lehnertz, Jay F.
1972 Juan Santos, Primitive Rebel on the Campa Frontier (1742–1752). XXXIX Congreso Internacional de Americanistas, Lima. *Actas y Memorias* 4: 111–126.
1974 Lands of the Infidels: The Franciscans in the Central Montaña of Peru, 1709–1824. Ph.D. dissertation. University of Wisconsin. Ann Arbor: University Microfilms.

Letts, Ricardo
1981 *La izquierda peruana: organizaciones y tendencias.* Lima: Mosca Azul Editores.

Levano, Cesar
1966 Lessons of the Guerrilla Struggle in Peru. *World Marxist Review* 9(9): 44–51.

Lincoln, Bruce, ed.
1985 *Religion, Rebellion, Revolution: An Interdisciplinary and Cross-Cultural Collection of Essays.* New York: St. Martin's Press.

Loayza, Francisco A.
1942 *Juan Santos, el invencible.* Lima: Los Pequeños Grandes Libros de Historia Americana.

López, Atanasio
1922 Las misiones de Cerro de la Sal. *Archivo Ibero-Americano* 18: 174–222.

McClintock, Cynthia
1984 Why Peasants Rebel: The Case of Peru's Sendero Luminoso. *World Politics* 37(1): 48–84.

Macdonald, Theodore, Jr.
1985 From Coca to Cocaine in Indigenous Amazonia. *Cultural Survival Quarterly* 9(4): 30–33.

McDowell, Nancy
1988 A Note on Cargo Cults and Cultural Constructions of Change. *Pacific Studies* 11: 121–134.

Macy, Christy, and Susan Kaplan
1980 *Documents.* New York: Penguin Books.

Mallon, Florencia E.
1985 *The Defense of Community in Peru's Central Highlands:*

Peasant Struggle and Capitalist Transition, 1860–1940.
Princeton: Princeton University Press.

Manrique, Manuel
1982 *La Peruvian Corporation en la selva central del Perú.* Lima:
Centro de Investigación y Promoción Amazónica.

Manrique, Nelson
1984 Las guerrillas en el Perú: El MIR de los sesenta. *30 Días,*
July: 8–10.

Mariátegui, José Carlos
1971 [orig. 1928] *Seven Interpretive Essays on Peruvian Reality.*
Austin: University of Texas Press.

Marzorati, Gerald
1989 Can a Novelist Save Peru? *New York Times Magazine,* 5
November 1989.

Mendoza, Samuel R.
1966 Personajes ilustres del Perú: Carlos Fermín Fitzcarrald.
Actualidad Militar, January: 16–17.

Mercado, Roger
1967 *Las guerrillas del Perú.* Lima: Fondo de Cultura Popular.

Mercado Jarrín, Edgardo
1967 La política y estrategia militar en la guerra contrasubver-
siva en la América Latina. *Revista Militar del Perú,*
November–December: 4–33.

Métraux, Alfred
1941 The Messiahs of South America. *The Interamerican Quarterly* III(2): 53–60. April.

Miller, Ryal
1975 The Fake Inca of Tucuman: Don Pedro Bohorques. *The
Americas* 32(2): 196-210.

Ministerio de Guerra
1966 *Las guerrillas en el Perú y su represión.* Lima.

Moncloa, Francisco
1977 *Perú: qué pasó (1968-1976).* Lima: Editorial Horizonte.

Morales, Edmundo
1989 *Cocaine: White Gold Rush in Peru.* Tucson: University of
Arizona Press.

Morón Ramos, Joaquín M.
1975 *Monografía de la Provincia de Satipo.* Satipo.

Morote Best, Efrain
1952 El degollador. *Tradición, Revista Peruana de Cultura* 2: 67–91.

National Human Rights Coordinating Committee (Peru)
1990 *Bulletin* No. 6, Working Group of the National Human Rights Coordinating Committee Against Disappearances and Political Murders in Peru. February 1990. Lima.

Neira, Hugo
1968 *Los Andes: tierra o muerte.* Madrid: Editorial ZYX.

New York Times
1965 Guevara Reported Seized in Peru. *New York Times* News Service, 9 October, p. 3, col. 1.
1990 U.S. Will Arm Peru to Fight Leftists in New Drug Push. 22 April 1990: 1, 18.

Niedergang, Marcel
1971 Revolutionary Nationalism in Peru. *Foreign Affairs* 49(3): 454–463.

Oliver-Smith, Anthony
1969 The Pishtaco: Institutionalized Fear in Highland Peru. *Journal of American Folklore* 82: 363–368.

Ordinaire, Olivier
1988 [1892] *Del Pacífico al Atlántico y Otros Escritos.* Monumenta Amazónica, Serie D, No. 1. Iquitos, Perú: Centro de Estudios Teológicos de la Amazonía. [Translation of original French edition.]

Orellana Valeriano, Simeón
1974 La rebelión de Juan Santos o Juan Santos el rebelde. *Anales científicos de la Universidad del Centro del Perú*, No. 3: 513–551. Huancayo.

Ortiz, Fr. Dionisio
1961 *Reseña Historica de la Montaña del Pangoa, Gran Pajonál, y Satipo (1673–1960).* Lima: Editorial "San Antonio."
1976 *Las Montañas de Apurímac, Mantaro, y Ene.* Lima: Editorial "San Antonio."

Ossio, Juan, ed.
1973 *Ideología mesiánica del mundo andino.* Lima: Ignacio Prado Pastor.

Páez, Angel
1990 Guerrillas del 65: la otra historia. *Diario La República*, 24 June 1990: 22–24.

Palmer, David Scott
1986 Rebellion in Rural Peru: The Origins and Evolution of Sendero Luminoso. *Comparative Politics* 18(2): 127–146.

Pérez Marcio, Manuel F.
1953 *Los hijos de la selva*. Buenos Aires: Casa Editora
Sudamericana.
Phelan, John Leddy
1970 *The Millennial Kingdom of the Franciscans in the New World*,
2d ed. Berkeley, Los Angeles, London: University of
California Press.
Portillo, Pedro
1901 *Las montañas de Ayacucho y los ríos Apurímac, Mantaro,
Ene, Perené, Tambo y Alto Ucayali*. Lima: Imprenta del
Estado.
1905 Exploración de los ríos Apurímac, Ene, Tambo,
Ucayali, Pachitea i Pichis por el prefecto de Ayacucho,
coronel don Pedro Portillo. In: *Colección de leyes,
decretos, resoluciones i otros documentos oficiales referentes al
Departamento de Loreto*, ed. Carlos Larrabure i
Correa, III: 463–509. Lima: Imp. de "La Opinión
Nacional."
Presente
1965 ¡Guerrillas en los Andes! *Presente* (September–October):
16–51. Lima.
Pumaruna, Americo [Ricardo Letts Colmenares]
1967 Perú: revolución, insurrección, guerrillas. *Pensamiento
Crítico* 1 (February): 74–128.
Punto Final
1967 Lobatón estaría vivo y preso. *Punto Final* 36 (July): 36.
Santiago de Chile.
Randall, Robert
1982 Qoyllur Rit'i, An Inca Fiesta of the Pleiades: Reflections
on Time and Space in the Andean World. *Bulletin de
l'Institute Frances d'Etudes Andines* 11: 37–82.
Reyna, Ernesto
1942 *Fitzcarrald, el rey del caucho*. Lima: Taller Gráfico de P.
Barrantes C.
Reynolds
1930 *Versiones incaicas*, Tomo I. Santiago de Chile: Casa
Amarilla.
Rodríguez Beruff, Jorge
1983 *Los militares y el poder: un ensayo sobre la doctrina militar en
el Perú, 1948–1968*. Lima: Mosca Azul Editores.

Roosevelt, Anna C.
1987 Chiefdoms in the Amazon and Orinoco. In: *Chiefdoms in the Americas*, ed. Robert D. Drennan and Carlos A. Uribe. Lanham, Md.: University Press of America. 153–185.

Rossa, Della
1963 A Peruvian Exile's Story. *The Militant* 27 (September 30): 6.

Rumrrill, Róger
1983 *Vidas mágicas de tunchis y curanderos*. Lima.

Sabaté, Padre Luis
1925 Viaje de los padres misioneros del convento de Cuzco a las tribus salvajes de los Campas, Piros, Cunibos, y Shipibos por el P. Fr. Luis Sabaté en el año de 1874. In: *Historia de las misiones Franciscanas*, vol. 10., ed. P. Fr. Bernardo Izaguirre. Lima: Talleres Tipográficos de la Penitenciaría. 11–317.

Sahlins, Marshall
1985 *Islands of History*. Chicago: University of Chicago Press.

Sala, Padre Gabriel
1897 *Exploración de los ríos Pichis, Pachitea, y Alto Ucayali y de la región del Gran Pajonál*. Lima: Imprenta La Industria.

Salazar Bondy, Sebastián
1965 Who They Are. *Atlas* 10(3), September: 170–171.

Santos Granero, Fernando
1986 Bohórquez y la conquista espurea del Cerro de la Sal. *Amazonía Peruana* 13: 119–134.

1988 Templos y herrerías: Utopía y re-creación cultural en la amazonía peruana (siglos XVIII-XIX). *Boletín del Instituto Francés de Estudios Andinos* 17(2): 1-22.

Schwartz, Hillel
1976 The End of the Beginning: Millenarian Studies, 1969–1975. *Religious Studies Review* 2(3): 1–15.

Scorza, Manuel
1983 *La danza inmóvil*. Barcelona: Plaza & Janés.

Scott, James C.
1985 *Weapons of the Weak: Everyday Forms of Peasant Resistance*. New Haven: Yale University Press.

Seligmann, Linda J.
1985 Mysterious Terror of the "Shining Path." *Washington Post*, 24 March 1985: C1–2.

Shafer, D. Michael
1988 *Deadly Paradigms: The Failure of U.S. Counterinsurgency Policy*. Princeton: Princeton University Press.

Shakespeare, Nicholas
1988 In Pursuit of Guzmán. *Granta* 23 (Spring): 151–195.

Sheehan, Neil
1988 *A Bright Shining Lie: John Paul Vann and America in Vietnam*. New York: Random House.

Shoemaker, Robin
1981 *The Peasants of El Dorado: Conflict and Contradiction in a Peruvian Frontier Settlement*. Ithaca: Cornell University Press.

Silverblatt, Irene
1988 Political Memories and Colonizing Symbols: Santiago and the Mountain Gods of Colonial Peru. In: *Rethinking History and Myth: Indigenous South American Perspectives on the Past*, ed. Jonathan D. Hill. Urbana: University of Illinois Press. 174–194.

Smith, Gavin
1989 *Livelihood and Resistance: Peasants and the Politics of Land in Peru*. Berkeley, Los Angeles, Oxford: University of California Press.

Stahl, Ferdinand A.
1932 *In the Amazon Jungles*. Mountain View, Calif.: Pacific Press Publishing Association.

Stern, Steve J., ed.
1987 *Resistance, Rebellion, and Consciousness in the Andean Peasant World, 18th to 20th Centuries*. Madison: University of Wisconsin Press.

Stoll, David
1982 *Fishers of Men or Founders of Empire?: The Wycliffe Bible Translators in Latin America*. London: Zed Press.

Swenson, Sally, and Jeremy Narby
1986 The Pichis-Palcazu Special Project in Peru—A Consortium of International Lenders. *Cultural Survival Quarterly* 10(1): 19–24.

Tarazona-Sevillano, Gabriela, with John B. Reuter
1990 *Sendero Luminoso and the Threat of Narcoterrorism*. The Washington Papers 144, Center for Strategic and International Studies. New York: Praeger.

Taussig, Michael
1987 *Shamanism, Colonialism, and the Wild Man: A Study in Terror and Healing.* Chicago: University of Chicago Press.

Thorndike, Guillermo, and Angel Avendaño
1976 *Abisa a los compañeros, pronto.* Lima: Mosca Azul.

Thurston, Herbert, S. J., and Donald Attwater
1956 *Butler's Lives of the Saints.* New York: P. J. Kenedy and Sons.

Tibesar, Antonine S., O.F.M.
1952 San Antonio de Eneno: A Mission in the Peruvian Montaña. *Primitive Man* 25: 23–39.

Trapnell, Lucy
1982 El Tambo: Por el camino del despojo a la destrucción. *Amazonía Indígena* 2(4): 22–29. Lima.

Uriarte, Luis M.
1976 Poblaciones nativas de la amazonía peruana. *Amazonía Peruana* 1: 9–58. Lima.

Valdez Lozano, Zacarías
1944 *El verdadero Fitzcarraldo ante la historia.* Iquitos.

Vallejo Fonseca, José A.
1957 La lucha por la independencia del Perú: la rebelión de 1742. Juan Santos Atahualpa. *Revista del Archivo Histórico de Cuzco* 8: 232–292.

Varese, Stefano
1967 Este mundo: la nueva conquista de la selva. *Amaru* 3 (July–September): 92–94. Lima.
1973 *La sal de los cerros.* 2d ed. Lima: Retablo de Papel Ediciones.

Vargas Llosa, Mario
1983 Inquest in the Andes: A Latin Writer Explores the Political Lesson of a Peruvian Massacre. *New York Times Magazine,* 31 July 1983.

Villanueva, Victor
1967 *Hugo Blanco y la rebelión campesina.* Lima: Librería Editorial Juan Mejía Baca.
1971 *100 años del ejército peruano: frustraciones y cambios.* Lima: Editorial Juan Mejía Baca.

Vinhas de Queiróz, Maurício
1963 "Cargo Cult" na Amazônia: Observações sôbre o milenarismo Tukuna. *América Latina* 6: 43–61.

Waggener, Lt. Col. John C.
  1968 East of the Andes: Internal Development Operations of
       the Peruvian Armed Forces. Student essay, U.S. Army
       War College, Carlisle Barracks, Pa.
Wallace, A. F. C.
  1956 Revitalization Movements: Some Theoretical Considera-
       tions for their Comparative Study. *American Anthropologist*
       58: 264–281.
Weiss, Gerald
  1975 *Campa Cosmology: The World of a Forest Tribe in South
       America.* American Museum of Natural History. Anthro-
       pological Papers, Vol. 52, Part 5.
  1986 Elements of Inkarrí East of the Andes. In: *Myth and the
       Imaginary in the New World*, ed. Edmundo Magaña and
       Peter Mason. Amsterdam: Centre for Latin American
       Research and Documentation. 305–320.
Wertheman, Arturo
  1905 Exploración de los ríos Perené, Tambo i Ucayali por el
       ingeniero don Arturo Wertheman. In: *Colección de leyes,
       decretos, resoluciones i otros documentos oficiales referentes al
       Departamento de Loreto*, ed. Carlos Larraburre i Correa,
       III: 174–204. Lima: Imp. de "La Opinión Nacional."
Wilson, Bryan
  1973 *Magic and the Millennium.* New York: Harper and Row.
Wolf, Eric
  1959 *Sons of the Shaking Earth.* Chicago: University of Chicago
       Press.
  1982 *Europe and the People Without History.* Berkeley, Los
       Angeles, London: University of California Press.
Wolpin, Miles D.
  1972 *Military Aid and Counterrevolution in the Third World.*
       Lexington, Mass.: D.C. Heath and Company.
Worsley, Peter
  1968 *The Trumpet Shall Sound.* 2d rev. ed. New York: Schocken
       Books.
Wright, Robin, and Jonathan D. Hill
  1986 History, Ritual, and Myth: Nineteenth-Century Millenar-
       ian Movements in the Northwest Amazon. *Ethnohistory*
       33: 31–54.

Zarzar, Alonso

1989 *Apo Capac Huayna, Jesús Sacramentado: mito, utopía, y milenarismo en el pensamiento de Juan Santos Atahualpa.* Lima: Centro Amazónico de Antropología y Aplicación Práctica.

# Acknowledgments

Here we would like to thank those who helped us along the path to completing this book. By recognizing the contribution of these friends, colleagues, and interviewees, we do not mean to imply that they necessarily agree with our conclusions or that they are in any way responsible for errors of fact or interpretation.

The following people consented to interviews or responded in writing to our requests for information. Unfortunately, Peru's political circumstances prevent us from identifying many interviewees who today live in Satipo Province and other parts of the Peruvian Amazon.

John H. Bodley
Albert Brun
David Chaplin
Javier Dávila Duránd
Jacqueline Eluau de Lobatón
Donald R. Finberg
Lt. Col. John T. Fishel
Jeanne Grover

Sara Beatriz Guardia
James C. Haahr
Søren Hvalkof
Isidoro Llano, O.F.M.
Milton Jacobs
Amb. J. Wesley Jones
Kenneth M. Kensinger
Willard Kindberg

David L. Laughlin
Donato Lecuona, O.F.M.
Ricardo Letts Colmenares
Amb. Frank Ortiz
Peter Matthiessen
Joseph B. Pent
Deborah Pent Hudson
Mack Robertson
Nélida Rojas
Della Rossa

Róger Rumrrill
Eugenio Sarove
Amb. Ernest V. Siracusa
Gavin A. Smith
Dagoberto Soto
Steve J. Stern
Stefano Varese
Victor Villanueva
Gerald Weiss

The book benefited from thoughtful readings of specific sections or, in some cases, the entire manuscript, by the following colleagues:

Jerry W. Carlson
Winifred Creamer
Gary M. Feinmann
Steven Feld
Ronald L. Grimes
Jonathan Haas
Judith Habicht-Mausch
Søren Hvalkof
Robert Jackall
Grant D. Jones
Robert L. Kelly
Sylvia B. Kennick
Kenneth M. Kensinger
Jane Kepp

Jerrold E. Levy
William L. Merrill
N. Scott Momaday
Molly H. Mullin
Joseph B. Pent
Lin Poyer
Anna C. Roosevelt
Douglas W. Schwartz
John D. Speth
David M. Stoll
Robin H. Waterfield
Robert Woodbury
Susan P. Woodbury
Bobby Lee Wright

We would like to acknowledge the support and tactical assistance of the following:

Félix Alvarez
Amb. Harry G. Barnes, Jr.
A. Carlos Egan
Fernando Fuenzalida

Nicole Garreaud
Ernesto Hermoza
Søren Hvalkof
Robert Jackall

Kenneth M. Kensinger

Irma Lostaunau

William L. Merrill

José Miguel Irizarri

Carlos Mora

Alfonso A. Ortiz

Alejandro Ortiz Rescaniere

David M. Stoll

Robert Woodbury & Family

Special thanks go to Katrina Lasko for preparing the book's maps, to Douglas M. Barnes for a photocopy of one of the few extant copies of Guillermo Lobatón's book *Secondo Fronte,* and to Rodger W. Davis for his research assistance. We are grateful to the newspaper *El Comercio* for permission to work in its archives and to Mario Vargas Llosa for permitting us to quote brief passages from an unpublished letter. We also wish to recognize the encouragement and editorial expertise of Stanley Holwitz and Paula Cizmar of the University of California Press.

Index

sion, 177–180; and peasants and Indians, xiii, 119, 140; shamanic interpretation of, 116, 118, 166; as supernatural figure, xi, 117–118, 120–121, 166; and tension among leaders, 140; and Vallejo, 101
Loret de Mola, Carlos, 195
Los Angeles, 155–156

McDonald (Pent alias), 155
Machiguenga (Indian tribe), 10
Majes (ethnic label), 10
Mangoré (Asháninka headman), 23
Manso de Velasco, José Antonio, 41
Maoism, in Shining Path, 4, 201
Maoists, 81, 197
Mao Tse Dung, 101
Mapitziviari, 183, 239 n.35
Marca, Juan de la, 27
Mariátegui, José Carlos, 81, 94, 95; Indian role in Peruvian socialism, 94, 95; *Seven Interpretive Essays*, 81
Marta (Bulner follower), on Bulner movement, 76, 167
Marthans, Hércules, 169
Martínez, Jaime. *See* Herrera, Froilán
Marxism, 4, 80, 94, 96, 102, 137–138, 158, 214; and MIR, 102, 214; and native peoples, 94, 96, 137, 138
Marxists, 1, 118, 197; criticize MIR, 118, 197; guerrillas, and Amazonian tribesmen, 1
Mashco (Indian tribe), 63
Masisea, 145
Mastrillo, Nicolás, 14
Matiandios, Santiago, 47
Mazamari, 108, 122, 130–132, 138, 142; SPEU site, 108, 130–132, 138, 142; Túpac Amaru base camp, 122
Mazaronquiari, 122
Mendieta, Fray Gerónimo de (historian), 46, 135
Menearos (ethnic label), 16
Mengele, Josef, Pent misidentified as, 157

Mercado Jarrín, Edgardo (general), 106, 194
Merino, Horacio, 73
Mesa Pelada (MIR "security zone"), 94, 141, 170–171
Metraro mission, 26
Meza, Antonio (MIR organizer), 7–8, 119, 203
Migrations, mass, and millennial movements, 211–212
The Militant, 155
Milla, Pedro, 36
Millennarianism. *See* Millennial movements
Millennial movements, xiv, 3–4, 13, 35, 46–48, 60, 62, 75–78, 120–121, 136–137, 146, 166–167, 192, 202, 211–217, 243 n.9; and Asháninkas, 3, 13, 35, 46–47, 75–78, 120–121, 136–137, 146, 166–167, 192, 211–217; and Bulner, 76–77; and Conquest, 212–213; and Fitzcarrald, 62; and Franciscan missionaries, 47; and Juan Santos Atahualpa, 35, 46; and Lobatón as Itomi Pavá, 120–121, 167; and mass migrations, 211–212; and MIR, 120–121, 137, 167, 192; and Pent, 146; and rubber boom, 60; and Shining Path, 202
MIR. *See* Movement of the Revolutionary Left
Miraflores, xiii, 8, 86
Missionaries, Franciscan, 12, 15–53, 56, 60–62, 67, 143, 167, 176–180, 212; and Asháninkas, 12, 19, 27, 29–30, 47, 52, 67, 212; and Juan Santos Atahualpa, 42; and jungle conquest, 15–53, 56; Lecuona in Gran Pajonál, 176–180; and millennial movements, 46–47, 143
Missionaries, other Catholic, 16, 22, 41, 43, 144
Missionaries, Protestant, xiv, 76–77, 144, 146–148, 160; Bulner, 76–77; Pent, 146–148, 160
Missions: Franciscan, 18–23, 25–31, 37, 52, 68–69, 74, 175; other, 21, 31, 74, 76
Mochobos (ethnic label), 17

Momoris (ethnic label), 17
Moncloa, Francisco, 170
Monobamba, 42
More, Thomas, 47
Movement of the Revolutionary
Left (MIR), xiii–xv, 1, 3, 6–8,
89–142, 144–145, 158–160, 164–
200, 203, 214, 228–229 n.35, 229
n.43, 232 n.3, 239 n.35; and
armed forces, 109, 112, 170–
172, 189–190, 193–194; and
Asháninkas, xiii–xv, 6, 95, 115–
128, 131–140, 158, 167–169, 192;
criticized by other leftists, 196–
197; and Cuba, xi, 92, 102; de la
Puente, death of, 171–172; guerrilla forces, size of, 228–229
n.35; Guzmán defects, 138, 214; and
Marxism, 138, 214; and millennial movements, 137, 168, 192,
214; and peasants, 98–99, 198–
199, 232 n.3; penetration by
CIA, 128–129; and Pent, 145;
survivors, 198–200, 203; use of
religious symbols, 95, 115–140;
U.S. embassy reports, 128, 179,
190. See also Lobatón Milla,
Guillermo; Túpac Amaru
Movimiento de Izquierda Revolucionaria. See Movement of the
Revolutionary Left
MRTA. See Túpac Amaru Revolutionary Movement
Murillo, Elías (MIR survivor), 96,
119, 125–126, 137–138, 140,
144, 168, 200, 229 n.43; on Asháninkas, 96, 168; describes Castillo ambush, 125–126; recalls
bombing, 127, 144
Mythopraxis, and Asháninkas, 6

Napalm, 113–114
National Institute of Flora and
Fauna (INFOR) report on Asháninkas, 207
Nationalization of oil companies,
114, 128
National Liberation Front (FLN),
154
National System of Social Mobilization (SINAMOS), 198, 206,
229 n.35

National University of San Cristo-
bal de Huamanga, 200
Nazis, 93, 157
Nevati, 183
New York Times, 141, 159–160,
187
Nicolás (Asháninka), 187
Nimuendajú, Curt, 211
Nomatsiguenga, xiii, xvi, 10, 167,
220 nn.12, 13
Núñez, Lorenzo, 40

Obenteni mission, 69, 176–180,
184; Peruvian Army at, 184; Tú-
pac Amaru rest site, 176–180
Ocoña, 8
Odría, Manuel A. (president), 89,
100
Odriist National Union, 193
Oil companies. See International
Petroleum Company; Standard
Oil of New Jersey
Ordinaire, Olivier, 24
Orlandini, Alva (minister of gov-
ernment), 172
Ortiz, Frank (U.S. ambassador),
193
Ortiz, Fray Dionisio, 52, 68–69
Orton, James, 66
Otsitiríko, 13
Oxapampa, 183

Pachacama, Romulo, 187
Pachacutec (MIR column), 170
Pachacuti (apocalyptic rupture of
time), 170
Pachitea River. See Río Pachitea
"Page eleven scandal" (IPC), 195
Paitití, 21
Pampachacra (Velando's village),
91
Panama Canal Zone, 106
Pangoa, 68, 117
Pangoas (ethnic label), 16
Panoan rebellion, 52
Paris Group, 170
Paucarcaja Chávez, Juan, 92, 116,
119, 122, 180–181, 209
Pautiques (ethnic label), 17
PCP. See Communist Party of
Peru
Peasant organizers, 73, 92

Designer:	Seventeenth Street Studios
Compositor:	Wilsted & Taylor
Text:	Bembo
Display:	Antique Olive
Printer:	Maple-Vail Book Mfg. Group
Binder:	Maple-Vail Book Mfg. Group